ALLIANCE
CURSE

ALLIANCE CURSE

How America Lost the Third World

Hilton L. Root

BROOKINGS INSTITUTION PRESS
Washington, D.C.

ABOUT BROOKINGS

The Brookings Institution is a private nonprofit organization devoted to research, education, and publication on important issues of domestic and foreign policy. Its principal purpose is to bring the highest quality independent research and analysis to bear on current and emerging policy problems. Interpretations or conclusions in Brookings publications should be understood to be solely those of the authors.

Copyright © 2008
THE BROOKINGS INSTITUTION
1775 Massachusetts Avenue, N.W., Washington, D.C. 20036
www.brookings.edu

Library of Congress Cataloging-in-Publication data

Root, Hilton L.
  Alliance curse : how America lost the Third World / Hilton L. Root.
     p.   cm.
  Summary: "Proposes an analytical foundation for national security that challenges long-held assumptions or outdated suppositions about foreign affairs. Presents case studies of American foreign policy toward developing countries, efforts at state building, and nations growing in importance. Concludes with recommendations designed to close the gap between security and economic development"—Provided by publisher.
  Includes bibliographical references and index.
  ISBN 978-0-8157-7556-0 (cloth : alk. paper)
  1. United States—Foreign relations—Developing countries. 2. Developing countries—Foreign relations—United States. 3. Democratization—Developing countries. 4. Nation-building—Developing countries. 5. National security—United States. I. Title.
  JZ1480.A5R66 2008
  327.730172'4—dc22   2008012055

9 8 7 6 5 4 3 2 1

The paper used in this publication meets minimum requirements of the American National Standard for Information Sciences—Permanence of Paper for Printed Library Materials: ANSI Z39.48-1992.

Typeset in Minion

Composition by Cynthia Stock
Silver Spring, Maryland

Printed by R. R. Donnelley
Harrisonburg, Virginia

While there is no human way to prevent a king from having a bad heart, there is a human way to prevent a people from having an erroneous opinion. That way is to furnish the whole people, as a part of their ordinary education, with correct information about their relations to other peoples, about the limitations upon their own rights, about their duties to respect the rights of others, about what has happened and is happening in international affairs, and about the effects upon national life of the things that are done or refused as between nations; so that the people themselves will have the means to test misinformation and appeals to prejudice and passion based upon error.

—Elihu Root
"A Requisite for the Success of Popular Diplomacy"
Foreign Affairs (1922)

To my father

Stanley

Contents

Preface, or the Genesis of a Perspective

Foreign policy is a matter of perspective, and my perspective changed decisively during the period in which the ideas expressed here germinated. As a senior U.S. Treasury official in 2001, I began with a front seat at the creation of the Millennium Challenge Account, the invasion and subsequent administration of Iraq, and U.S. development policymaking under the Bush administration, more generally. But just like those celebrities who enjoy front-row seats at the theatre or ballet, I could see only part of the action. Although dramatic impact is maximized, proximity can be distorting and shadows can pass for reality. How all the parts fit together is obscured—a reason the critics prefer the front balcony seats. Nevertheless, the front-row-seat location enjoyed by elite spectators can influence how others appreciate the show, and their reactions can become part of the spectacle itself. When they clap, the rest of the audience soon follows their lead.

In 2002 I moved to the back of the auditorium and resumed my career as an academic international policy specialist. My response to events no longer had any hope of influencing others in the audience. The media were no longer interested in what I had to say; public-opinion makers were less likely to seek me out; and invitations to the homes of ambassadors came less frequently. But I enjoyed other advantages, particularly those of being able to read and reflect. I started by reading the works of other scholars on U.S. foreign policy while in residence at California's Claremont colleges. But the literature on international relations seemed too often influenced by passion and partisanship, much of the writing geared to supporting one side or the other, expressing admiration, disapproval, or contempt.

Still unsatisfied, I explored another perspective after joining the faculty at George Mason University in 2006. I immersed myself in studies of complexity in various sciences often far removed from current events. What I offer here is an adaptive evolutionary perspective in which dispersed and decentralized networks of agents interact constantly and strategically. The agents are not the states as unitary actors of traditional international relations theory but are representatives of firms, ethnicities, or individuals that compete or cooperate among themselves, forming new rules in anticipation of what the other agents will do. The order that emerges is an irreversible outcome of continuous feedback and communication among the agents.

People who care about foreign policy care about it passionately and that passion was clearly evident in the support I received writing this book. Enthusiastic yet exacting research support came from a cohort of dedicated young professionals that included Philip Baxter, Drew Edge, Ayesha Hashim, Yan Li, Somjita Mitra, Shaijumon C. S., Cheryl Van Den Handel, Ha T. T. Vu, and Chunjuan Wei.

The Mercatus Center at George Mason University organized a one-day seminar that transformed the manuscript into a book. The participants were Paul Dragos Aligica, Ray Bowen, Patrick Cronin, Steven Hook, Maryann Cusimano Love, John Mueller, Henry Nau, Margaret Polski, Joseph Siegle, Mario Villarreal, Ming Wan, Richard Wagner, and Ronald Wintrobe. Special thanks to Jack Goldstone, my colleague at George Mason, for moderating and Claire Morgan and Rob Herritt for administrating and organizing the event.

International policy specialists Jacek Kugler, Jack Goldstone, Carol Lancaster, Robert Looney, Hung M. Nguyen, Nancy Overholt, Karti Sandilya, Rachel Stohl, and Melissa Thomas read and commented on all or part of the manuscript. An article that appeared in *National Interest* has become chapter 11. I thank the editors for permission to use the material. I also owe a considerable debt to Dinah McNichols, who substantively edited the entire manuscript, and Susan Steiner, who helped find the right tone at a very early stage in the writing. At Brookings Institution Press, Christopher Kelaher and Janet Walker have been delightful to work with.

I thank them all for keeping my spirits up during a period of isolation, concentration, and self-absorption and, of course, self-doubt—hazards that all writers face.

*The Legacy of the Cold War
and Instability in the
Twenty-First Century*

Economic Logic of the Alliance Curse

We have as our grand strategy only the arms race and the cold war.
—John F. Kennedy, *The Strategy of Peace* (1960)

American globalism requires a new script. During the cold war that script was motivated by grand theories of social change that failed to establish correlations between what actually occurred and what we had grounds to expect.[1] Yet cold war perceptions of threats and opportunities were built so well into our culture that they are repeated by today's policymakers.[2] We are prevented from seeing gaps between our vision and the effects of our actions because we continue to base perceptions of our own security on models of containment that were originally designed to prevent the spread of Soviet power across Europe and throughout the third world.

America's cold war foreign policy was characterized by alliances with autocratic leaders such as China's Chiang Kai-shek, South Vietnam's Ngo Dinh Diem and Nguyen Van Thieu, and the Philippines' Ferdinand Marcos, to name a few. These alliances, ostensibly of mutual benefit, instead resulted in political and social instability and in failures to sustain economic development. The domestic failures of those governments dragged the United States into regional conflicts and two wars, in Korea and Vietnam, in the name of containing Communism.

The U.S.-backed leaders considered in the case studies in Part 2 of this book overstayed in office without creating adequate public goods or social policies. They ruled personally and autocratically, creating neither parties nor bureaucracies to ensure a smooth succession nor policy continuity after stepping down. They eliminated secular opposition so that civil society never emerged or matured.[3] They did little to create thriving, competitive economies. Nor did they provide equality, meritocracy, or upward opportunities for their people. They built armies based on personal loyalty rather than competence. Yet time and again, the United States overlooked these liabilities in its ambitious campaign to fight the spread of global Communism. When those rulers became targets of resentment by their own populations and fell, the alliances sent blowback to U.S. shores in the form of unanticipated threats.[4] In some situations, violent anti-American policy setbacks created security risks that were even greater than those the alliances were designed to offset. Jihadism has emerged among those nations considered to be the staunchest allies against global Communism, as has the proliferation of nuclear weapons by Pakistan and state-sponsored terrorism by Iran.

If, as has been proved through history, an alliance between a greater power and a weaker but strategically significant dictator traps the dominant partner into unnecessary conflicts and moral compromises, why has the United States forged so many such alliances since 1945? Why did regimes that are rated as highly corrupt receive a disproportionately large share of U.S. overseas assistance during the cold war? What drives democratic policymakers in the United States to support leaders who plunder their own countries, and why does the war on terror compel the United States to again ally itself with regimes that discredit America as a leader of progressive social reform? Are U.S. alliances with third world nations a possible contributor to global corruption? Have policymakers misapprehended the underlying causes that may explain the correlation of aid and corruption? What remedies can be taken today to correct mishaps of the past?

Consequences of the Alliance Curse

Asymmetric alliances between first and third world countries are easily formed because in theory they appear to improve the well-being of both parties.[5] The more powerful partner benefits in the short run, extending its political and military influence and gaining policy concessions such as cheap oil or UN votes that are appreciated by the home electorate. The weaker state gains a benefactor, as well as protection, aid, and abundant credit. But what may at first seem a fair and cooperative mutuality of interests invariably turns out to be unfair to the disenfranchised populations within the weaker state. Because the asymmetrical alliance may create a "development trap" and reduce the incentives of local leadership to govern for prosperity, the political status of already marginalized segments is likely to diminish as regime longevity increases.

When aid from foreign taxpayers substitutes for domestic resources, the reforms and policy strengthening necessary for long-term viability can be neglected, leaving a recipient state with diminished social and institutional capital to resume a developmental path once a corrupt regime's grip is removed. When leadership in the weaker country depends for legitimacy on the benefactor for resources such as foreign aid, abundant credit, and military assistance, the government can neglect building its own predictable system of laws, policy, procedural transparency, and political accountability. U.S. assistance was often a reason that authoritarian rulers who exercised power unchecked by law or other institutions enjoyed great longevity in office.[6] The aid plays a particularly critical role if they have little popular support, because their political tenure depends on a small, exclusive coalition to whom they extend access to private goods and for whom disloyalty can be costly.[7]

Many third world recipients of alliance rents suffered governance failures as a result. In fact, during the final years of the cold war (1985–89), when cross-country data on corruption became available, developing countries within the lowest 20th percentile of the corruption ranking received two-thirds of U.S. aid. Only 7 percent of all U.S. aid went to the least corrupt quintiles among low-income countries. After the cold war, the bulge of U.S. assistance that went to countries with high levels of corruption was reduced and less than 10 percent of U.S. foreign aid was distributed to the most corrupt regimes (lowest 20th percentile) of the developing world. The attacks of September 11 produced another shift in the data, and the amount of aid given to the most corrupt quintile went back up to 39 percent. One recurrent pattern emerges: the bulge of U.S. assistance persistently flows to the more corrupt regimes of the developing world (figure 1-1).

Between 1985 and 1989, among the eighty developing country aid recipients, twenty out of the most corrupt thirty-two governments are classified by Polity IV as complete autocracies. Another six were autocracies that transitioned during the period; only six were consistent democracies. These deficits of democratic accountability were ignored when U.S security concerns were raised. Many of the countries that were highly corrupt but democratic after 1985, such as Pakistan and the Philippines, were major aid recipients before holding elections and had only recently—during the late 1980s—become democracies. Thus, we can assume that if these major aid recipients are counted, the lavishly funded countries among the corrupt bottom throughout the cold war were primarily autocratic regimes or regimes whose institutions were corrupted by a long period of autocratic rule. After they transitioned into democracies their systems of public finance remained riddled with avenues for corruption.

During the cold war, while the United States touted itself as the world's greatest promoter of democracy, 53 percent of U.S. aid went to autocracies. This distressing pattern will be explored in chapter 2. The small winning

Figure 1-1. *Concentration of U.S. Assistance to Corrupt Low-Income Countries*

Percent of assistance

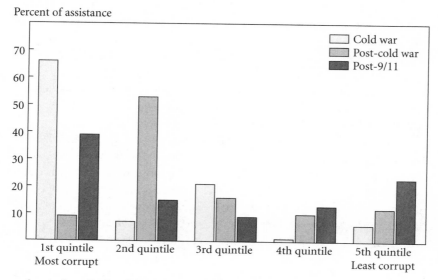

Source: Green Book and the PRS Group International Country Risk Indicators.

coalitions that controlled these recipient governments did not desire transparency, for it would have exposed the kickbacks and corruption that perpetuate the system. Because of abundant U.S. aid, accountability mechanisms to local constituents could be sidestepped. Autocrats attempt to keep their supporting coalitions as small as possible so that rents from collaboration can be concentrated among essential supporters.[8] Predictable contract enforcement and reliable information about the government's economic plans were averted because they would reduce dependence on the government's role as the economy's pivotal deal maker. Building an effective bureaucracy or the judicial and educational systems necessary for a strong state could represent threats to the incumbent.

Because the ruling party fails to build broad-based institutions, political and social development are stunted and the client nation is likely to manifest lower levels of social organization than are warranted by its income levels. In the extreme case, public goods, transportation, or communication networks can improve the conditions for revolutionaries to be active. Political mechanisms to reach compromises between the conflicting aspirations of citizens fail to develop. The opposition, unable to openly court broad-based support,

Figure 1-2. *Concentration of Aid to Internally Conflicted Low-Income Countries*

Percent of assistance

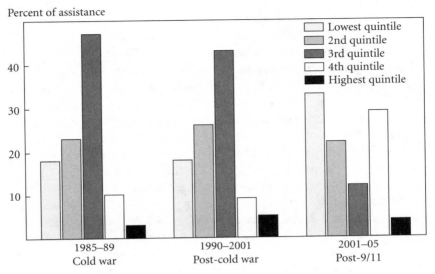

Source: Green Book and the PRS Group International Country Risk Indicators.

will focus its efforts on grabbing control of the governmental apparatus rather than on adapting skills of coalition formation and policy advocacy.

With a flow of resources from the outside, a leader can sacrifice policies needed to ensure growth in order to redistribute more income to key supporters. The concentration of economic opportunities in the hands of government gives the incumbent the tools to create a loyalty premium, making the defection of dissatisfied coalition members costly.[9] Abundant external resources also strengthen a tyrant's resistance to domestic restructuring or redistribution, which causes preexisting social rifts to fester and become poisonous. These alliance-twisted incentives are among the primary causes of development gaps that trigger regional tension, resentment, and instability. In fact, U.S. aid is skewed toward internally divided governments to ensure that domestic conflicts end with a pro-American outcome. But the availability of aid often fanned internal political tensions and often extended and intensified conflict (see figure 1-2).[10]

Unlike their political rivals, leaders that obtain alliance status with a wealthy sponsor can afford to reward their coalition members well. This makes it harder for rivals to survive, and forces opposition groups into subversive activities as the only course to challenge the incumbent. When the incumbent and the regime become one and the same, the opposition must target the entire apparatus of government in order to overthrow the leader, heightening political volatility and the risk of violent overthrow.

An autocrat who has consolidated a coalition and survived an initial period of instability can enjoy a much longer survival rate than can a successful democratic leader, whose political survival depends on the support of a large coalition.[11] But the former is likely to face a much more disagreeable end. All dictators fear being deposed or killed in a revolution or a coup d'état, so they set aside funds as secret insurance for new payoffs or possible exile.

Fearing that its own benefits are in jeopardy, the sponsor nation may intervene on behalf of the regime. This places the sponsor nation in opposition against the local population, producing a commitment trap that arises time and again in U.S. relations with third world dictators.

Inevitably, in this kind of alliance, the aid cycle, along with the alliance, will enter a downturn. Foreign aid comes in boom-bust cycles and produces countercyclical investment patterns that leave the weaker country with debt burdens that cannot be repaid once the alliance-driven aid cycle slows down. Just as resource abundance may not generate healthy economic growth, the resources that autocrats gain from an alliance with a first world benefactor can create an "alliance curse." This curse has political-economy consequences that resemble the better-known resource curse.[12]

Pakistani–U.S. relations in the wake of September 11, 2001, exemplify the economic consequences of the alliance curse. A frontline country in the war on terror, Pakistan received $10 billion in U.S. assistance in exchange for its commitment to fight the Taliban and al Qaeda at home.[13] That aid, however, has not targeted the sectors where it would have the largest long-term payoffs for the nation: rural health, education, agriculture, manufacturing, and infrastructure. Instead, the funds have been channeled into subsidized industries controlled by the military brass such as luxury construction, inciting a real estate boom, and into the purchase of sophisticated weapons systems for combat against state-based forces, not jihadists. In this sense, Pakistan, like every country that has experienced an alliance curse, concentrates its newly acquired resources on ephemeral sectors that benefit the regime and reward its backers. The economy's long-term production potential remains underexploited. Because uncertainty exists about the durability of alliance-cursed regimes, businesses tend to invest in sectors and projects from which rapid withdrawal is an option, and neglect investments that will come to fruition in the future.[14] Since the most important contributor to growth is investment, the client nation will be economically impaired and unlikely to remain a stable and reliable ally. When the marriage arranged on the basis of short-term objectives is disrupted, the client nation is likely to become a security liability or even hostile to America. A change in geopolitical priorities will leave the country with long-term debts it cannot repay because the alliance curse has left it without resources that can be replenished from sound investments.

U.S. policy planners are generally unaware of the corrosive effects of asymmetrical alliances.[15] This lack of awareness results in a commitment trap in which the United States supports the status quo for fear something worse might arise in its place—a situation that will be discussed at greater length in chapter 11. The uncertainty that emerges when the patron fears that change could produce a greater evil seals the commitment trap. In fact, the very nature of the alliance (not the threats from domestic rivals or fear of the patron) is sufficient to cause an incumbent autocrat to disregard domestic accountability, equity, and transparency. The result is alienation of the domestic population, which may then harbor enemies of the tyrant and of the United States.

Such alliances deflect the focus from long-term development and allow preexisting social fissures such as inequality and ethnocentric- or class-based discrimination to trigger social conflict. In the end, the inadequacy of inclusive policies that yield rewards for the general population reproduces the security dilemmas we sought to preclude in the first place. Yet again, when facing an entirely new system of threats and warfare, the United States resorts to supporting frontline dictators, and we are surprised to be the target of a global jihad.

Since September 11, 2001, dozens of countries that promise to join the "global war on terror" have been provided with U.S. weapons and training. Many of the recipients are autocratic governments that are extremely corrupt, hostile to democracy, and dismissive of human rights. The Center for Defense Information has tracked twenty-five frontline states and found that more than half were cited by the U.S. State Department as having serious human rights abuses.[16] Six of the twenty-five were ranked among the most corrupt in the world by Transparency International. One of the countries not covered by the study, Sudan, is receiving assistance despite allegations that government forces have abetted genocide in Darfur.[17] Yet since declaring support of U.S. counterterrorist activities, the twenty-five countries have received eighteen times more total U.S. assistance than they received before September 11. The report's lead author, Rachel Stohl, warns, "The unprecedented level of military assistance is short-sighted and potentially very dangerous. . . . Selling arms for short-term political gains undermines long-term U.S. national security and strategic interests."[18]

The arms sales create future liabilities for several reasons. The weapons are difficult to control once delivered. Sending military assistance to regimes that abuse human rights makes us enemies of the very people we are trying to defend. As long as the United States builds military capability where developmental conditions are ignored, the people in those countries will view the war against terror as a U.S. war. Under such conditions these armaments may someday be used against Americans.[19] Today's terrorists will end up leaders of tomorrow's local insurgency movements.

Both Congress and the State Department recognized the danger that the United States might lose control over the weapons it sent to coalition members. Before September 11 Congress had imposed oversight through the budgetary process. The State Department established guidelines to ensure that arms were not sent to human rights violators or to regimes that weaken democratic processes, practice terrorism, or threaten neighbors. Long lists of such countries were sanctioned before September 11 to prevent arms sales from endangering long-term U.S. security.

But on September 12, 2001, the U.S. government lifted all previous sanctions, even though conditions that led to the sanctions had not changed. It established new programs outside of the foreign operations budgets overseen by Congress.[20] Countries barred from receiving arms because of violations are now eligible merely by promising to help stamp out global terrorism. And by reclassifying as terrorist groups insurgencies that those countries had been fighting for years, the U.S. government greatly expanded the list of eligible arms recipients.

As a result of the lifting of sanctions and the creation of new accounts, the United States recently became the world leader in transferring arms to the developing world at a time when arms sales to developing countries are mounting dramatically. Between 1999 and 2006, arms transfer agreements with developing nations constituted 66.4 percent of all worldwide arms agreements, and in 2006, 71.5 percent of all agreements. In 2005 the arming of the third world generated $31.8 billion in agreements, and in 2006 it generated another $28.8 billion.[21] As the growth in arms sales to the third world grows, so do the risks that previous safeguards were designed to offset. Viewing counterinsurgency as counterterrorism, we interfere in domestic conflicts in which we do not have a role. Many recipients for arms are likely to use the weapons in conflicts with neighbors, making unstable regions less stable. Thus Pakistan, Azerbaijan, and Armenia, among others, have been able to fill their shopping carts with arms they had been seeking for years. Who would be surprised to learn that some of the weapons that the State Department considers important to control have found their way into the arsenals of countries still under sanctions, such as Iran and China? Yet the greatest danger of overriding the previous safeguards is rarely mentioned. Repressive regimes that do not enjoy support at home are being strengthened, triggering a downward spiral in domestic governance that ultimately represents the greatest threat to future stable relations.

In essence, September 11 allowed the Bush administration to return to four priorities of early cold war U.S. foreign policy:

—Agreement on the need to contain the Soviets has been converted to a consensus on the global war against terrorism.

—Agreement on the need for active globalism during the cold war was characterized by the Marshall Plan and a network of alliances to contain Communism; again after Sept. 11 the arming of emerging nations and expansion of U.S. military capacity have created arms clients in all corners of the globe.

—The agreement on the primacy of presidential leadership was modified after the fall of Communism by greater attention given to voices from civil society; the war against terrorism, however, gave the president a rationale to close out civil society and tighten access to strategic information.

—Briefly during the Clinton administration international trade and commerce took priority over security in foreign policy. Clinton strengthened the international policy role of the agencies concerned with economic policy, bringing economics to the center of foreign policy.[22] After September 11 the "economic complex" comprising the Treasury and Commerce Departments and the Office of Budget and Management once again has been subordinated to security.

U.S. Popular Sentiments That Facilitate the Alliance Curse

The United States sees itself as a benign superpower that maintains world stability, discourages regional conflicts, and facilitates democracy and economic growth.[23] In the words of former President Clinton, "There are times *only* America can make the difference between war and peace, between freedom and repression, between hope and fear."[24] Such an optimistic self-portrait is not widely shared by the leaders of developing democracies, who must also seek to satisfy constituent goals of national pride, identity, and interest.

As we will see in the next chapter, third world democracies rarely enter alliances with first world patrons. Why? Because their home constituents want widely distributed public goods. This feature of competitive politics makes democrats of the developed world incompatible with their developing world counterparts. It also underscores one of the regularities of cold war geopolitics: the tolerance expressed by first world nations toward compliant repressive regimes that serve entrenched elites at the expense of broader social interests. Many of the developed nations' interventions, both political and economic, lower the competitiveness of those we try to assist. This puts us into conflict with our idealization of open-market liberalism and with successful developing democracies such as India and Brazil.

We not only ignore the negative fallout from our policies, we also exaggerate our role in the downfall of our socialist enemies. The demise of the Soviet Union reinforced our belief in containment as a dominant factor in the geopolitical decline of socialism. Yet containment may have played a smaller role than we are willing to acknowledge.[25] Its impact was greatest in stopping a possible Soviet advance into Europe. But even the ultimate failure of the Soviet regime cannot be attributed directly to containment. The Soviet system failed in part because entrenched internal problems impeded economic and political reforms, and because of its ambitions in Afghanistan and Eastern Europe.[26] The evolution of socialist planning models and capitalist entities have both been deeply influenced by global forces that left centrally controlled hierarchies in the dustbin of history. The United States takes credit for precipitating the fall of the Soviets without acknowledging that the same foreign policy planning apparatus failed to anticipate the rise of China's market economy—grown out of socialist institutions and practices. That planning apparatus also produced unsustainable alliance partners in the Islamic world that today harbor our most virulent foes. Surrounding the Soviet Union with an Islamic "green field" created a hospitable environment for the spread of Taliban-style Islamic revolution.

Clearly, the United States should have sought alternatives to the alliance curse. However, the political process has a limited capacity to anticipate or respond to the blowback effects triggered by overseas interventions. Elected officials use foreign policy as a tool to obtain such public goods as security and cheap natural resources that their constituents desire at home. Public opinion surveys consistently show that voters place democracy building and development low on their lists of foreign policy priorities. These items rate below emergency humanitarian assistance, which only helps reduce short-term problems rather than build durable overseas economies.[27] Foreign policy debates invariably focus on convincing domestic audiences that their elected leaders deserve credit and reelection for having brought home valuable resources and investment opportunities, policy concessions, and the political and military influence cited earlier. As a result, system-level social and political transformations occurring in the third world are generally ignored in U.S. policymaking.

Reframing Our Global Agenda

Dynamic changes throughout the world suggest that U.S. policymakers have fundamentally misapprehended the relationship between global economic development and political stability. So off-balance has been our understanding of this fundamental relationship that we failed to anticipate the most consequential transformations of the cold war—the peaceful dissolution of the Soviet Union and China's rapid rise from a Communist past. Efforts to graft policies and practices from the first world onto the third world in order to stimulate growth and progressive social change produced meager results. Ironically, allies that we bolstered with military and economic assistance in the Philippines and Pakistan are politically unstable, socially volatile, and economically stagnant. Meanwhile, American businesses seek opportunities among our former geopolitical enemies, China and Vietnam. In South Asia anti-U.S. terrorist cells thrive in allied regimes such as those of Pakistan, the Philippines, and Indonesia. Yet China and Vietnam, our former adversaries, stand firmly in the antiterrorist camp. No one could have anticipated that the world's most tenaciously Communist country is the leading creditor of the world's largest capitalist nation. Or that Vietnam's middle class in 2007 is broader and the gap between rich and poor narrower than in the Philippines, our cold war ally.[28] Nevertheless, almost two decades after the demise of the Soviet Union, the strategies designed to counter another global menace are constructed using a cold war model that planted the seeds of much subsequent instability.

During the cold war, we chose allies simply because of their anti-Communist credentials and ended up being defeated by Communists in China, North Korea, and Vietnam. Today we support regimes that are anti-jihadist, regardless of their repressive policies and dubious domestic support. Insensitivity to the negative consequences of asymmetrical alliances has biased our effectiveness on many issues and leads us to an insufficient understanding of local and regional economic realities. This foreign policy downplays the social and economic challenges faced by the populations whose trust our security ultimately requires. Yet even so, the relevance of global economic development to U.S. security and of sound relations with the major developing powers appears to be counterintuitive to U.S. strategic culture. To fight the new enemy, both the administration of President George W. Bush and the political opposition accept the logic of propping up autocratic leaders with high-tech weapons and training in exchange for short-term strategic services. Our triumphalism—and the militarism it provokes—are so deeply embedded in our institutions that we are unable to see that we can sometimes be the author of the very evils that we seek to overcome.

In place of transferring weapons to regimes that violate the rights of their citizens, an alternative strategy is needed that ties security to economic development. This book attempts to focus attention on general global forces that underscore geopolitical order and stability. Third world reconstruction requires that we pay more attention to the principles of self-organization and the fact that our actions often create the environment that determines the strategies of third world adversaries and allies alike. Because foreign policy, national security, and development policy are generally taught, studied, and managed through largely separate entities, they produce fragmented policy recommendations. This book aims to unify the three to bring about an integrated approach to the political economy of U.S. foreign relations.

2

Democratic Paradoxes: Institutional Constraints on U.S. Democracy Promotion

> The small state should avoid taking predetermined positions on all international issues on the basis of identification with one Great Power as against another, for the sake of fleeting material benefits or because its regime in power believes that it is being propped up by a Power without whose support it would be liquidated by its own people.
> —Zulfikar Ali Bhutto, *The Myth of Independence* (1969)

> Almost all the defects inherent in democratic institutions are brought to light in the conduct of foreign affairs.
> —Alexis de Tocqueville, *Democracy in America* (1863)

When the United States engages in foreign policy, it must confront two paradoxes: many people who hate the United States want to live here and, in contrast with the ideals and principles that Americans profess, their government supports repressive, even brutal regimes that enjoy little popular support. The following chapters provide a theoretical and historical framework in which to examine these paradoxes through the case studies of China, the Philippines, South Vietnam, Iran, India, and Pakistan that will appear in part two. These chapters also look at why foreigners who identify with American ideals are ready to resist U.S. political influence on their soil.

Other current approaches to U.S. security dilemmas of the twenty-first century tend to examine conflicts with emerging powers in the context of recent events, which is like watching the last twenty minutes of a feature film. This book will trace the character formation of the principal players to their sources. It will reveal that current U.S. foreign policy dilemmas and America's consequent inability to sustain long-term security relations with developing countries are more often than not the unintended consequences of cold war strategies and priorities. The failures of policy, organization, and cognition that are responsible for these consequences derive from institutional constraints central to the functioning of American democracy.

Many U.S. political leaders and ordinary citizens believe that the United States embodies democratic ideals and is therefore a model of sociopolitical development. Those democratic ideals, they claim, form the moral basis for U.S. global leadership. Indeed, they are often stunned and confused by the visceral criticism leveled against this country from abroad.

As a young man in the 1970s, I visited West Bengal and remember being similarly stunned by the anti-American sentiment I found. Almost daily, friends and colleagues treated me to rants about the evil effects of American power. Yet these same people welcomed me into their families. Many sought visas for themselves or relatives hopeful of working, studying, or even living in the United States. Later, in graduate school I met young Iranians who had stood before the White House shouting "Death to America!" while family members queued for visas at the U.S. embassy in Tehran to acquire residency permits.[1]

As a student in Paris I shared an apartment with an individual who later played a prominent role in Nicaragua's Sandinista insurgency. An admirer of Thomas Jefferson, he knew the American Constitution and the writings of the Founding Fathers better than I did. Several years after we met, his photograph appeared in the *New York Times* with those of four others, all wanted for violent anti-American activities in Central America.

It took me a long time to understand fully the source of these contradictions. Certainly, American political rhetoric did not provide the answers. Administration after administration has maintained that American ideals form both the paradigm for global development and the moral foundation for U.S. leadership in progressive policy change overseas. As a result of this unflinching confidence in America's benevolent influence on the affairs of others, presidents and their cabinets and advisers can only imagine one explanation for anti-American criticism overseas: envy. They reason that even allies such as Saudi Arabia and Egypt, or formerly allied nations such as Iran and Iraq, rail against us because they envy our success, because America is rich and modern, democratic and powerful.

Democrats and Republicans use the same language. "Americans are targets of terrorism in part because we act to advance peace and democracy," said President Bill Clinton.[2] Richard Haas, a senior State Department official in the George W. Bush administration, explained that "it's not anything we're simply doing. It is who we are. It's the fact that we're the most powerful country in the world."[3] Such conventional answers that attribute the motive of envy to our critics' actions are not only inadequate and dangerous; they inhibit true understanding and corrective action. The discrepancy between how we see ourselves and how others see us has become an obstacle to the leadership that America seeks to project and a threat to global stability. After we infuse the colonized people of the third world with enthusiasm for controlling their own government and destiny, our failure to live up to the rhetoric inflames anti-U.S. passions around the world.[4]

I knew that my friends did not hate America because of its wealth. Nor did they resent America because, as both Presidents George W. Bush and Clinton have insisted, it stands for democracy and human rights. My friends were idealists too. Their ambitions for themselves and for their loved ones were the same as ours—the guarantee of human and democratic rights. But their experience of U.S. power was sharply at odds with the values America espoused and guaranteed for its own people. As they saw it, the way America governed itself was incompatible with the power projected when making antidemocratic interventions in others' domestic affairs. For my friends, liking Americans and liking America were two different matters.

How did the ideals that hold American society together become so removed from the perception outsiders have of America's role in the world? Why do others see the United States as a threat to the very values it champions? Why do the majority of Egyptians, Jordanians, Pakistanis, and Saudi Arabians have a negative image of America while being among the largest recipients of U.S. aid? Why do countries like India, Vietnam, Burma, Ethiopia, and Kenya exhibit less anti-Americanism than countries that Washington has helped finance and arm, such as Egypt, Jordan, Pakistan, and Turkey—where favorable views of the United States are held by 21, 20, 15, and 9 percent of the population, respectively?[5]

At the end of World War II all parties agreed to focus U.S. foreign policy on the reconstruction of Europe and Japan. Later, as the cold war progressed, both Democrats and Republicans were primarily concerned with containing Soviet Communist influence abroad. They did this by building defensive military capabilities along Soviet borders and by ensuring that the nations with the industrial capacity to threaten U.S. security did not fall in with the Soviets. Later the focus to contain the Soviets shifted to the third world and would-be Soviet allies. Angola, China, Cuba, Chile, Congo, Egypt, and North Korea, among others, received stern warnings that neither conventional nor guerrilla warfare, neither the encouragement of insurgency nor the subversion of pro-Western regimes, would succeed. Between 1949 and 1965 American foreign policy enjoyed a rare consensus across the entire political spectrum.

U.S. policy declarations always clearly supported and encouraged democracy, national independence, and the welfare of the citizenry. However, cold war presidents emphasized policies that subordinated the promises that America expounded to protect people living in third world nations from the injustices of colonialism and social inequality. Friendly regimes, especially those near Soviet and Chinese borders (such as Iran, Pakistan, the Philippines, and South Vietnam) and therefore considered crucial to the containment of Communism, received aid to strengthen their domestic security services in order to resist domestic or external challenges. The methods, both covert and overt, were in fact applied so indiscriminately to cement alliances that they corrupted the very regimes being protected. As noted in chapter 1 (figure 1-1), two thirds of U.S. assistance to developing countries at the end of the cold war went to countries in the lowest quintiles of corruption. In many cases, autocratic leaders used domestic security forces strengthened with U.S. aid to repress or plunder their own populations. They also did so with full concurrence of their American backers. And as we shall see, the dictators themselves frequently turned on America.

At the end of the cold war, between 1985 and 1989, 51 percent of U.S. assistance went to forty-seven autocratic regimes. No wonder the populations in those countries grew embittered and mistrustful (see figure 2-1). When the cold war ended the number of autocratic regimes in the sample declined from forty-seven to twenty (see figure 2-2). Yet this smaller number of countries continued receiving 45 percent of total U.S. assistance to developing countries (see figure 2-1). The persistence of the flow of aid to regimes in the autocratic category was due largely to support of U.S. allies in the Middle East. U.S. support of friendly autocrats in the Middle East sharply contrasts with efforts to encourage democratic strengthening elsewhere and it is one of the reasons that the most virulent forms of anti-Americanism took root in this region. After the September 11 attacks U.S. policies were unmoved and the autocratic stalwarts received ample supplies of U.S. assistance despite the aggressive rhetoric from the administration in Washington in support of global democracy.

Unlikely Partners

If we are to guard against unsustainable and often fatal partnerships (as with Iran, Iraq, and the Palestinian Authority), it is essential to understand how they came about in the first place. Why did cold war foreign policy depart from the principles of American traditions and ideals that shone brightly during two world wars?

Figure 2-1. *Concentration of U.S. Assistance to Developing Country Autocrats*[a]

Percent of assistance

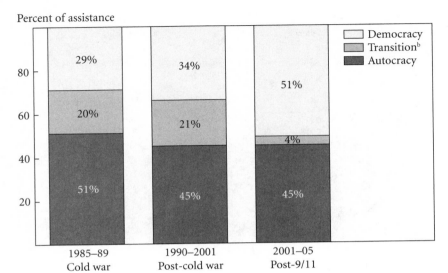

Source: Green Book, Polity IV.
a. Regime type is defined by polity score.
b. Transition refers to regimes:
—changing from autocracy to democracy,
—changing from democracy to autocracy,
—going through a period of interregnum, during which there is a complete collapse of central political authority, or a period of interruption, during which there is either foreign occupation or short-lived attempts at the creation of ethnic, religious, or regional federations.

Mobilizing comprehensive governance reform in overseas partners ranks very low among the foreign policy goals of American voters.[6] Thus, U.S. presidents find they can provide the public goods that their constituents demand—allies, intelligence posts, military bases, trade access, strategic raw materials, and votes in international organizations—by enticing autocrats with aid, even when this means that values back home are compromised.[7]

In the most comprehensive study ever conducted of the foreign policy preferences of the American public, Page and Bouton found the number one foreign policy preference of the public to be security from attack. Citizens also want foreign policy to protect U.S. economic and social well-being. "There is no escaping the fact that most Americans put their own well-being and their own country's welfare ahead of the welfare of people who live

Figure 2-2. *Number (Percentage) of Low-Income Countries Receiving U.S. Assistance, by Regime Type*[a]

Percent of assistance

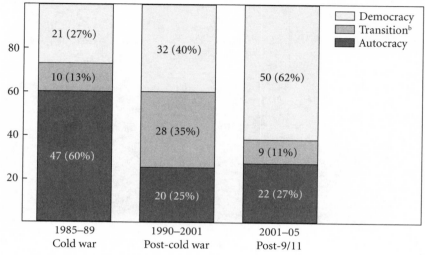

		Democracy
		Transition[b]
		Autocracy

1985–89
Cold war

1990–2001
Post-cold war

2001–05
Post-9/11

Source: Green Book, Polity IV.

a. Regime type is defined by polity score.

b. Transition refers to regimes:

—changing from autocracy to democracy,

—changing from democracy to autocracy,

—going through a period of interregnum, during which there is a complete collapse of central political authority, or a period of interruption, during which there is either foreign occupation or short-lived attempts at the creation of ethnic, religious, or regional federations.

abroad."[8] Justice-related goals are a lower priority. In descending order is support for humanitarian foreign aid, which ranks higher than "helping to bring a democratic form of government to other nations. . . . Promoting market economies" abroad was ranked near the bottom. Dead last among the priorities of the American public are helping to improve the standard of living of less developed nations. Page and Bouton found that the basic foreign policy objectives of the American public were virtually unchanged by the end of the cold war.[9]

To satisfy the needs of various constituents, an incumbent administration will prioritize partners overseas, knowing that the demand for security and affordable natural resources is much greater than the demand to monitor democratic norms. Thus, being a good president at home does not necessarily mean that the president is a good global citizen or an advocate of good government abroad. In fact, Page and Bouton found a striking disconnect between public opinion and expert opinion, which emphasizes military and economic security and underestimates public receptivity to humanitarian programs. No one captured this irony better than Franklin Roosevelt, who remarked of America's friend Anastasio Somoza García in Nicaragua, "He may be a son of a bitch, but he's our son of a bitch." In a similar vein, Roosevelt entered into an alliance with Stalin to defend democracy against Nazism. He entered into these alliances because Somoza and Stalin were willing to carry out the policy preferences of U.S. voters.

When formulating foreign policy, incumbents need not look beyond how their domestic audience values the consequences of their actions. Their ratings do best domestically when they are seen as effective at gaining policy compliance from foreign leaders. If a president believes or convinces Americans that national security is at stake, the malleability of a foreign regime is more important than its internal political structure.

Throughout the cold war it was convenient to ignore the connections between the length of client regimes' political tenure, the nature of governance, and the flow of foreign aid. Data collected by Bueno de Mesquita and colleagues confirm that the survival prospects for autocrats who received aid but did not promote growth were considerably higher than those for democrats with below-average growth. In fact, aid helps corrupt dictators more than it helps corrupt democrats to stay in office. The survival prospects for autocrats without aid and below-average growth converge with the survival prospects of democrats with no aid and below-average growth.[10]

The prospect of ruling through the disbursement of private goods to select clients is often possible because democratic regimes in the West provide those autocrats with resources for which no domestic substitute exists. This improbable partnership occurs because democratically elected leaders in rich countries find that their counterparts in poor countries who rule at the pleasure of a small, exclusive group of loyalists are likely to make policy concessions in exchange for aid as long as those concessions do not threaten their core base of supporters. Only when the pool of necessary supporters is allowed to expand, and more contenders for power emerge to put pressure on diminishing reserves, do agreements with autocrats become less effective and begin to break down. The geopolitical loyalties of successor regimes are likely to be unpredictable and difficult to influence.

Those who point out that aid constitutes a small component of a nation's total economy may find that argument counterintuitive. However, although aid may constitute only a few dollars per capita and may have small overall impact on a national economy, it is a political bonanza for autocrats, who only have to pay off a small following. The privileged domestic supporters whom they patronize in exchange for loyalty usually include those who control the military, the civil service, the communications and information infrastructure, and the economy. The more external support is allotted to these regimes, the easier it becomes to exclude the many from sharing in power, diminishing prospects for reforms and a more inclusive, democratic orientation.

Furthermore, receipt of early aid can stabilize a ruler's tenure because it frees up money to buy support. Even small amounts of aid can provide the novice autocrat with the revenue to outbid political rivals, gain the support of essential partners, and deter defection. In this way, rulers do not have to raise wealth through an inclusive process. Once the budget is depleted the loyalty that was purchased is dissipated, as occurred to South Vietnamese leader Nguyen Van Thieu. He lost his ability to stay in power once he lost access to American aid.

In addition, a quid pro quo strategy can be effective only with dictators who maintain tight control by being able to claim strong loyalty from key supporters. To obtain concessions, it is advantageous to keep otherwise unacceptable partners in power for as long as possible. Thus, autocratic regimes with little or no public debate or transparency in the collection or disbursement of revenues, no free press, and no civil liberties become the partners of choice for Western democracies seeking to buy influence. Repressive overseas regimes can disperse aid selectively with little risk of public exposure or censure.

The incentives offered by external assistance will generally be insufficient to bring about an alignment of geopolitical policy when significant extraneous influences such as the press, public opinion, celebrities, and an inclusive bargaining process are present. When foreign aid or public disbursement is subject to debate in legislatures, in the press, and in the ballot box, public exposure can make survival difficult for incumbents who accept aid but do not produce growth and popular public policies. Thus, democratic leaders in both donor and recipient countries face the same political incentives. To gain constituent support they must adopt policy positions aligned with majority preferences. Uncertainty exists as to whether elected leaders of developing country democracies would support Western security objectives (such as military bases or air routes).[11] Therefore, leaders of wealthy countries with functioning inclusive political institutions rarely form alliances with democratically elected leaders of developing countries, as we shall see in the relationship between the United States and India.

In a competitive democracy, a leader quickly depletes his budget by distributing public resources, including foreign aid, to large numbers of voters. Successful democratic leaders end up competing for support by creating public goods that can assist the poor—health, education, agricultural services, and rural credit—and that enjoy broad support. Such goods are hard to provide through bilateral or multilateral overseas assistance, because their dissemination is labor-intensive, requiring extensive distribution and administrative linkages with the capital.

Aid bureaucracies have a weak track record in being able to support small or young firms or in directing government credit to innovators. Most foreign aid goes toward the government itself or to established incumbents. In both donor and recipient countries aid constituencies are beneficiaries of capital-intensive allocations such as infrastructure or defense contracts. This means that both the poor and the emerging or dynamic sectors of the population rarely benefit from externally provided assistance. Aid goes instead toward supporting incumbent interests, linking the reputation of the donor with the incumbent. No wonder the left has tended to critique aid for being biased toward the status quo.

It is cheaper to co-opt leaders who rule through the disbursement of private goods to small coalitions. Thus, the global powers of both blocs—America, Britain, and France, as well as the Soviets and the Chinese—found it cost-effective to back autocratic leaders who built support for their regimes by selectively distributing aid to ensure that the well-being of an influential few depended on connections to the regime. Since fewer concessions can be made by democratic recipients of aid, the motivations of democratically elected leaders at home are more difficult to align with those of democratically elected leaders overseas. This mismatch underlies the preference of leaders of large winning coalition systems to form alliances abroad with leaders of small winning coalitions. The consequence is an enormous bad governance overhang in client regimes that often can be attributed to a history of external interventions and alliances.[12]

Third world government alliances with the United States differ little from alliances with other donors, but the U.S. footprint is larger. By virtue of the scope and size of its aid programs, the United States attracts more recrimination. This is especially true in the Middle East, where much of the divide between Muslim and non-Muslim communities is over strategies for empowerment.[13]

The Middle East has received more per capita support than other region, yet the U.S. has been less active in governance-related assistance there than in other parts of the world. Outside of the Middle East U.S. assistance programs generally included support for public-sector reforms and results-based management. Despite the high degree of U.S. involvement and support for regimes such as those of Jordan, Egypt, and the Palestinian Authority, essential public-sector reforms have not received priority in U.S. assistance programs.[14] Power, control, and information concentrated in the executive have produced deep structural inefficiencies that interfere with the functioning of administrative services. The gap between administrative performance and people's expectations causes Middle Easterners to "perceive their public institutions as corrupt and oppressive entities that only serve their political masters and try to preserve themselves."[15]

Public-sector employment as a proportion of total employment is higher in the Middle East and North Africa than in other regions. Government administration constitutes more than 10 percent of total employment. Examples of an effective government-business interface cannot be found in the region. Yet the lack of accountability or limits on executive discretion were ignored because donor concerns, primarily security, were more effectively addressed when authority emanated from the executive. Security attained via central control was more important than good governance in building a strong, effective state.

Instead of embracing the idea that Arab leaders must be accountable, the United States extended support to leaders who are estranged from their societies and employ repression and harsh security measures. Leaders expanded government employment as a means to build support among the population, but that strategy weakened civil service discipline and impeded the delivery of public services, resulting in the undermining of policy credibility. Fiscal deficits funded by loans from international lenders, external assistance, or oil enabled sitting regimes to postpone or ignore governance reforms. When, after the cold war, international donor attention shifted to state building, Islamist political organizations were the only alternatives to the extreme centralization of sitting pro-Western regimes. Expressions of civil society discontent ended up passing through a religious filter.

After 2002, President Bush emphasized that the nations of the Middle East needed constitutions, separation of powers, rule of law, and transparency. Yet historically, when anti-Western governments such as Algeria's and Lebanon's were expected to prevail at the polls, the United States and other Western allies undermined democratic processes. By contrast, U.S. aid has helped autocrats in Morocco, Tunisia, Saudi Arabia, Jordan, Uzbekistan, and Pakistan to remain in power, which only lends credence to Islamist anti-Western rhetoric. Military base rights and cheap resources acquired by the West from friendly tyrants overseas continue to create a perception that nourishes extremism and disillusionment among those countries' citizens.

The external assistance that can still make a key difference in securing an autocrat's hold on power would only marginally improve the fortunes of a democratic leader, one who depends on broad-based support. An instructive case can be found in the deeply troubled relationship between the United States and its oldest third world ally. Historically India has been the fourth-largest recipient of U.S. overseas development assistance, but American economic aid has never been sufficient to gain substantial policy concessions from that country.[16] India's elected leaders are beholden to a large winning coalition. If aid were dispersed as private goods to all Indian voters, it could never buy enough influence to make the broad electorate partial to American interests.

While espousing democracy, secularism, the rule of law, and development, U.S. foreign policy makers disseminated far more aid on a per capita basis to Pakistan than to India. And Pakistan's autocratic regimes received more support than was provided to its democratically elected leaders. India's democratically elected leaders, needing support from large electorates at home, would not accommodate America's geopolitical objectives. By the 1980s, the economic and strategic preferences of the Indian electorate drew further away from those being espoused by the United States, and India voted more frequently against the United States in the United Nations than did the Soviet Union. Pakistan, on the other hand, allowed America to extract a large quid pro quo from its leaders in exchange for assistance needed to keep that leadership in power. In effect, foreign aid relieved the incumbent Pakistani regime of having to build institutional mechanisms for gaining the assent of political constituencies outside government. Similar situations occurred with China before 1949, Iran and South Vietnam in the 1960s, and the Philippines in the 1970s. Yet little has been learned from these cold war mishaps. Exports of high-technology weapons and training are being extended to allies in the war on terror even when the recipients fail to meet established criteria for long-term security set by the U.S. Department of State. A long history of aiding autocrats who failed to promote the development of their own countries, while disregarding all democratic processes and values, is one reason that America today finds itself confronting indignant populations across the developing world.

Democratic Narcissism

This book argues that U.S. political ideals—the nation's commitment to democracy and the rule of law—are not the causes of embittered relations with many third world countries. In trying to understand why some of America's worst enemies are found in allied nations such as Saudi Arabia and Egypt, or formerly allied nations like Iran and Iraq, this study finds that the range and depth of antipathy reflect a lack of convergence between U.S. ideals and actions abroad. That lack of convergence is being replicated by deals made with reprehensible regimes that sign up to fight on the U.S. side against terrorist threats.

Between 1972 and 1986 four U.S. administrations essentially collaborated with Ferdinand Marcos in the destruction of Philippine democracy, demonstrating to Filipinos that good government and their own national development were of secondary importance to U.S. security interests. That behavior caused disappointment. Filipinos are clear about their feelings toward the United States. Amina Rasu-Bernardo, a civil society activist, wrote in 2004, "In general, we love the United States. We love the American people, and we love the American way of life. However, Filipinos are also becoming more critical and distinguish the difference between the American people and American policy."[17]

Although the United States was instrumental in Marcos's removal, this did not erase the memory of fourteen years of solid U.S. backing for the dictator. Plus, the image of America offering a safe haven to Marcos, as it had earlier offered to Iran's shah, further inflamed nationalist indignation. In 1991 the Philippine senate ordered America to close its bases on Philippine soil, bases that had become symbols of the era of U.S. complicity in the destruction of Philippine democracy.

The deterioration of U.S.-Philippine relations is only one more example of the gap between reality and ideals in U.S. actions abroad. The problem is that democratic narcissism, what author Richard Kerry has described as the "star-spangled mirror," prevents Americans from seeing themselves as others see them.[18] It is increasingly dangerous for the United States to ignore this gap and the negative impact of U.S. policies overseas. Without a compact that provides obligations and rights to each side, American foreign policy is self-destructive and naïve. Democratic narcissism and self-admiration prevent Americans from seeing the effects of their policies on populations beyond U.S. borders. The continuing influx of foreigners seeking a better life in the United States only reinforces national vanity and assumptions of moral righteousness and cultural exceptionalism. International public diplomacy continues to focus on rhetoric that lauds the ways in which America conforms to democratic ideals, yet it ignores the impact of harmful overseas policies.[19]

The democratic decisionmaking process—the most cherished feature of the American political process—is at the root of the country's poor performance in foreign policy and has extreme consequences for its capacity to sustain global leadership. What gets presidents elected at home, and the effects of their policies overseas, have become the source of hostile relations with many third world populations. If U.S. policies are to change, we must recognize that the interventions overseas and the ideology that sustains them are inseparable from the incentives American leaders face to build viable domestic coalitions to survive in office.

The real danger is this: policies that are democratically constructed at home and produce outcomes injurious to majorities in other nations inevitably create risks to long-term security. America's political leaders must learn to appreciate and manage the risks to long-term security posed by democratic narcissism. As improved relations with India since 2001 demonstrate, anti-American sentiments are not immutable. Strategic coordination is possible once adjustments are made in U.S. policy toward accepting the emergence of alternative power centers. When trust is based on the durability of interdependency, even former antagonists can learn to cooperate.[20]

At her Senate confirmation hearing, Karen Hughes, the nominee for under secretary of state for public affairs, appraised her mission as "helping others understand our policies and values."[21] Such a remark points straight to the problem America faces overseas—the gap in moral perception and the clash between values and action. It is not the message but the action that must be adjusted. The task ahead is to reconcile the democratic practices of America's domestic policies with the democratic aspirations of the world's emerging populations. The challenge for U.S. global leadership is to discover an intellectual basis for foreign engagement that allows future foreign policy to be steered by America's moral compass and that leads a community of nations toward enhanced global citizenship.

Military Interventions and Adverse Effects

It is much less costly to win over small coalitions through payoffs and threats than to gain the allegiance of large overseas majorities. One harmful consequence of this democratic paradox is revealed in the U.S. strategies used to overthrow foreign governments in Nicaragua, Guatemala, Honduras,

Grenada, Panama, Chile, Iran, South Vietnam, and most recently Iraq.[22] However, such interventions to align foreign governments with U.S. policy goals inevitably reproduce all the undesirable consequences of small-coalition rule, especially its most significant determinant: the capture of the state to dispense rewards to coalition members in the form of private goods. Regimes installed by force or violence have little potential to evolve into systems that nurture broad-based participatory governance; such regimes typically reinforce a cycle of instability.[23]

A major power can easily take out a corrupt and uncooperative regime. Inexpensive coups seem initially successful because they offer a cheap and efficient mechanism to bribe a small subset of a poor nation's population to do the bidding of a wealthy external power. For thirty years the U.S. foreign policy community thought that replacing Mossadegh with the shah of Iran in 1953 was a foreign policy success. We now can see that accountable governance is not the logical outcome of such interventions. Accomplishing regime change through inexpensive coups like those that brought Shah Reza Pahlavi to power in Iran and General Thieu to power in South Vietnam also accounts for the long-term inability to transform such regimes into responsive democracies.

Outside assistance allows autocrats to circumvent the need to gain financial support and leverage from their own populations, and in turn makes the United States dependent on unstable individuals and regimes rather than on popular support. Regardless of the ideological, political, or economic reason for overthrowing a foreign government, putting into place a system that ensures durable large-coalition rule is unlikely.

When misguided U.S. interventions fail, a common response is to hold intelligence services responsible for providing inadequate forecasting. But it is not clandestine intelligence collection and counterespionage that fail us. Rather, inadequate models of socioeconomic development, uncorrected, lead to flawed advice. Calls for reorganization of the intelligence services follow when a major foreign initiative collapses, but competent counterespionage is not the solution when unsound models or systems of belief produce mistaken policies. Mistaken policies, of course, are the far more intractable problem, and cannot be overcome by eliminating incompetencies in data mining. An inability to create dynamic models of adaptive social and economic processes results in short-term interventions that diverge from long-term national interests. Remedies are needed that will establish international relations rules, procedures, and institutions that will reverse the tendency for high-income majorities in developed countries to link with high-income minorities in the third world.

Democratic Sources of Policy Failure in International Development

Ironically, when the incentives of political leadership are aligned with large coalitions, as in Western democracies, the commitment to democracy promotion in the third world is undermined. The very exclusivity of autocratic regime constituents makes them targets for alliance building by wealthy democracies. Enriching a handful of influential families is the best and easiest way to ensure the political loyalty of such governments. This regularity of third world politics is generally not the result of U.S. machinations. But U.S. policymakers have learned to manipulate local politics to keep autocratic regimes in power and be assured of dependable allies when America needs favors such as military bases, UN votes, or scarce natural resources. Ensnaring foreign elites in a web of entitlements that secure their loyalty and dependency is a proven way to gain the policy concessions that Americans covet.

This manipulation of third world political vulnerabilities comes at a price. Accommodating odious regimes

—causes economic conditions to deteriorate, increasing the dependency on external assistance and making the country more prone to crisis,

—reduces the accountability of leaders to their own citizens,

—leaves U.S. overseas assistance with few channels to reach broad segments of recipient populations, forcing it instead to be disseminated as consumption to regime supporters,

—creates a legacy of resentment and bitterness, making it likely that reformist leaders will be compelled to prove themselves through anti-American postures,

—allows autocratic partners to dictate their interests to the United States, playing on U.S. national security fears,

—discredits both the United States and its economic model, because America's uncritical belief in the efficacy of private markets makes us party to the entrenchment of corrupt regimes and their cronies, and

—reinforces the powers that established oligarchs can exercise over weak institutions of emerging economies.

These outcomes occur because democratic idealism blinds us to a very inconvenient reality: the private incentives of democratically elected U.S. politicians align with the private incentives of autocrats overseas. The results are alliances that sustain small, winning-coalition systems facilitated by the assistance that America gives to their police and armed forces. Another misconception follows: the democratic values we espouse raise hopes among third world populations that our actions offset. We mistakenly assume that, as the world's greatest advocate of democracy, America is also the most convincing example of the system's success. However, democratically elected leaders in the United States have weak political incentives to align themselves with democratic reform movements overseas. The democracy we preach arouses aspirations and attracts immigrants and visitors, but those same individuals become our sternest critics. Having learned to admire U.S. values, they end up deploring U.S. policies toward their own countries.

3 The Dangers of Triumphalism

We are "fit" only as long as the network exists in its current form. We tend to see fitness as something absolute, perhaps because we view the present period of stasis as permanent, with a preferential status.
—Per Bak, *How Nature Works: The Science of Self-Organized Criticality* (1996)

When "triumphalism" fosters complacency, it goes too far. It obscures the fact that victories, more often than not, carry within themselves the seeds of their own undoing.
—John Lewis Gaddis, *Strategies of Containment: A Critical Appraisal of American National Security Policy during the Cold War* (2005)

According to U.S. triumphalism, American resolve turned the tide of international Communism, brought down the Berlin Wall, and propelled the United States into its role as the world's sole superpower. This belief appeals to collective pride and suggests a reassuring message for policy specialists and proselytizers in both parties. On the right, triumphalists maintain that U.S. military strength won the arms race and accelerated the fall of the Soviet Union, which brought an end to the cold war. Donald Rumsfeld, Dick Cheney, and Paul Wolfowitz, triumphalists all, opposed détente and the presumption of peaceful coexistence. Triumphalists on the left, meanwhile, hold that American ideals won ascendance for the West. "We defeated Communism ideologically," said General Wesley Clark, who ran in the 2004 Democratic presidential primaries. John Kerry, who eventually won the party's nomination, often made the case that America won the cold war not with armaments, but on the strength of its values.

Both parties seriously misread history. Both equate the demise of Communism with the fall of the Soviet Union. And both overlook the devastating consequences of that fifty-year conflict between the U.S. and the USSR. Having partitioned the cold war world into hostile blocs, the United States suffered impaired relations with postcolonial developing countries and ignored governance failures in seemingly loyal states that had served as bulwarks against Communist expansion. If triumphalists are to take credit for the fall of the Soviet Union, they must also accept responsibility for the enduring casualties of the conflict—corruption and inequality in regimes that enjoyed Western support, and radicalism that has spread and deepened over successive generations of repression.

In fact, the U.S. installation and support of pro-capitalist dictatorships frequently created more problems than were solved.[1] It was U.S. backing of Cuba's Fulgencio Batista, after all, that nourished the grievances that eventually brought Fidel Castro to power. The emergence of the Sandinistas in Nicaragua can be attributed to the U.S. support that Anastasio Somoza enjoyed, despite his hideous record of abuse and mismanagement. Were it not for the cold war logic that led the West to arm Saddam Hussein, it would not have been necessary to go to war against him twice. From Panama to Pakistan, the United States has been forced to react, with sanctions or soldiers, against regimes it once considered useful and compliant. And where America intervened to prevent populist candidates from taking power, or subverted those already in office (in Indonesia, Chile, Guatemala, the Dominican Republic, and Nicaragua), it incurred the wrath of citizens who saw their hopes for self-governance clipped by the world's greatest democracy. The negative legacy of past behavior is thus often behind negative interpretations of current intentions.

Falling Victim to Success

The members of the foreign policy team that President Bush selected and that produced the U.S. response to September 11 all had their views shaped by prior service to Republican administrations in which they served the Pentagon.[2] These "cold warriors"—Donald Rumsfeld, Dick Cheney, Paul Wolfowitz, John Bolton, Richard Armitage, and Colin Powell—came to their thinking not by doctrine, but through experience and the lessons they took from three watershed events: the U.S. defeat in Vietnam, the destruction of the Berlin Wall and subsequent demise of the Soviet Union, and the collapse of Iraqi forces in the first Gulf War. Their viewpoints and the way they framed foreign policy follow triumphalist cold war lines: without continued superior military strength, America will lose its ability to influence world events in a way that serves its interests.

Colin Powell and Richard Armitage served in Vietnam and accepted Colonel Harry G. Summers's acclaimed assessment that U.S. military forces failed because the war was conducted without tangible and obtainable political goals.³ "Many of my generation, the career captains, majors, and lieutenant colonels seasoned in that war," wrote Powell in his memoir, "vowed that when our turn came to call the shots, we would not quietly acquiesce in halfhearted warfare for half-baked reasons that the American people could not understand or support."⁴ But America's political goals in Vietnam were, in fact, substantive—the establishment of a democratic, capitalist South Vietnam allied with the United States in the battle against Communism. And these goals were accepted by the public, at least initially. The goals ultimately proved unrealistic, given the inadequate assessment of military intervention necessary to defeat a nationalist struggle. But to insist that Vietnam was lost because of a failure of purpose presumes that America can succeed at any foreign policy goal it sets, as long as it is willing to stay the course.

The tearing down of the Berlin Wall, the dissolution of the Soviet Union, and the stunning success of the first Gulf War offered a more positive reading of the same lesson: make the armed forces popular, advance democracy, and overwhelm the enemy with military strength. Thus, the Bush administration has maintained a cold war preoccupation with the stability of client regimes such as Pakistan and Saudi Arabia. It has focused on forging alliances, preventing military threats (by making efforts to influence APEC and ASEAN to prioritize the global battle against terrorism), and emphasizing military security over economic and developmental objectives. To this end, the administration is unwilling to acknowledge that American military dominance may be a source of apprehension for other countries, and therefore may be a strength that undermines America's security.

The cold war model of foreign policy also disregards some of the most important forces shaping the world today: the institutional transformation of Europe, the economic rise of the East Asian tigers including China, and the emergence of India from the slumber of state control. And that model underestimates the most important threats facing America, which are the "great uncertainties and dangers from regions outside its empire, not of the traditional military and economic sort, but rather of the kind that comes from incredible poverty, social disorders, disease, and extremely weak governments."⁵ Add to this the proliferation of nuclear weapons; the breakdown of intellectual property rights; illicit trade in drugs, arms, and human beings; environmental degradation and global warming; and the risk of pandemics. None of these dangers has a military solution. None requires increased military strength. Each demands sound and effective connections with institutions in developing countries. Fighting emerging pandemics, for example, requires the ability to cultivate international alliances, transparent reporting systems, and a permanent professional public health corps in emerging nations. The fight against terrorism similarly entails capacity building in developing nations that are likely to be the bases of terrorist groups.

Yet the foreign policy triumphalists' seductive logic, which creates revisionist illusions about the cold war, produces inappropriate doctrines for dealing with current security threats. Perhaps unaware of its triumphalist bias, which derives from a belief that heightened virtue accounts for America's ascendancy, the Bush administration has already subjected the nation to a number of dangers. These include a weakened ability to assess the morality of America's actions overseas, a diminished motivation for seeking innovative solutions to foreign policy dilemmas, a blindness to the virtues of others, and an unrealistic sense of the inevitability of triumph in conflict. But triumphalism's greatest danger by far is that colossal self-confidence dictates that the use of force can, in the last resort, compensate for any failure in judgment or for any unseen contingency.

On October 6, 2005, President Bush offered a comprehensive foreign policy formulation of his administration. In a speech at the National Endowment for Democracy the president explained the war on terror using phrases rife with cold war echoes. The enemy is not a country with particular interests, he noted, but a "global campaign of fear," a universal ideology. "In many ways this fight resembles the struggle against Communism in the last century. Like the ideology of Communism, Islamic radicalism is elitist, led by a self-appointed vanguard that presumes to speak for the Islamic masses. Like the ideology of Communism, our new enemy pursues totalitarian aims," he said. "Its leaders," he warned, "have endless ambitions of imperial domination, and they wish to make everyone powerless except themselves. Like the ideology of Communism, our new enemy is dismissive of free peoples, claiming that men and women who live in liberty are weak and decadent."[6]

Such rhetorical strategy speaks to the fears of the American public, as does the president's frequent invocation of good against evil when describing the war on terror. The declared war and the language used to frame it are also pretexts to revise and even obliterate history. Those same charges of endless ambition and a self-appointed vanguard dismissive of free peoples have been made against the United States for its support of dictators in the same Islamic world—in Morocco, Egypt, Saudi Arabia, Uzbekistan, and Pakistan. Both Iran and Iraq were once recipients of U.S. arms, training, and funding. The U.S.-backed anti-Communist jihad in Afghanistan became the training ground for much of the subsequent terrorist activity in the Islamic world today.

The president's speech failed to distinguish external influence from indigenous politics. "These operatives," he said, referring to al Qaeda, "fighting on separate battlefields, share a similar ideology and vision of our world." It was enough that "these extremists want to end American and Western influence in the broader Middle East because we stand for democracy and peace." He made no effort to explore the local factors that foster violent uprisings and breed terrorists, nor did he promote solutions specific to local problems, many of which have gone without remedy for decades. The president's speechwriters overlook that terrorism is not an enemy but a tactic, and that anti-Americanism is not a rejection of American ideals but of American policies.

America will fight back, Bush declared, with a "global campaign of freedom," adding that "we will not tire or rest until the war on terror is won." But can Bush lead the world to freedom if the world will not accept his leadership? Can America lead the people of Egypt, Saudi Arabia, Jordan, or Morocco to democracy when those populations hold America responsible for the tyrants and regimes that deny their civil and personal rights?[7]

The president used another tactic in which his administration has become practiced—rationalizing action ex post facto. "We must recognize Iraq as the central front in our war on terror," he said in October 2005, even though before the U.S. invasion Iraq had few, if any, known links to al Qaeda or to radical Islam. Under Saddam Hussein, Iraq was neither a religious battlefield nor a place where terrorists stood much chance of gaining access. If Iraq is the front line now, then why not Iran and Syria and a dozen other places where terrorists are active? In chapter 8 we will encounter the same explanations that justified the U.S. intervention in Vietnam.

The president, as well as triumphalists in both the Democratic and Republican parties, continues to make assumptions about jihadist intentions without adequately assessing their capabilities. In his same 2005 speech, Bush declared,

> We're facing a radical ideology with inalterable objectives: to enslave whole nations and intimidate the world . . . and no concession, bribe, or act of appeasement would change or limit their plans for murder. The militants believe that controlling one country will rally the Muslim masses, enabling them to overthrow all moderate governments in the region and establish a radical Islamic empire that spans Spain to Indonesia. With greater economic and military and political power, the terrorists would be able to advance their stated agenda: to develop weapons of mass destruction, to destroy Israel, to intimidate Europe, to assault the American people, and to blackmail our government into isolation.

To reach these ends the terrorists would require the loyalty and support of large numbers of people, plus the ability to govern, to mobilize armies, to

promote trade and investment, and to collect taxes. To do all this the terrorists would have to form a government, at which point they would cease being
terrorists.

Terrorists do have the potential to capture existing state structures, and
this is the great uncertainty facing the Middle East, where most moderate
factions have been eliminated.[8] Kenneth M. Pollack explains that during the
Iranian revolution the virtual absence of moderate, secular organizations
eventually facilitated Khomeini's grip on power. "The mosque was one of the
few places in Iran where people felt they could speak their minds and 'breathe
freely.' . . . And since the shah had prohibited political parties and otherwise
emasculated the secular political opposition, all that remained were the
mosques and the mullahs."[9] It was left to "the seminary students and the
clergy themselves [who] established a nationwide network to try to commu-
nicate their message to the Iranian people, which in time became a network
to mobilize their followers to spread their ideas." As Gary Sick points out,
American hopes to counterbalance the radical Islamic forces represented by
Khomeini were foiled because there was no longer any independent power
base.[10] What was left was too weak to mobilize against Khomeini's organized
followers and the mosque. Likewise in Iraq, the only organized groups that
survived Saddam's crushing of civil society were the Islamists.

The Hamas victory in the January 26, 2006, Palestinian parliamentary
elections illustrates again the damage to civil society caused by decades of
political repression. For years the United States and Israel tolerated Yasir
Arafat, believing he could constrain Hamas and other extremist groups. In
reality, he suppressed all opposition to his rule; the military wing of his Fatah
party assassinated many moderate Palestinians. At the same time he patronized Hamas to strengthen his position with the West, suggesting that Hamas
would be a much worse alternative to Fatah rule. Coddled by the United
States, Arafat made it impossible for democratic alternatives to his rule to
solidify, and he enabled political and financial corruption to proliferate.
Given a chance to voice their disgust with the status quo, Palestinians finally
rejected Fatah after years of misrule. But the damage to Palestinian civil society that was created by Arafat's strategy, which both the U.S. and Israel
embraced, will take years to undo.

What Triumphalism Gets Wrong

The debate over whether we won the cold war through our actions has
become a major subfield within the study of international relations. Even if it

could ever be confirmed that military confrontation with Soviet forces in Europe was brought to a successful conclusion by massive infusions of allied resources and will power, the question of why the Soviet Union failed to keep up with Western resources has many dimensions. Furthermore, even if we could confirm that military confrontation in Europe resulted in a successful outcome, extending the cold war outside of Europe is an entirely different question. The success of the latter enterprise is much more difficult to confirm, as we will see in Part II of this book.

In contrast to triumphalism, modern economics views internal contradictions that prevented adaptation to postindustrial information technology as a contributor to the Soviet Union's demise. This view refocuses the question of why Soviet spending and technology fell further and further behind the technological capacity of Western arms. Looking back to the early days of containment, even George Kennan, its architect, argued in 1947 that "Soviet power bears with it the seeds of its own decay."[11] The Soviet capability in military command-and-control activities was not matched by an economy that manufactured products that its own people wanted.

Communism improved productivity of activities in which the roles of individual units were easily described and codified, as in the manufacturing of a single product through a set of repetitive activities. Its principle of central control could not adapt to the diversity of tasks required by a new information environment in the global economy. Specifying individual roles over long periods of time, Communism directed armies of workers toward the completion of simple tasks. But once the global market began to demand products with complex specifications and manufacturing sequences that were not amenable to a simple assembly line, Communist control systems became redundant. A hollow economy caused the Soviet bloc to collapse.

The Western corporation's hierarchical control models also failed to deal with the increasingly complex demands of the new global marketplace for goods and services. Modern information-driven economies both facilitate and require independent actions of many individuals. Hierarchical control systems of the past were not designed to deal with the increasing specialization in the sources of information or with the broader democratic access to that information. Accordingly, many of the hierarchical firms that dominated U.S. industry during industrialization's first century also failed, as corporate America experienced comprehensive reorganization on a firm-by-firm basis, just as the Soviet Union did on a systemwide basis. A breakdown occurred in the Soviet Union because the firm was the entire political system. Even though increasing global interdependence of the global economic system caused the decline of Communism as a system of production, as an expression of human aspirations for equity the values of the Communist system continue to be present in the emergent world order.

The triumphalist view also disregards Soviet accomplishments in its misreading of many crucial facts about the cold war. This disregard has prevented U.S. policymakers from understanding that many of the aspirations that shape today's world are the same as those that led people to seek solace in Communism's message. Triumphalism prevented U.S. policymakers from realizing that the goal of Chinese Communism and that of U.S. development policy was to liberate productivity and innovation from traditional cultures. The Soviets intervened in Afghanistan to bolster a modernizing socialist regime against the growth of Islamism that threatened to destroy it. The United States defined its interests in opposition to both efforts without realizing the deep affinity its own policies had with the core beliefs of international socialism. Both the Soviets and the Americans were convinced that the very concept of modernity based on rational action sprang from their own historical experiences. In hindsight we can see that Communism, which took its institutionalized structure from components available within the Soviet Union and later in China, was a local manifestation of a critical global process. That process continues today, assuming new forms now that Communism is gone.

Soviet Communism had many geopolitical, social, and human successes, and its collapse created a new set of social problems. It is true that Soviet citizens were denied political and civil rights such as participating in antigovernment demonstrations or exercising press freedom. Unlike citizens in traditional autocratic regimes, however, Soviet citizens enjoyed a reliable social safety net: they had significant access to public goods such as public transportation; housing; free primary, secondary, and higher education; and health care. They had leisure to pursue state-supported arts and sports. Soviet socialist regimes were generally successful at promoting social goals such as gender equality in education and in the workplace. These regimes therefore must be distinguished from autocracies in South America, Burma, Egypt, and Pakistan, where human resource development poses a threat to the regime. The Soviet state emerged as a vehicle to bring about Russia's industrialization, providing it with legitimacy and making its behavior more predictable than that of other autocracies, in which theft by the leadership was a regime's only legacy.[12]

In both post–cold war Russia and China, the market economy diminished the status of women in the workplace; and in both, access to primary education and health care also declined. The Soviet legacy explains why the people of Kazakhstan, Kyrgyzstan, and Uzbekistan still enjoy the highest literacy rates, evenly distributed between men and women, among all Muslim countries.

Just as triumphalism disregards the Soviets' values and accomplishments, it trivializes the accomplishments of China's transition to a market-based economy. China's poverty reduction accounts for most of the global poverty reduction in the last twenty years. Triumphalists ignore this accomplishment, as well as the spread of primary health care and education and the affirmation of gender equality in a country that traditionally has had very little regard for these kinds of social programs and services. Viewing democratic capitalism as the goal of history, triumphalists can see only one dimension of China's dynamism and strength. In keeping with this line of reasoning, they insist that China's most important step since 2001 has been the inclusion of the business elite into the ruling party. Yet Bruce Dickson's 2003 study of the recruitment of business leaders into Communist Party ranks demonstrates that the recent emergence of entrepreneurs has not created a force independent of the state. Entrepreneurs in China are dependent partners of the state and are unlikely to act as an independent opposition force.[13] Third world business elites are often nationalists first and free traders only when options for privileged access are closed.

With the need to satisfy a party that comprises more than 70 million Chinese, Communist Party leadership invested in building human capital, allowing the population to participate in many of the industries that thrive in the global economy. The major failure of triumphalists' conceptions of China lies in ignoring that nation's accomplishments prior to liberalization.[14] Before liberalization Beijing eliminated preexisting social imbalances, putting into place foundations that allowed people to benefit from market reforms. For example, female literacy went from 20 to 40 percent between 1950 and 1970, whereas in India female literacy was just 22 percent in 1971 and only reached China's 1970 levels in 1991. By 2004 male and female literacy levels were roughly equivalent in China (about 95 and 86.5 percent, respectively). "Basic education ensured wide participation in the benefits of a market economy, and eradicating illiteracy helped promote market opportunities. What good is a machine worker who cannot read the instructions to make it run?"[15] Today 44.2 percent of Indians live below the poverty line, while only 18.5 percent of Chinese are at that level. The literacy rate of adult females in India stands at only 34 percent, whereas this number is 68 percent in China. Chinese adolescents report even higher literary rates, with 97 percent for males and 92 percent for females.[16]

Social polarization explains why market reforms yield social unrest instead of growth in many Latin American countries. How can liberalization be a unifying ideology when one segment of the population cannot satisfy its own basic needs? By correcting some of these imbalances prior to opening its market, China did not have to face major conflicts of class and ethnic tensions that can result when some groups experience larger benefits than others.

Learning from the Cold War

The inability of U.S. forces to make progress in Iraq will eventually highlight the need for an intellectual revolution in how Americans perceive our own security in the twenty-first century. We must first accept that the heft of the world's economy will shift increasingly to former third world nations. Then we must acknowledge how a psychology of triumphalism steers current foreign policy to dubious conclusions. That psychology has a corrosive effect by rationalizing policies that are inconsistent with our values. It leads us to inadequately assess our own experience and to disregard how different our situation is from that of the world's poor, emerging nations. The narratives that shape our views of recent global history are rarely shared by others. For example, the bipartisan consensus that interprets the decline of Communism as a validation of America's culture, thereby projecting cold war triumphalism on the war on terror, actually marginalizes support for U.S. market and political models.[17]

When the cold war began, third world contributions to world GDP were negligible and its contribution to the well-being of America as a marketplace for U.S. goods and services was generally insignificant. Today, expanded third world economic significance has considerable impact on the well-being of Americans, and the developing world's relationship to U.S. security has likewise changed. The cooperation of the third world is now crucial to solving the major challenges to future U.S. welfare.

As such, the cold war must be avoided as a model for future actions. Triumphalism allows the United States to exaggerate the nation's virtues and to overlook its abuses. It creates the feeling of omnipotence that deludes Americans into believing that U.S. foreign policy success rests solely on political will and support for the president. If this country is unwilling to acknowledge its part in why others feel indignation, the tensions between America and other countries will only be exacerbated.

It is unrealistic to think that America's ability to shape the world according to its interests or ideals is limited only by its own resolve. Believing that the wrath of others cannot harm us is dangerous. Contrary to what the triumphalist right believes, the United States was not responsible for the fall of Communism. Contrary to what the extreme left believes, the United States is not responsible for all the unfortunate outcomes in the third world. The cold war model not only misreads the past, it leads to poor policy planning.

Many of the inappropriate international policies with which the Bush administration's war on terror will be identified stem from the choice of the wrong metaphors, beginning with the administration's modeling of the post-cold war security environment on the cold war. The belief that U.S. resolve defeated Communism in the last century and, God willing, will help defeat jihadism, deeply oversimplifies a complex environment that is shaped by the interactions with other agents in the system. Another blindness is a failure to see U.S. power as part of an interlocking, ever-changing, nonlinear network that requires constant co-adaptation. We cannot optimize our security based on notions of duality between the U.S. and the rest of the world. In biology, when one gene of a species is altered, other species in the same ecology are affected. The frog's fitness depends on its own genetic code and that of the fly. When the frog's tongue becomes stickier, the fly's legs become more flexible. The limits of American power come not only from the skills of the U.S. population and the effectiveness of its domestic institutions. Many interacting agents determine the limits of U.S. power. The strategies of our adversaries co-evolve with our own plans. Covering the globe with U.S. bases influences the plans, strategies, and preferences of our adversaries, coloring their response and sometimes making terrorism their only perceived option.

4 | *Incompatible Missions*
and Unsuitable Organizations

The major foreign policies must be made by the man charged with the
responsibility in the Constitution, the President. He rarely came to his task
trained in foreign affairs, nor did his personal entourage. What he needed
was communicable wisdom, not mere conclusions, however soundly based
in experience or intuition, what the man in the street called "educated
hunches." I saw my duty as gathering all the wisdom available and
communicating it amid considerable competition.
                                    —Dean Acheson, *Present at the Creation:*
                                    My Years at the State Department (1969)

Perhaps the most costly miscalculation in American foreign policy is
a failure to appreciate how the private interests of politicians affect their
choice of public policies. One body of literature in economics known as *pub-*
lic choice teaches that foreign policy serves the same electoral objectives for an
incumbent administration as does domestic policy. Public choice allows us to
view the president as the first customer and principal consumer of foreign
policy, and to apply the same utilitarian calculations that we apply to consumer behavior. By linking the chief executive's private interests with his
choice of public policies, we gain a useful perspective on the political constraints that shape U.S. foreign policy. The insights gained may even help illu-
minate the sources of the most expensive miscalculations in American foreign policy.

Keeping the First Customer Happy

The president is the decisive actor in the formation of American foreign policy. He sets the tone and the agenda, and takes the lead on strategy. He is also
the only political actor whose electoral fortunes depend on his foreign policy successes. Yet a president's previous experience rarely equips him with

expertise in foreign affairs, and the Constitution confers little power for executive action in that sphere. The president has more responsibility than authority.

Presidents are further hindered because they are served by institutions that have made cold war–era military and security imperatives the basis for U.S. foreign policy toward developing nations. This bias has often eclipsed the longer-term issues of social and political change that are essential for national security. The government departments that determine foreign policy priorities and the structure of foreign aid can trace their status, norms, and relative standing to geopolitical imperatives that these agencies were designed to handle during the cold war. After five decades they have cultivated a following both in Congress and with policy-aware elites such as arms manufacturers, importers of natural resources, expatriate members of deposed regimes, and evangelist religious sects. These elites, as partners in crafting foreign policy, are often the recipients of hidden subsidies and preferences that their partnerships with these agencies bestow. The influence of foreign policy elites is rarely subjected to public scrutiny, and therefore does not affect electoral politics except in very general terms. They surface only in cases of high domestic policy salience, particularly when U.S. blood has been shed or when a news topic such as Israeli-Palestinian relations, constantly in the news, is discussed. The sprawling network of overseas connections and bases maintained through these channels is rarely subjected to electoral accountability.[1] Presidential effectiveness is made still less probable by institutions, agencies, and advisers whose overlapping and poorly defined responsibilities cannot separate domestic and foreign concerns. Turf wars between the Department of State and the National Security Council and between the CIA and the FBI, for example, are well documented.

Efforts to reorganize those institutions carry few political benefits to the president, whose constituency for foreign policy has traditionally been so weak that such efforts generally fail. Jimmy Carter tried and failed, and Richard Nixon just circumvented regular channels. Legislatures, bureaucrats, and the armed services, meanwhile, have their own constituencies whose self-interests may not be served by restructure and reform and who may work to prevent change. It took several decades, in fact, to reform the Joint Chiefs of Staff as an efficient central command structure for the armed services. Restructuring occurred within the intelligence services only after the tragedy of September 11, 2001. The U.S. Agency for International Development (USAID) has long resisted reorganization, as has the State Department, despite numerous studies that agree on the urgency of reform.

Gaining congressional approval for agency restructuring, even within the executive branch, can prove difficult. Jimmy Carter noted that Lyndon Johnson, one of the most effective congressional arm twisters, "was never successful at getting more than one-third of his proposed reorganization plans through Congress." Carter lamented, "If you win this argument over the legislation, you still won't have anything to show for it."[2] If they are to succeed, attempts to measure the success of our policies through systematic program evaluation must grapple with the origin of agency biases. If proper identification and attribution of motives and practices are not taken into account, we will be disappointed in expecting our government to accomplish tasks it is not capable of accomplishing.

Foreign Aid That Does Not Work

Americans are not against assisting overseas, but the same dollars can always find their way to more salient domestic use. The formulation and implementation of U.S. overseas assistance is constrained by institutions that do not separate domestic and foreign policy effectively.

Individual members of Congress use aid to serve the interests of their electoral constituency, for whom aid is an instrument to be used to bargain for unrelated domestic priorities. Every dollar in the U.S. budget is subject to competition and is fungible, so that, for example, congressional committees see paying United Nations dues as interchangeable with tax relief or prescription drug reform.

Former President Bill Clinton is reported to have remarked that there is virtually no congressional district in which a candidate can gain votes by saying, "We live in an interdependent world; we have to make it more integrated. I want to see us pay our fair share to the United Nations . . . They won't get any benefits for doing it."[3]

After 9/11, President Bush tried to impose unity of purpose in intelligence gathering, the lack of which had been revealed as a national security weakness. Yet overseas development assistance, despite an equally poor track record, remains without a unified internal organizational structure and is subject to disagreements among competing branches of government over its shape and function. Worse, its procedures are poorly designed to enhance the well-being of aid recipients, and the failure of foreign aid to attain its stated purposes has serious consequences for the effective conduct of foreign policy. Aid that only strengthens the political and economic hegemony of autocratic elites produces a legacy of deep resentment in resident populations and destroys confidence in the integrity of American assistance efforts.

Competing government departments and agencies that distribute foreign aid are overseen by diverse congressional committees. Oversight of overseas development strategy is dispersed through a labyrinth of independent and often competing government departments and agencies. The chief administrator for USAID reports to the secretary of state. Farm surpluses fall under the purview of the Department of Agriculture. Overseas food aid is managed by the Senate Foreign Relations Committee, the House Agriculture Committee, and the House Foreign Affairs Committee. Foreign military assistance is subject to Defense Department oversight. The Commerce Department coordinates foreign aid with trade issues and private investments. The Treasury Department oversees the funding of international financial institutions. The House Banking Committee considers multilateral aid programs in consultation with the Senate Foreign Relations Committee. Final authority for the approval and allocation of economic aid resides with the House and Senate Appropriations Committees, which first receive recommendations from their respective foreign operations subcommittees.[4] The maze of overlapping jurisdictions is memorialized in the 1961 Foreign Assistance Act, which established more than 2,000 pages of political strings that manipulate both the setting of objectives and the evaluation of outcomes. The White House Peace, Prosperity, and Democracy Act of 1994, which called for repealing the 1961 Foreign Assistance Act and centralizing U.S. aid oversight, never made it out of committee.

A second problem lies in the lack of firewalls to keep foreign aid funds from being targeted by powerful domestic interests. The same dollars are politically more valuable to incumbent politicians if they are used to satisfy the agendas of domestic constituents. Procedures subject overseas assistance to acrimonious domestic policy debates such as whether abstinence is the cure for global AIDS epidemic, or how to allocate funds for population and gender issues, or whether there should be tariffs on fish or enforcement of quotas on textiles. Such domestic policy concerns intrude into the disbursement and management of foreign aid, and ultimately interfere with the goals of that aid.[5]

Because the institution most directly responsible for managing foreign aid, the State Department, relentlessly blocks efforts to subject aid to any kind of performance evaluation criteria, assessments are left to legislators in the House and Senate, and to a public that is increasingly skeptical about foreign aid's overall effectiveness. Liberals have argued that support of economic assistance must be rationalized in terms of recipient well-being. However, they have been unable to show a systematic linkage between aid and development or to demonstrate that the level of development assistance creates major differences in inter-country economic growth.[6] (As a result, there is only limited domestic political support for recipient-oriented programming, which deprives America of a basic tool needed to forge cooperative relationships with developing countries.)

Conservatives, on the other hand, insist on justifying overseas aid in terms of U.S. economic or strategic interests, but they, similarly, have been unable to show direct linkage to enhanced security. Vernon Ruttan's comprehensive study of U.S. assistance concludes, "The power of the American government to act in the national interest is so influenced by parochial interests and by cycles in popular sentiment that the capacity to pursue longer-term national interests lies effectively outside the competence of those charged with the shaping and execution of foreign policy."[7] Such opposing political perspectives preclude the resolution of differences between "short-term donor strategic objectives" and the needs of "longer-term recipient political development."[8] Although Ruttan correctly identifies the domestic issues that affect foreign policy, he suggests the existence of some American national interest other than what a broad sample of Americans want, a notion that disregards the essentially political origins of foreign policy discussed in chapter 2.

The authority to determine the size and content of the bilateral economic support fund, relative to the development assistance budget, allows the State Department to eclipse the USAID's leadership, preventing the agency from piloting the nation's foreign assistance program. A 1994 report, *Strategy for Sustainable Development,* submitted to Congress by USAID to address the problem of leadership, was rejected by Senate appropriations committees that preferred to commit most of the aid budget to "earmarked" programs of special interest to specific legislators and to strategically important recipients. Such constantly shifting aid programs signal to recipients that their welfare is secondary to donor objectives. For example, to mollify America's sense of humiliation after the Iranian hostage crisis, Ronald Reagan tied overseas aid to policy compliance, which aroused resentment in recipient populations. The short-term gain in domestic public support was won at the expense of compromised diplomatic credibility. Aid that misses its target produces neither security nor development.

Many critics have argued for a cabinet-level department with the exclusive mandate for international development to rationalize the dissemination of aid and ensure accountability for the desired impact. Again, the State Department has generally sided with those who would coordinate aid with security priorities. Thus, foreign aid, despite its poor track record, remains without a coherent structure and is subject to disagreements among competing branches of government over its shape and function.[9] Sweeping institutional changes are necessary to eliminate overlapping jurisdictions by congressional subcommittees.

Linking Foreign Aid with National Security

U.S. aid flows rarely correspond to needs, as revealed by human development indicators.[10] Instead, the primary recipients of assistance are determined by their strategic importance, even if this means reinforcing small, winning coalitions.[11] Within those countries the smaller the winning circle, the easier it is to obscure the hand of a donor and keep information hidden about the distribution of benefits from foreign collaboration. As a result, foreign assistance has not gone where it performs best in reducing poverty, and those most in need rarely are the recipients of aid.

Aid flows have been shown historically to fall short of benefiting the poorest segments of the global population, as William Easterly has passionately argued.[12] Even more disturbing is that the poorest segments within recipient countries such as Pakistan or the Philippines, to name but a few, rarely benefit. When public officials and bureaucrats are corrupted by incumbent leaders who represent a narrow social or ethnic class, they have no incentive to provide the populace with education, clean water, primary sanitation, and adequate calories. An unfortunate match occurs. Projects such as airports, dams, armaments, and power stations, which engender large kickbacks to regime loyalists and fiscal deficits among recipient nations, are consistent with the political incentives of U.S. politicians as well.[13] American politicians appear successful at home when they can trumpet concessions obtained overseas. Such concessions are less likely from nations seeking loans for educational and health facilities for the downtrodden. And even if the president succeeds in successfully eliminating poverty in a client regime, the reward is unlikely to be policy concessions that the U.S. electorate is seeking.

When a recipient society at large benefits, no single agent exists with whom the United States can barter for policy concessions. It is easier to allow a few dozen families to control the economy and government, even if they overlook deficits, avoid fiscal austerity, and deprive the poorest citizens of health, education, and social services. This is why our alliances in the Third World frequently leave behind bitter legacies of poverty, violence, and pollution, even in those countries where significant GDP growth can be measured, such as Iran, Indonesia, and Pakistan. Today the global deficit of good governance—often the residual effect of foreign policy during and after the cold war—-is a warehouse of grievances that destabilizes international relations.

Incompatible Institutions

The strength of the State Department lies in its network of ambassadors and career foreign service officers, who are recruited through a rigorous exam process. Nevertheless, every president since John Kennedy has depended on the National Security Council, rather than on the State Department to attune foreign policy to domestic politics. Coming to a consensus with the State Department would improve the implementation of a president's foreign policy agenda, since the National Security Council has no apparatus to carry out its programs overseas. Moreover, NSC personnel are not career officers; NSC recruitment occurs through presidential fiat. Every new administration selects NSC members according to its political and ideological predilections. NSC advisers know that the president will pay for their foreign policy failures at the polls, ensuring that foreign policy issues of high salience to the public will be politically managed. Congress exercises very limited oversight of the NSC. Even during the height of the Watergate and Iran-Contra hearings, Congress was able to wrest very little intelligence from NSC staff.

> McGeorge Bundy [JFK's NSC director] and his successors have clearly seen themselves as the president's men; they have engaged in policy debates, offered policy advice, and managed the NSC process in ways that serve the particular political interests of the president and no one else. Beginning with the Kennedy administration, all national security advisers have had offices in the White House, close to the Oval Office. All have enjoyed frequent informal contact with the chief executive. And all have played a central role in designing and articulating the administration's foreign policy.[14]

In 1956 the State Department played the dominant role in advising President Dwight Eisenhower on the Suez crisis, but by the October War of 1973 the State Department was out of the picture. The shift toward the National Security Council occurred during the Kennedy administration, largely to facilitate White House activism in foreign affairs. The NSC enables the president to tighten his political grip on the management of foreign policy, to rough-ride over bureaucratic opposition within the State Department, and to connect foreign policy decisions to electoral outcomes.

Problems that arise due to the marginalization of the State Department are well documented. A stunning breakdown occurred during the final days of the shah of Iran (see chapter 9). Kissinger has concluded that:

I have become convinced that a President should make the Secretary of State his principal adviser and use the national security adviser primarily as a senior administrator and coordinator to make certain that each significant point of view is heard. If the security adviser becomes active in the development and articulation of policy, he must inevitably diminish the Secretary of State and reduce his effectiveness. Foreign governments are confused and, equally dangerous, given opportunity to play one part of the government against the other; the State Department becomes demoralized and retreats into parochialism.[15]

Whenever a new administration comes to Washington, hopes are revived for a restoration of the State Department's authority that was pilfered by the previous administration. Every major bipartisan study has recommended moving policy decisionmaking authority back to the Department of State so that its expertise can play a more decisive role in policymaking. However, under the pressures of day-to-day decisionmaking, the management of national security eventually reverts to the NSC. As Rosati and Twing conclude:

Regardless of how decentralized and open a policy process that presidents may initially prefer, the historical record since World War II suggests that within a short time presidents quickly come to rely on a small number of advisers who tend to be part of the White House staff and agencies within the executive office, such as the National Security Council. This occurs because of time constraints, increasing familiarity between the president and his advisers, and questions of trust and loyalty. Therefore, it is not surprising that presidential management of foreign policy tends to revolve around a White House-centered system that becomes more centralized and closed over time, for it is most responsive to presidents, and their policy agendas and personal styles.[16]

The president always faces the risk of becoming a prisoner of his own beliefs and of his narrow circle of advisers.

An Absence of Jointness among the Chiefs

Until it underwent major restructuring in 1986 the Joint Chiefs of Staff, created like the NSC by the National Security Act of 1947, were considered unimaginative, unhelpful, and obstreperous. In times of urgency, the Joint Chiefs lacked coherent strategy and were hampered by interservice rivalries and poor communication. Flawed since inception, the JCS were perhaps the most criticized component of the president's foreign policy arsenal. In contrast to the NSC, the Joint Chiefs did not offer effective presidential control over the behavior of its members.

Although the JCS were established as a way to curtail the administrative autonomy of the Army, Navy, and Air Force, they did not receive primary budgetary authority. JCS members rarely thought in joint terms owing to an inherent conflict of interest between their roles as joint chiefs and loyalty to their services. This permitted parochial concerns to prevail. Appointees to the JCS viewed their tenure as an opportunity to better serve their home service rather than to advise the president independently. Eventually, presidents tried to strengthen civilian control of the armed services by shifting more responsibility to the secretary of defense or by inviting military brass to join the NSC. But these presidents were unable to sidestep the JCS.

The wastefulness caused by insufficient integration was especially evident during the war in Vietnam, when the three services spent time and money in disputes among themselves over jurisdictions and power. An array of fiefdoms within the armed forces prevented ambitious generals from interfering with civilian control, but also made finding a political solution to war virtually unattainable. The divided services were unable to offer a coherent alternative strategy for victory, and none of the services was able to demonstrate a connection between its activities and a larger strategic outcome. The White House feared that if the services were unified, adventurous military operations might have been more difficult to control. But the result was a counterproductive rivalry. Procurement was tailored for each service. The planning, execution, and evaluation of wartime activities were carried out by each service independently, resulting in divided and redundant efforts and an absence of economies of scale.

The 1986 Goldwater-Nichols Act completely reorganized the military command structure. It modified the deficiency of central organization and bolstered the power of the JCS chairman, who acquired responsibility for strategic plans, military contingency plans, and budgets. The law established a vice chairmanship that was empowered to promote staff over objections from the parent service. It also centralized the chain of command from the president through the secretary of defense to unified combat commanders. The unified combat commanders gained enhanced autonomy over their units, thereby loosening the services' grip on field commands.

The forty years of stagnation that preceded these reforms exemplify how innovations in organization have a low probability of success, despite the imperatives of national security.

The Central Intelligence Agency

If any agency of the U.S. government can be described as out of control, it would be the Central Intelligence Agency, created in 1947. For starters, it is not central at all, but actually two agencies operating in isolation from each other. Two distinct activities—special operations, and research and analysis—were placed under the same roof. The CIA's mandate was never distinguished from that of the intelligence activities of the three armed services, or from that of the State Department. Prior to post–September 11 reorganization, each had its own intelligence service and none had oversight over rival bodies. Each was barred from investigating the integrity of information from the other agencies. The CIA director was the titular head of the fourteen other intelligence agencies, but lacked oversight of their budgets or personnel. In effect, no one was in charge of the intelligence community.

Throughout the cold war the CIA enjoyed a more influential role in the U.S. government than did any intelligence service in any other world government. The CIA had its own channels of dialogue with many foreign leaders. Its budget was at least 60 to 65 percent higher than the State Department's, with personnel strength of 15,000 in Washington and several thousand overseas. The agency was criticized for employing more analysts and operatives than it could monitor. A budget that was only partly audited gave the CIA great flexibility and many means to gain approval for projects, so that it could evade formal controls. Its secrecy and flexible budget made meaningful oversight impossible. No continuing outside review process of overseas intelligence staff existed. The CIA's mission became vague and difficult to define. It took the tragedy of the Sept. 11 attacks and the flawed diagnosis of Iraq's weapons of mass destruction before these failures were finally addressed through wholesale institutional reform that tried to coordinate what had become shapeless and redundant.

Reform Failures

Compared to domestic policy issues, national security issues enjoy weaker interest group support.[17] As we have seen, domestic interest groups are too loosely connected to effectively influence national security, which is guarded by barriers of extreme secrecy erected by tightly connected bureaucracies.

Although the president can find domestic support for his espousal of principles and policies to govern multilateral organizations, the unity of domestic interest groups weakens on questions of general national security, and these groups are not able to exercise much impact on the general outline of foreign policy or the institutions that shape it. Registered groups that do organize effectively, such as expatriate Iranians who harbor illusions of restoring the Pahlavi monarchy, are concerned with gaining resources for their pet foreign policy issues. Similarly, advocates for Cuba, Israel, and Taiwan are extremely well organized. Yet even when they succeed in gaining congressional backing for their demands, they do not contribute to more effective representation of third world interests. As Jürgen Ruland observes:

> Representatives and senators normally respond only to issues that help them in their reelection bids, that is, issues that generate publicity or have an immediate bearing on the interests of their constituents and their campaign financiers. Given the limited interests of the American public in foreign policy and in regions where no or only marginal American interests are at stake, Third World affairs normally attract only limited attention in Congress.[18]

Only a small constituency exists for discussion of general foreign policy. The important battles to shape the broad contours of security policy are waged within the government itself, but the consequences can have a direct impact on the electoral fortunes of an incumbent administration. The consequences for American foreign policymaking are a highly politicized set of policies influenced by the themes of domestic politics, in tune with domestic electoral cycles with short-term focus.

The Need for a New Institutional Environment

The overlapping and poorly defined responsibilities of the foreign policy bureaucracy frequently result in incoherence, as when the State Department in 1969 and 1970 launched peace plans for the Middle East that the White House did not endorse, or when the State Department opposed the tilt to Pakistan advocated by the White House during the Bangladesh crisis of 1971. Stanley Hoffman comments, "Nixon and Kissinger, exasperated by the bureaucrats' lack of imagination, frequent resistance, and propensity to leaks, reserved more and more control over key issues to themselves, but this only compounded the problem, since the execution of policies had to be largely entrusted to departments that had not been consulted or even informed."[19]

Decisions are not carried out effectively without engaging the initiatives of the career civil services. Building a policy consensus across the foreign services is a task that presidents frequently wish they could dispense with during times of emergency, only to regret this neglect when they need the services to carry out the daily drudgery of implementing policy.

Although foreign policy is an activity that takes place outside U.S. territory, its legitimacy primarily depends on whether it is valued within the overall context of domestic politics. Adjusting his foreign policy message to his domestic audience, the president is likely to be misconstrued abroad. When his message is adjusted for the ears of an overseas public, it is likely to be rejected at home. Rarely are international and domestic opinions shaped by the same forces and guided by the same ideas or interests. Presidents who lose support for their foreign policy are likely to see the consequences at the polls; accordingly, few are willing to compromise domestic popularity to garner international support for their programs. Each party since the cold war has suffered electoral setbacks attributable to public dissatisfaction with its foreign policy. Foreigners who assume that the presidency wields great power are baffled by the difficulty presidents actually have in gaining optimal and coordinated support for their policies.

U.S. voters are accustomed to the radical rejection and wholesale review of an incumbent's foreign policy by an incoming administration. But despite the presumptions of a wholesale shakeup, the basic assumptions that have guided American foreign policy since the end of World War II resist the complex changes around the globe. Where is the innovation that characterizes so many other realms of democratic politics? Why, after sixty years, does the presidency, regardless of who occupies it, resort to the same rhetorical devices in the conduct of foreign affairs? Because the president has inadequate authority or control over the foreign policy apparatus, he often turns to the public—his constituency—and employs "declaratory history" or "declaratory principles of persuasion," as happened after Truman's so-called "loss of China," when cold war rhetoric became the most effective way to gain public support at home. In fact, perhaps the greatest privilege of the office is the power to shape the nation's sense of historical memory. But cold war rhetoric and "declaratory history" left few opportunities to address developing countries on their own terms. Likewise, contemporary cold war rhetoric results in oversimplified and irrelevant responses and in overseas hostility. This is one reason why, despite all the power of the presidency and all the energy that presidential candidates expend convincing the public that they will avoid the mistakes of their predecessors, their promise of transformation rarely survives a single term. With the influence of the bureaucracy and private interests difficult to surmount, the president has to speak as if what is done is in the general interest. Reliance on past cold war anti-Communist rhetoric and today on post–cold war antiterrorism rhetoric is a tool for the chief executive to satisfy the broad mass of voters.

No one has exploited this tool more purposefully for enhancing executive power for partisan purposes than George W. Bush. The war against terror was central to the president's strategy to recruit Republican candidates and mobilize support during the 2002 and 2004 electoral campaigns. The primacy of national security made the presidency the pivot of government action, so that the congressional campaign of 2002 became a celebration of presidential leadership. The White House urged congressional candidates to run on the war. Thus the president transformed the salience of international threats into loyalty, facilitating an enormous increase in executive power. The 2002 Republican landslide in Congress was a great victory for the presidency itself. However, the landslide linked future electoral outcomes to the president's approval ratings, which caused the Republican candidates to lose much of what they had gained in 2006 from their prior loyalty. By escalating the rhetoric about the menace of global terrorism, the president was able to gain significant partisan advantage while reducing the limits on presidential action.

Social Bifurcation and Ultimatum Bargaining: The Vision Gap in U.S. Reconstruction Efforts

The most common and durable source of factions has been the various and unequal distribution of property. Those who hold and those who are without property have ever formed distinct interests in society.
—James Madison, *Federalist* No. 10 (1787)

American presidents are compelled to tailor their appeals to the electorate in a language that draws from domestic experience. Unfortunately, the domestic models and belief systems on which U.S. foreign policy are based diverge from the experience of developing nations. Worse, U.S. models and assumptions have created a gap between American conceptions and the imperatives of social change faced by third world populations. U.S. policies end up appearing simplistic, misdirected, and hypocritical, generating deep aversion instead of trust among potential partners.

To understand how the most salient foreign policy issues are defined, we must first understand America's historical imagination and the public beliefs that shape it. The president must create broad consensus among citizens yet still cater to elites and interest groups—Congress, federal departments and agencies—for foreign policy support. Richard Melanson has written:

Presidents and their foreign policy advisers try to provide interpretive images of the international situation that are compatible with domestic experience to justify the necessity, urgency, and character of their actions. Legitimation establishes the broad purposes of policy by translating its objectives into an understandable and compelling reflection of the domestic society's dominant norms. As such it represents a political act within the context of national politics and characteristically relies on politically potent symbols to link foreign policy and these internal norms.[1]

Drawing on America's legacy, U.S. politicians use cultural and historical models of social progress and political processes that are familiar to Americans but rarely are comparable to the experiences of third world peoples. The relationship between U.S. social institutions and economic development is unrecognizable to most developing nation populations. Even ideas that Americans take for granted, like the primacy of property rights, assume different political meanings in other historical and social settings. As a result, efforts to harmonize foreign policy goals with beliefs endorsed by the U.S. public are frequently at cross-purposes with the imperatives faced by third world governments.

State Building in Europe and the Third World

Gradual industrialization in the United States has endowed policy planners with models that reflect poorly the full context of economic change in the developing world. For example, America never had to achieve a political-social transition at the same time that it transformed its industrial structure.[2] Even America's revolution and break from Britain are often represented, in both contemporary and historical accounts, as expressions of continuity rather than a wrenching break with the past.[3] In America the institutions of the capitalist marketplace emerged in tandem with the institutions of democratic politics. Such co-evolution is not universal.

A common standard of civic ethics or shared moral standards to facilitate arm's-length market transactions is unrealistic in regions where, for instance, states were organized around artificial national borders drawn by colonialists,[4] or where social organization is derived mostly from interactions with the same people in a small group.[5] The identities of third world populations are frequently independent of formal institutions. South Vietnam had no social contract—a large body of laws or social institutions—that applied to groups sharing a standard of civic ethics. This is one reason that America's most expensive effort at state building failed. John D. Montgomery, one of the most perceptive early analysts of U.S. foreign aid in Vietnam, explained in 1962:

> American values such as efficiency, responsibility, and professionalism
> have dominated all efforts to improve foreign aid procedures, although
> they are values which are at times irrelevant or even run counter to
> those of most traditional societies. "Efficiency," a Western and especially
> American value, calls for the abandonment of many taboos and social
> traditions, including forms of favoritism that are essential to the family

and elite systems of most of the underdeveloped world; "responsibility" implies a delegation of authority and specialization of function that are impossible in much of the world; "professionalism" requires forms of training, the development of a career service, and the introduction of standards that few nonindustrial nations can support.[6]

By the early 1950s U.S. policy planners assumed that the Marshall Plan in Europe (1945–49) offered the format for successful policy transformations worldwide. But unlike the Marshall Plan in Europe and the rebuilding of Japan (1945–52), U.S. policies in pre-Communist China, the Philippines, South Vietnam, Iran, and Pakistan, to name a few, were set back by corruption and favoritism.[7] The protocol of a modern bureaucracy was established in Germany and Japan before World War II. The ambitious scope for U.S. foreign policy defined by the Marshall Plan assumed preconditions that could not be extended to nation building in third world countries.

By the latter half of the twentieth century, European countries had already undertaken the cultural, social, and political reforms necessary to carry out industrial processes. Formal institutions to facilitate cooperation and trust had replaced informal institutions as the glue of the social order. The agrarian family system as a model for social production was disrupted. Champions of reform seeking their own constituencies on which to stake claims to authority were already well organized. With the administrative infrastructure of a modern state already in place, the U.S. occupation of both Germany and Japan was able to effect economic reconstruction by using the apparatus of public administration, which had survived the war. U.S. policy specialists were therefore able to manage the Marshall Plan by using institutional capacity that is absent in developing countries, where bureaucratic norms clash with vested interests and local traditions. Where the preconditions for bureaucratic social organization have not previously been established, an extensive program of reconstruction such as the Marshal Plan will conflict with existing concepts of status, class, and identity. This important difference between Europe and the third world is one of the reasons that America's efforts in state building have generally ended unsuccessfully.

Industrialization and the Social Origins of Bureaucracy

Bureaucratic norms of social organizational had overtaken rural hierarchies in all of the countries—Great Britain, France, Germany, and Japan—in which the United States can claim success for its reconstruction efforts. A critical issue in the reconstruction of nonindustrial regions is to understand how the adherence to bureaucratic definitions of legitimacy matured. How do we relate bureaucratic universalism as a global outcome to the adaptive behavior of myriad individuals? Where did the behavior come from and why is there similarity across all successful industrial nations? How does the process of bureaucratization interact with other social and economic pressures? What signs indicate that the process is under way? Is it a slow change marked by the "long lapse of ages," as in Darwin's view of evolution, or is it a consequence of a rapid mass transition?

The systematic emergence of bureaucratic responsibilities and authority was a key component of state building that began even before industrialization in seventeenth-century Western Europe.[8] The notion that officials would be rewarded on the basis of fixed salaries that were graded by rank, and that individuals had to separate their private from their public responsibilities, redefined authority and therefore social relations. The transformation away from household authority systems first took hold in the organizations of the state—the exchequer, the courts, and finally the army. For example, English kings turned the management of the exchequer over to financial professionals.[9] The French kings dispatched *intendants* to the provinces to supplant the authority of traditional noble families. The process of eroding traditional seigneurial authority that was started by the French kings ended with the French Revolution in 1789. The revolution ended the legal protection of patriarchal authority. It replaced forever the great feudal provinces such as Burgundy with departments that were of uniform size and were governed by identical protocol. Napoleon's army became a template for a new form of social organization in which competence trumped birth. As this bureaucratic format spread to the workplace, it facilitated and legitimized the vast centralization of power, enabling industrialized societies to assemble unrivaled power in the hands of the state. But such centralization is only possible once the criterion of bureaucratic universalism has emerged as a societywide norm.

Bureaucratic universalism as a legitimating norm seems to be a key outcome related to the emergence of the factory system. The rules of conduct that define how people interact changed as a result of technological transitions such as subordination of fixed agriculture by factory employment. The bureaucratized workplace was the product of new rules in which rationality and legality combined to ensure that individual employees received equal treatment. Positions were defined in terms of relevant skills and experience. Positions belonged to the organization and were not for personal use. Personal relations were subordinated to a universalistic standard—matching a person's ability with a job description. Work standards were explicitly specified and recorded. Rules that served the interests of the organization bound managers and employees, and each side could hold the other to the terms of the employment contract.[10] Thus, industrial manufacturing transformed the organizational rationality of society at three levels: the structure and function of organizations were altered, individual effort was rewarded on a meritocratic basis, and individual rights were protected by rules that ensured a separation of the interests of the person from those of the organization. Several generations of factory-floor experience provide a framework of social leveling and mobilization that can sustain new systems of authority. By the early twentieth century complex U.S. organizations were to some degree bureaucracies.

Economies throughout the developing world comprise organizations in which a redefinition of traditional authority according to a universal criterion of organizational efficiency has not occurred. The simple erection of look-alike institutions will not prevent officials from running an organization as an extension of their households, where familiarity and loyalty rather than competence are the criteria for exercising power. When traditional and bureaucratic norms meet, as in India or Pakistan, a hybrid structure emerges. Rather than following the principle of bureaucratic efficiency, specific groups end up using public resources to promote their own interests.[11] In Pakistan interpersonal distrust within government is so great that leaders are unable to obtain the information required to make proper decisions.[12] Until the requirements of bureaucratic rule setting are met, officials can pursue unofficial over official goals and can even use the power vested in new institutions to prevent the goals of the institution from being met.

Preindustrial societies coordinate complex tasks without reference to the same universalistic equity norms that are essential to both factory production and transparent governance. The persistence in developing countries of the status quo, including entrenched patron-client networks, limits prospects for change. The structural lacunae most harmful to development overseas are not missing market laws such as property rights or missing political institutions such as elections. The most harmful gaps are inadequate social complexity and engineering to support those institutions once erected. Social complexity depends on self-organizing processes that are not easily transplanted or imposed by outsiders.

The Challenge of Social Asymmetry

The fear of fostering revolutions in strategically important third world countries inspires amnesia about America's own past. America's founders expressed concern that heterogeneity caused by inequality might make society ungovernable. Throughout American history, enormous civic, symbolic, and cultural resources have been invested to overcome the risks of social polarization caused by heterogeneity of interests and identities.

Likewise, the need to establish social legitimacy for new political institutions has been off the cognitive map of the U.S. public for a long time. This makes Americans insensitive to the vacuum of ideological, moral, or ethical coherence that new leaders must fill in the third world. After the Truman administration, sustained support for social change in third world client countries was virtually unavailable. The United States blinded itself to the asymmetry in wealth and power, putting its faith in private-sector trade and in transplanting Western institutions to third world environments.[13] But asymmetrical social reciprocity supported by the patron-client model can be an insurmountable obstacle to the functioning of formal institutions. Where deeply entrenched traditional and hereditary inequality is prevalent, new institutions are likely to succumb to preexisting social inequality. Adam Przeworski demonstrates that poor countries, in which inequality and asymmetry are the norm, cannot sustain democracy.[14] Owen Harries further points out that when a society is divided by extremes of wealth, both the haves and the have-nots will have few qualms about resorting to violence. It then becomes difficult for a third, moderate force to find stable support from either segment; such a force will be tugged to one extreme.[15] Power asymmetries ultimately cause a breakdown in the norms of voluntary exchange. When one group loses too much too often, the political and economic system will destabilize, as has been the case in Latin America, the Philippines, and in prerevolutionary China and Iran.[16]

People often adapt to polarized social conditions through clientelism. Reciprocal relationships between two entities that differ greatly in size, wealth, and power arise because weaker individuals typically need and seek patronage to obtain assistance and protection against adversity. The purpose of clientelism is to create personal obligation and to ensure loyalty in exchange for providing private goods such as jobs in state-owned industries or subsidies for private producers. The purpose is not to develop social overhead or to encourage investments that build social welfare.

Politicians who engage in clientelism prefer to offer their constituents tangible rather than intangible rewards, personalized favors, factional rather than public goods or national economic policies.[17] Such politicians discourage independent organizations such as charities, credit unions, or advocacy organizations that act in the name of public policy. Not surprisingly, the result in such countries is a short supply of roads, public transportation, general health, and education. The incentive in patronage systems is for politicians to manipulate control over public budgets in order to fix the gutters along the streets of particular voters only. Clientelism politics generates bloated and inefficient public sectors in which business profit is a direct consequence of government concessions rather than the outcome of good management skills. The pursuit of political protection diverts investment away from competitive business models. If regime cronies can outbid their more efficient rivals and drive them out of the market, capital will take flight to more congenial markets. Property rights are often altered when a regime changes hands. The result is usually macroeconomic instability, as government budgetary problems are transformed into public-sector deficits.

The bosses, meanwhile, need weaker allies in order to obtain goods and services below market prices and to ensure political support in elections or maintain local political dominance. Clientelism is hardly limited to the third world. In New York's nineteenth-century Tammany Hall, for example, the bosses were proxy social welfare workers, using patronage to protect their supporters from calamity and indigence. In actuality, they robbed the poor of future opportunities.

The effects of clientelism on public policy cut across political institutions without regard to distinctions between autocratic and democratic regimes. When formal institutions are superseded by personal exchanges between patrons and clients, the government capacity to implement its policy objectives is weakened and the formal organizational structure of government is circumvented.

Clientelism is a pattern that persists microscopically and macroscopically, operating in the international system, within a country, a party, a family, or a personal entourage. Consider relationships in which the United States is patron. In such cases the typical client is a regime leader or an elite group, easily defined and courted. Clientelism usually includes the following client perks: selective benefits and special treatment, sweetheart access to silent partnerships with large U.S. investors that are seeking to open operations in the client country, easy access to long-term U.S. visa and educational opportunities at elite U.S universities, support for security services that keep elites in power, and assistance in eliminating regime opponents. In return, the United States seeks special access to resources, protection of its investments by the host country security service (especially investments in mineral resources, mines, or pipelines), and support for U.S. geopolitical objectives through permission to host troops and through UN votes that back U.S. initiatives. Just as in the case of domestic clientelism, the key to the relationship is loyalty in exchange for private benefits to select groups. In a relationship of codependency, even groups that cannot survive in power without U.S. assistance end up being able to manipulate the United States to their own advantage.

Arrangements that focus on collective benefits for the client population at large do not yield such a direct quid pro quo (see chapter 10 discussion of Pakistan and India). As a result, the typical client is most often a small country or a small winning coalition within a larger nation. The smaller the winning coalition, the easier it is for the United States to gain the policy concessions it seeks. But the United States in turn becomes dependent on regimes that are unstable and that require increasing inputs of U.S. resources to ward off domestic challenges.

Economic Change and Social Bifurcation

Economic history makes great leaps with epochal innovations in technology that often change a society's social organization. The dramatic discontinuity caused by today's technology innovation is much greater than that of the West's Industrial Revolution, when growth rates rarely surpassed 2 percent. A globalizing world is not getting flatter. The bifurcation caused by today's high-speed growth augments the inequality between and within countries. South Korea has accomplished in forty years what took the United States a century; China's transformation is still more rapid than that of South Korea. The speed of these changes, Paul Collier has noted, leads to dramatic increases in the growth gap between the bottom billion and the next billion.[18] The Human Development Report of the United Nations in 2007–08 notes that more than 80 percent of the world's population live in countries where income differentials are widening.[19] Yet conventional conceptions of rapid economic change rarely anticipate the destabilizing and potentially polarizing consequences for social and political structures. In fact, the assumption that economic expansion is the way to manage unrest, promote democracy, and spread prosperity has proved inaccurate.[20] Productivity gains can be destabilizing in the context of prior inequality imposed by colonialism or traditional social hierarchies. John D. Montgomery has written:

> Uneven growth benefiting certain segments of the economy more than others leaves dissatisfaction, and 'misdirected' aid (and most aid may seem misguided to those who themselves do not benefit from it) sometimes arouses more resentment than no aid at all. Economic

development tends to create new economic or bureaucratic elites who may exploit foreign aid to weaken traditional forms of leadership; other dynamic new classes that arise as a result of greater educational and economic opportunity naturally reach out for political power. These new forces are well able to bring about chaos in the course of their struggle to replace existing regimes.[21]

Although penned to describe U.S. support to Diem's coalition of northern Christians in South Vietnam, Montgomery's analysis is applicable to the sources of discontent that caused the regime of the shah of Iran to crack despite record high growth.

What Montgomery is describing is that people feel strongly about payoffs that others receive. They respond to unfair behavior by harming those who treated them unfairly, something commonly observed in "ultimatum bargaining" in the world of analytical game theory.[22] An ultimatum game typically involves three parties. The first player offers a sum to the other two players on the condition that they can reach an agreement on how to split it. The second player will offer terms to divide the sum with the third player. If the third player accepts the offer, both will keep their portions. Both get nothing if the offer is rejected. Economists rarely anticipate that people will incur costs to punish others; they typically assume that people will accept any offer that makes them better off, because getting something is better than getting nothing. The game offers a building block for modeling complex situations like the fall of the shah of Iran and the disintegration of Cambodia, where in both cases growth measured in GDP terms actually preceded social cataclysm. The results of the game do not vary according to culture or participants' relative wealth. The game has been played among rich and poor and among participants of diverse cultures. The game always ends with the same result. If economists were right, participants should always take a payment that makes them better off, even if by only a small amount. Instead, participants accept only relatively equitable divisions. Grossly unequal divisions result in rejection—a form of punishment that prevents both sides from enjoying any possible gain. Traditional economic models assume that people care about what they personally gain or lose. The ultimatum game provides evidence that people care just as much about the result for other people, and that once fairness is violated people punish those who treat them unfairly.

Understanding this behavior is essential for making sense out of the divergent performances of Latin America versus East Asia or China versus South Asia. The size of the social networks in which reciprocity was sustained is a cornerstone of wealth creation. Repeatedly, when there is a one-sided distribution people will defy their own self-interest and forgo potential gain by taking costly actions that express their preference for fairness.

GDP as a metric of development has been criticized for being blind to the social costs incurred during economic transition. GDP does not record losses to social capital, nor does it capture difficulties that arise in the dynamic sequencing of adjustments to change, when gross inequalities of income distribution can arise.[23] Sequencing problems that disrupt traditional livelihoods are not easily measured.[24] Damages to community social capital that are embedded in traditional risk-management regimes do not show up as losses in GDP data. If technological and economic growth fails to produce new jobs, as in the Philippines or Venezuela, the losses may grow before economic winners emerge. In Pakistan and Iran, for example, capital-intensive, large-scale agriculture displaced farm workers before opportunities for absorption into new occupations arose. The effect of new agricultural practices on income distribution was adverse, harming independent family farmers and herders.[25]

Innovations that increase agricultural incomes have inadvertently increased the percentage of poverty-stricken households, as in Nicaragua. There, the Alliance for Progress helped fund agricultural modernization. Large agricultural export enterprises displaced traditional subsistence farmers from their lands, transforming peasants into laborers for coffee- and cotton-growing agribusinesses. Nicaragua's economy grew during the 1960s, but so did its total number of poor. Migration from the fields to the cities depleted social capital while swelling urban centers that grew lawless and could provide neither protection of property rights nor personal security. Similarly, independent traders of Iran's traditional bazaar economy suffered relative deprivation as a result of the shah's push for heavy industrialization. Growth that undermines the social fabric and strains society's institutional and ideological frameworks is likely to be contested. The regimes that served as sponsors of such growth may be the final casualty.

Growth without Ultimate Bargaining: East Asia

The most prosperous developing nations during the cold war made economic doctrine adjust to politically sustainable policies by linking economic growth with equitable distribution and poverty reduction. High-performing South Korea, Taiwan, Singapore, and Japan emphasized policies and institutions that ensured shared growth with dividends accruing to all social strata.[26]

Balancing gains in productivity with concessions to the poor preserved social cohesion and made rapid growth socially sustainable.[27] Democratic institutions require democratic social conditions. This explains why some of the most promising emerging democracies are clustered in East Asia, where conditions for basic human development and broadening social equality occurred before elections were introduced. East Asian leaders who felt the least secure of American support were the most socially innovative. South Korea, Taiwan, Malaysia, and Singapore—all frontline nations in the battle to contain Chinese Communism—built inclusive regimes. Their leaders were nationalists who feared the need to depend on the West for political survival. Taiwan's Chiang Kai-shek adopted inclusive governance only after losing mainland China. In contrast, South Vietnam's leaders failed to build internal resilience to Communism via social justice. Sustainable industrial transitions have occurred primarily in nations where the winners enter into agreement with those who would bear the costs.

Markets are understood by economists to be the best way to ensure that resources are used in activities that make the best economic use of them. At some point in every society, however, social hierarchies that enjoy political favor exercise great influence over market outcomes. The first task in building efficient economies is to shift resource allocation away from hierarchical patron-client networks and toward broad-based decentralized markets that satisfy the welfare of the people participating in them.[28] Policies that disregard the role that clientelism plays in sustaining traditional economic inequality inadvertently perpetuate prior unequal conditions.[29]

Social Mobilization and Economic Discrimination

Economic policies designed to reduce Communism's reach blindly subordinated people to data (about consumption and income). These policies ignored the fact that underdevelopment often had its origins in governing institutions that kept people powerless to influence the most important household decisions. Such policies ignored the dangers of winner-take-all outcomes. Growth that compounded entrenched historic inequality resulted in systemic instability, as occurred in China under Chiang Kai-shek, in Pakistan in the 1960s, in Iran under the shah, and in the Philippines under Marcos. If economic policy is to close the gap between first world rhetoric and third world reality, it must acknowledge the deep consequences of historically constructed inequality. Social discrimination obstructs the efficient use of society's resources and prevents the emergence of bureaucratic universalism. Inattention to the heavy hand of past discrimination diminishes the appeal of U.S. economic models to third world populations.

In third world societies traditions often exist to ensure that individuals of like competence are tagged by class, color, or ethnicity to allow for the allocation of lower compensation to some groups for the same job. Discriminatory tags culturally transmitted from generation to generation form expectations that can persist for long periods, even if they produce large-scale economic inefficiencies.[30] South Asia's caste system persists into the twenty-first century; discrimination in North America and South Africa once required one group to sit in the back of the bus, drink from separate wells, or use separate toilets. Such inequalities although inherently unstable and prone to evolutionary upheaval can survive for long periods of time. The longer the oppression, however, the more likely a regime's legitimacy will implode when the repression is slightly released.[31]

A popular economic theory (the Coase theorem named after Ronald Coase) argues that transaction costs matter because they prevent inefficient distributions of property rights from being corrected by market competition. In developing countries social endowments that bestow status are barriers that prevent society from reaching production frontiers. When such barriers are considerable, they influence the speed by which economic growth reduces poverty. However, economic policy transplanted from more egalitarian industrialized societies often neglects the ubiquity and magnitude of unequal social endowments in developing countries.

Patterns of cultural discrimination arise without colonization or conquest, and make it easy for a divided underclass to be governed by oppressive elites. These patterns are often the reason that victims cannot mobilize to resist outside domination. Deep-seated intergenerational discrimination can prevent the coherent organizations or norms that are needed for large-scale collective action to overcome an invader or oppressive ruling class. America's iconic cold war enemies Joseph Stalin, Mao Zedong, and Ho Chi Minh used one-party states to overcome historic barriers to collective action that were posed by past discrimination. These social revolutionaries had to overcome political rivals that also promised such measures. Mao's rival Chiang Kai-shek, for example, espoused gender equality but was much less effective than Mao was at implementing it. South Vietnam's Diem thought of himself as a nationalist revolutionary, as did Ho Chi Minh, but Diem was far less successful than Ho was at implementing nationalist objectives. Communism has retreated as a system of production. But the quest for a unifying equity norm around which to motivate collective action is a continuing dilemma of development.

This quest seeks new leaders, ideologies, and expressions among the world's emerging nations.

Economic Policy as an Ideological Dark Force

Will the logic of economics be the salvation of foreign policy? Surprisingly, when economic theory and foreign policy converge, the result rarely is propitious. In fact, cold war foreign policies and international economic policies suffer from many of the same deficiencies, including insensitivity to the deep structural features underlying long-term societal and historical change. Both foreign policies and international economic policies artificially separate micro and macro factors and fail to see how micro-level transformations are linked to larger global patterns. Both sets of policies shift the causes of major transitions to exogenous factors. Both fail to see the interconnectedness of downward and upward change cycles, and fail to see the self-transforming dynamics of large social transitions. Both fail to anticipate the barriers that well-organized social discrimination can pose to competition. Both underestimate the link among patronage, asymmetry of power, and illiberal institutions and fail to anticipate the regularity of crises, revolutions, and great transformations that punctuate history.

Economic policy is rarely based on a scientific understanding of dynamic processes such as how and why industrialization happened. It has ignored the conundrums that developing countries commonly confront, such as how complexity is created from the bottom up or why wealth grows in an explosive manner. Absent adequate theories about growth and change, the unrealistic assumptions underlying international economic policy limit its empirical success. Designed to deal with systems in equilibrium, most current economic models will fail to prepare Americans for the abrupt transformation of power relations with emerging developing giants including Brazil, China, and India. Significantly, conventional economic analysis ignores the punishment strategies that arise from the enormous social bifurcations both within emerging nations and between those nations and the industrial giants. The ultimatum bargaining that is triggered by grossly unequal payoffs in the global economy is a reservoir of resentment that threatens our own security.

The narratives that follow explore how U.S. security dilemmas are often failures of economic development. All five of the case studies are examples of failed models of economic development that directly or indirectly put U.S. security at risk.

*Alliance Rents and
the Economic Failure
of Client Regimes*

The United States and China:
The Power of Illusion

with Chunjuan Wei

> The failure of those in authority to implement existing United States policy brought about the downfall of an ally [Chiang Kai-shek] and jeopardized the very security of our nation. We have seen the growth of a Communist enemy where we once had a staunch ally. We have watched Communist imperialism spread its influence throughout the world.
>
> —General Douglas MacArthur, *Reminiscences* (1964)

> After U.S. efforts to mediate a truce between Chiang Kai-shek and the Communists failed in 1947, General Albert Wedemeyer took a different position stressing the need for reform in Chiang's government: "The existing Central Government can win and retain the undivided, enthusiastic support of the bulk of the Chinese people by removing incompetent and/or corrupt people who now occupy many positions of responsibility. . . . The Central Government will have to put into effect immediately drastic and far-reaching political and economic reforms. . . . It should be accepted that military force in itself will not eliminate Communism."
>
> —"China—Names for a General," *Time*, September 15, 1947

> Stillwell could see only one solution. "We ought to get out [of China]— now," he wrote firmly on August 19, [1945].
>
> —Barbara Tuchman, *Stillwell and the American Experience in China* (1970)

To stabilize China, Chiang Kai-shek had two options: eradicate Communism or work with the Communists to build an inclusive modern state. U.S. assistance allowed Chiang to concentrate on the first and ignore the second. Emboldened to think that he could count on unconditional American support to win China's civil war, Chiang had no incentive to form a coalition government. The generous U.S. aid allowed him to neglect land reform and avoid building the tax base that the fiscally weak Chinese state needed. This opened up an opportunity for the Communists to create a fiscal base for their insurgency in the countryside, something Chiang could afford to disregard because of his reliance on U.S. aid. Another critical element for developing a modern Chinese state was a meritocratic army, with promotions based on battle-tested competence. But Chiang promoted people on the basis of personal loyalty and their ability to speak English because he needed officers who could impress the Americans. Mao promoted officers who earned soldiers' trust and respect. These officers' competence was to be revealed when Communist Chinese forces confronted the United States during the Korean War. The ultimate result of U.S. support of Chiang Kai-shek was to give him the means to create a small winning coalition without deep mass roots. Mao took the opposite approach, building strong support among peasants through distributional policies that reduced inequality and minimized the effects of relative deprivation. Thus, in China the United States started a pattern that was to be perpetuated throughout the cold war: supporting dictators sustained by closed state-centered economic systems while preaching democracy and open markets.

America's Options in China

Douglas MacArthur, Albert Wedemeyer, and Joseph Stillwell—the three World War II generals with the greatest influence on U.S. China policy in the 1940s—expressed radically divergent views on the Sino-American relationship and the role for America in China's civil war. MacArthur advocated bolstering Chiang Kai-shek as an ally against global Communist conspirators in Asia. Wedemeyer believed that Chiang should be protected but forced to control the endemic corruption of his officials. Stillwell recommended strict neutrality once defeated Japanese forces left China.[1] Of the three, Stillwell was the most knowledgeable about China—he spoke fluent Chinese, had served as a military attaché at the American Embassy in Nanjing from 1935 to 1939, and was Chiang's chief of staff during most of World War II—yet his views had the least popularity at home. The notion that China should determine its own destiny found limited acceptance in the United States.

The U.S. victory in the Pacific theater launched what Henry Luce called "the American century" in a 1941 essay in *Life* magazine. He believed that Chiang and his wife would be the catalysts for a Christianized, democratic, capitalistic China.[2] When Chiang Kai-shek's Kuomintang (Nationalist Party) fell, many Americans believed that their own government's absence of will had permitted the Chinese Communist victory. Triumphalist visions of history privileged the idea that if only the United States had made greater investments in Chiang, the civil war would have ended as America wanted.

The views of MacArthur and Wedemeyer defined the mainstream and became the only politically feasible positions in U.S. politics throughout the cold war, not only concerning China, but ultimately the third world.

The "China lobby," led by the publisher of *Time* magazine, Henry Luce, tried to "convince Americans that a strong and friendly China under Chiang Kai-shek was essential to their own security . . . [and] that their representatives had failed to support Chiang to the desirable and necessary extent."[3] They "created a misplaced faith in the Nationalist regime as an efficient and reliable instrument of government"[4] and believed that the emergence of "Red China" was the betrayal of America's interests.[5] A national hysteria emerged amid fears of Communist sympathizers undermining American values, and led to dire consequences for loyal Americans who held opposing views.[6]

The political debate focusing on who lost China ignored evidence that the United States had pledged support to a leader who endangered his country's security for his own partisan interests. Hindsight suggests that America's China policy decisions in the 1940s were grounded in a series of illusions about China, Chiang Kai-shek, and Chinese Communism. The most unrealistic were the beliefs that the defeated Chiang could retake the mainland and that the regime he established in Taiwan was the real government of China's 400 million people. A consequence for the U.S. of this foreign policy staple was the enmity of a quarter of the world's population, two of the least successful wars in U.S. history (Korea and Vietnam), and a decade of anti-Communist witch hunts in America.

Illusion 1: With Military and Economic Aid, Chiang Kai-shek Could Reform His Army into an Efficient Force against the Japanese

The U.S. hope that Chiang Kai-shek could transform his Kuomintang troops into an efficient anti-Japanese force was based on the illusion that he had the will to do so. Although China's national interest lay in the defeat of Japan, Chiang had an agenda unknown in the West.

In contrast to his mentor, Sun Yat-sen, whose goal was constructive relations with the Chinese Communists, peasants, and workers in the interests of national unity, Chiang sought subjugation and ultimately destruction of those with whom he had differences. Blinding himself to Japanese military aggression, while Japanese generals were urging the emperor to conquer China, Chiang made plans against his own countrymen: the purge of Communist colleagues and leftists from the Kuomintang was his priority, followed by "punitive" expeditions against northern warlords.[7]

When Japan invaded Manchuria in 1931 and created a vassal state called Manchukuo in March 1932, a faction of Chiang's troops—the Nineteenth

Route Army—defended Shanghai against Japanese invasion. The Communist Jiangxi Soviet Republic responded in April 1932 by declaring war on Japan.[8] Yet Chiang claimed that the country was too weak and too poorly prepared to defend itself. Instead of bracing for a war against external aggressors, the Nanjing government under Chiang proclaimed that "internal security must precede foreign aggression" (*rang wai bi xian an nei*)—a slogan he used to move against Communists and Kuomintang dissidents. In December 1933 Chiang suppressed the Nineteenth Route Army while conducting his annihilation campaigns against Communist rivals. He "fought against them with all the resources at his command—armies, saboteurs, blockhouses, German military advisors, [and] money."[9] His fifth encirclement was so successful that he sent the Communist remnants to a bitter retreat, called the Long March, during which his enemies suffered an 80 percent attrition rate. Chiang signed the He-Umezu Agreement of 1935, recognizing Japanese occupation of Hebei and Chahar, promising to suppress anti-Japanese activities in China.[10] "Don't talk about the Japanese menace now," he declared in a speech to his soldiers in October 1936 during his sixth "bandit annihilation" campaign in Xi'an. "Anybody who speaks of fighting Japan now and not the Communists is not a Chinese soldier. The Japanese are far away. The Communists are right here."[11] Chiang's policies were resented by field officers assigned to suppress the Communists in the northwestern region. These officers kidnapped Chiang and released him on condition that he join forces with the Communists in fighting against Japan. Ironically, the man who indirectly saved Chiang's life was his archenemy, Mao Zedong.[12]

Full-scale war broke out in 1937, when the Japanese invaded Beijing, Shanghai, and Nanjing. Chiang fielded 500,000 troops to defend Shanghai and lost half of them. Nanjing, the capital, was captured and suffered extensive civilian casualties.[13] Yet Japanese advances still did not completely stop the Kuomintang generals from attacking the Communists[14] or prevent them from imposing an economic blockade on Mao's Yan'an border government.[15] Chiang did not declare war on Japan until after America issued its own war declaration in the wake of Pearl Harbor; Mao had done so nearly ten years earlier.

The United States regarded Chiang Kai-shek as an important ally against Japan and provided grants and loans in Lend-Lease supplies to his government with no strings attached. In addition, Roosevelt sent General Stillwell to China as Chiang's chief of staff in February 1942 to strengthen Chiang's army and improve its combat capability against the mutual enemy. Growing deeply frustrated that Chiang's armies were inadequately trained and overstaffed with officers, and that his administration was "a one-party government, supported by a Gestapo [Dai Li's organization] and headed by an unbalanced man with little education,"[16] Stillwell commented in 1943 that to reform such a corrupt system, "it must be torn to pieces."[17] America's support of "this rotten regime" was misguided, he wrote in his journals.[18]

A separate diplomatic mission of the U.S. Army Observation Group, known as "the Dixie Mission,"[19] was dispatched to Yan'an to assess Mao's military capability against Japan, establishing the first official contacts between the Chinese Communist Party (CCP) and the United States. The mission, under Colonel David Barrett, presented a favorable image of the Communists: "The CCP seemed less corrupt, more unified, and more vigorous in its resistance to Japan than the Kuomintang."[20] The colonel's cautious recommendation—to equip the poorly armed Communist forces with some weapons initially and larger amounts once the CCP's efficiency and effectiveness in fighting the Japanese could be assessed—was submitted to Chiang, who responded, "You cannot arm my enemies!"[21] According to Stillwell, Chiang did not want to exhaust his forces against the Japanese; he wanted to reserve their strength in order to attack the Communists when the war ended. Despite Stillwell's warnings that Chiang was hoarding munitions for future civil war rather than for the ongoing war against Japan, Roosevelt (and later Truman) continued to supply armaments to the Kuomintang under the Lend-Lease program.[22]

Human suffering during the war years changed the Chinese people's views about Chiang Kai-shek's leadership. His intolerance of internal division and his weak response to foreign aggression eroded his moral support among the populace. Just four months after Japan's surrender in 1945, U.S. forces allowed the use of Japanese troops to protect lines of communication on behalf of the Kuomintang government.[23] It was humiliating to Chinese eyes to see a quarter of a million Japanese soldiers, commanded by Japanese generals, serving Chiang as policemen against Communists and other guerrillas. Chiang's decision to keep Japanese soldiers for domestic purposes helped him lose the propaganda war against the Communists. His decision was consistent with the famous statement he made to a journalist in 1940 that "the Japanese is the disease of the skin, and the Communist is the disease of the heart."[24]

Illusion 2: Chiang Was Christian and Democratic;
Defending Him Was Defending Democracy

During the 1930s and 1940s American media described Chiang as a Christian and democrat, which captured domestic public affection for him and his

U.S.-educated wife, Soong May-ling. This description gave rise to the illusion that America had a moral imperative to support his regime.[25]

Chiang Kai-shek's two-decade reign on the mainland was characterized by indifference to rural poverty and to China's highly unequal land distribution.[26] He did not introduce any meaningful land redistributive policy or rent reductions to minimize the peasants' plight. Instead, forced conscription and high farm taxes alienated peasants, who constituted 70 percent of the Chinese population. These policies limited his power base to wealthy landlords, industrialists, financiers, and foreign nations with business interests in China. Yet the Chinese dictator was portrayed in America as a great general and his army as loyal soldiers. *Time* noted that "Chiang has not only used a peasant army but he educated it, as he went along, taught it to fight and taught it the elements of democracy."[27] U.S. mainstream media were silent on Chiang's mistreatment of his army, even when the conscripts' desertion rate reached 50 percent during the war.[28]

Chiang was also depicted as a devout Christian in "whose heart is no bitterness and no spirit of unforgiveness."[29] Such accounts overlooked his faithful "claws and teeth," the Blueshirts (*lan-yi she*) who exercised political repression and intellectual intimidation. Radical students and faculty were often searched and arrested in predawn university raids. Chiang's secret police under Dai Li[30] murdered civil rights leaders, newspaper editors, and university professors believed to oppose his leadership,[31] as well as generals who expressed dissatisfaction with his regime's inefficiency, corruption, and cronyism.[32]

When World War II ended, an article in *Time* proclaimed, "The Generalissimo was pledged to establish the social and humanistic democracy envisaged by Sun Yat-sen. He no longer sought unity by the sword."[33] Once order was restored, *Time* predicted, Chiang would rule in an era of peaceful democracy. Yet in 1946, under his orders Dai Li, the head of the secret police, murdered Li Gongpu and Wen Yiduo, two leading members of the Chinese Democratic League who opposed Chiang's domestic policy but disagreed with Communist objectives as well.[34]

The Communists have been rightly criticized for their use of undemocratic methods when they came to power in 1949, but Chiang's government was hardly more tolerant of party rivalry. Much contemporary research points out the similarities between the two camps, as well as the Kuomintang practices that the West had often associated with the Communists. Both parties conducted attacks on traditional values and religion and sought a future free of foreign interventions, and both shared the belief that Tibet and Taiwan belonged to China. Both adopted Leninist models of mass organization, a party-controlled army, censorship, and national education to mold citizen behavior. In fact, when Chiang withdrew to Taiwan he refused to allow multiparty democracy and ruled the island in white (as opposed to red) terror. Joseph Esherick concluded that "Kuomintang rule was as much the precursor of the Chinese Revolution as its political enemy."[35] Evan Luard pointed out that "in essence that contest [between the Kuomintang and the Communists] was a power struggle between factions that were equally authoritarian, equally nationalistic, and in the final resort, equally antipathetic to much that the West represented."[36]

Illusion 3: A Unified China under Chiang Was Destined to be Pro-American, While Mao Was a Russian Puppet

The United States long enjoyed the illusion that a unified China under Chiang would have been a loyal ally, contributing to U.S. security. But a strong and unified China under Chiang might have hesitated to cooperate with the United States. In his *Myth of Independence*, Zulfikar Bhutto noted that Chiang took an interest in India's independence and discussed with Nehru "the affinities between the ancient Indian and Chinese civilizations and outlined a plan for a federation embracing India, China, Persia, and other smaller countries, with the object of maintaining their independence and contributing to world peace."[37] Instead of becoming an active instrument in the cold war, Chiang might have proclaimed China's neutrality and aspired to lead the third world nonalignment movement.

It was equally a mistake to assume that China under Mao Zedong would have become a Russian puppet. Believing that they did not understand his peasant revolution, Mao did not trust the prescriptions of Soviet representatives in China. When Chiang was captured in Xi'an, Mao shrugged off Stalin's instructions to release the generalissimo unconditionally. Stalin did not have faith in the Communists and thought their victory in the civil war was "fake."[38]

In fact, Moscow recognized that the Communist Party, rather than Chiang, embodied the potential for modernizing China and its people, but. fearing a strong, independent China on its southern border, Russia was often reluctant to support the Communists. On August 14, 1945, for example, Moscow signed a treaty of friendship and alliance with Chiang's government and urged the Communists to defer to the Kuomintang. Mao's biographer, Ross Terrill, reports Stalin as saying that "we considered that the development of the uprising in China had no prospects," and that "the Chinese comrades should seek a *modus vivendi* with Chiang Kai-shek [and] that they should join the Chiang Kai-shek government and dissolve their army."[39] Even when the Communists were about to win the civil war, in 1949, the Soviet ambassador ignored the fact that half of China was under Communist control, but retained diplomatic recognition of Chiang's government from Nanjing to Guangdong, even while the United States briefly hesitated to do so.[40]

In addition, Soviet ambitions conflicted with Chinese interests. Financially strapped, at Yalta in 1945 Moscow managed to obtain a secret accommodation with the United States. The agreement granted the Soviets special administrative and military rights that were enjoyed by the defeated Japanese and that trampled on Chinese sovereignty. While in control of Manchuria, the Soviets systematically dismantled the entire Manchurian industrial plant (estimated to be worth $2 billion) along with the steel from the rail lines, and shipped it back to the Soviet Union.[41] As Hans Morgenthau and Kenneth Thompson have correctly pointed out:

> While Chinese Communism is the ideological vassal of Moscow, its rise to power within China owes little to the Soviet Union, nor will it need to rely upon Russian support to maintain itself in power. This fundamental difference between Chinese Communism and the Communist parties of Eastern Europe, which would never have come to power and could not stay in power without Russian military help, allows the Communist government of China a freedom of action in international affairs which the Communist governments of Eastern Europe entirely lack.[42]

The Russian objective of controlling this southern neighbor ran counter to China's dream for more than a century of resuming great-power status. In fact, Mao Zedong's most meaningful accomplishment was his successful transformation of the nationalist ambitions of the humiliated Chinese— beleaguered by civil unrest, military defeats, and foreign occupation—into a state that could mobilize the resources of the entire nation and that would be an equal of the superpowers. The China that met U.S. forces in Korea had a highly trained and efficiently organized modern army, something Chiang never accomplished during his mainland rule. Too weak to stand up for its own interests, Chiang's China was a friend that could neither protect itself nor be of much help to the United States. Communism, on the other hand, gave the nation a unified government free from foreign domination for the first time since the Opium War of 1840.[43]

Chinese nationalists remember with pride that at one time their civilization surpassed that of most of the world in the arts and sciences. Through

Communism, China traveled further toward statehood, international citizenship, and respect among nations than it had in its recent history of mixed regimes. For this reason Mao remains the father of modern China, in spite of his many flawed, disastrous economic and social policies.[44]

Illusion 4: A Marshall Plan Could Have Saved China from Communism

Unwilling to accept the Kuomintang defeat on the mainland during the Chinese Civil War, Chiang's U.S. allies argued for a Chinese Marshall Plan to temper the appeal of Communism. But Chiang had never built the administrative apparatus to meet the needs of the majority of the Chinese people.[45]

A 1946 report on UN relief aid published in *Time* foreshadowed how successful a Marshall Plan would have been had it ever happened:

> In Hunan and Kwangsi, China's sadly famed domains of hunger, 16 million people last week were suffering from what UNRRA [United Nations Relief and Rehabilitation Administration] experts termed "sudden and acute starvations." In Washington, D.C., UNRRA Chief Fiorello H. LaGuardia, with a sudden and acute stroke of his bristling pen, halted all but emergency shipments to China. . . . On the face of it, that did not make sense. But behind the tragic discrepancy of the two stern facts loomed an old, notorious situation; since November 1945, UNRRA had poured $132,250,000 worth of food, machinery and various relief supplies, from fishing boats to water buffaloes, into the country. But only a trickle had got where they were needed most. The bulk of the supplies piled up in warehouses, filtered down into the depths of the black market, and enriched the morass of government corruption and "squeeze" (China's term for "honest graft"). . . . The task of getting the supplies from the ports where UNRRA delivered them to the starving interior was up to China's own CNRRA (Chinese National Relief & Rehabilitation Administration). But CNRRA was paralyzed, not only by transportation shortages but also by towering inefficiency, "squeeze," and partisanship. Samples: in Kwangsi Province, thirteen junks loaded with medical supplies for Mme. Sun Yat-sen's "Peace Hospital," inside the Communist lines, were diverted to the Nationalists. Flour supplied free by UNRRA was being sold far above the average Chinese means. UNRRA Ford trucks were selling at $3,750 (gold).[46]

China's considerable economic growth during the half-century preceding World War II failed to reach millions of poor people, according to the economic historian Thomas Rawski, and its management created the perception of unfair access to influence.[47] Government patronage put China's economy under the control of a group of businessmen who depended on licenses to convert public resources into personal fortunes. From this perspective, Chiang's economic policies fit the description of "predatory capitalism" coined by the Communists, rather than the decentralized market capitalism idealized by his American apologists.

Chiang's monetary policies during and after the war did not promote the interests and well-being of private entrepreneurs, and explain why many middle-class groups ultimately turned against him. In order to finance the war against the Communists and the Japanese, he placed strict regulations on Chinese currency. He also arranged for the state to monopolize the banking sector, crowding out private financial institutions and forcing the closure of 80 percent of Shanghai's banks.[48] Chiang appointed his relatives and cronies as directors of the surviving institutions to enforce regime policies and allocate bank funds to political loyalists. His brother-in-law T. V. Soong was made premier and foreign minister, second in power only to Chiang himself.[49] In the wake of the war Chiang named himself chairman, and Soong vice chairman, of the joint administration office of the four government banks (the post had been held by his ailing brother-in-law H. H. Kung).[50] Chiang's arbitrary exchange rate of one yuan in gold for 3 million *fabi* (the legal currency in Chinese) compelled commercial banks and individuals to turn in their possessions of silver, gold, and foreign currency. The policy negatively affected the lower and middle classes in favor of those who had connections with government officials. In 1946 Chiang signed the Sino-U.S. Commercial Treaty, prompting criticism that it gave American businesspeople an unfair advantage over their Chinese counterparts. The deal proved to be politically shortsighted and further reduced support for Chiang among the merchant interests.[51]

Under Chiang the weak Chinese state lacked civil service capacity.[52] These failures reflected the fragility of the Kuomintang's claim to national governance. A Marshall Plan would have required the administrative apparatus of a modern state, something that Chiang's China did not possess. Postwar China suffered from endemic corruption at all levels of civil and military administration. Aid did not reach the people; food, medicine, and other materials intended for troops were diverted by officials seeking bribes for the most rudimentary activities of government. Pervasive corruption made economic programs difficult to implement; thus it was unrealistic to assume that more aid could be effectively channeled to China's population.

Commitment Trap

U.S. partisanship during the Chinese Civil War significantly prejudiced the outcome of relations with an entire generation of China's Communist leaders. In the latter's view, the United States played a double game after World War II: it maintained nominal neutrality in order to broker a peaceful negotiation by General Marshall between the CCP and the Kuomintang in 1946. However, the United States provided $600 million worth of arms to Chiang at bargain prices, ordered Japanese troops not to surrender to the Communist forces, and airlifted nearly half a million Kuomintang troops from Chongqing to Manchuria and coastal cities so that Japanese-controlled assets could remain firmly in Chiang's hands. In addition, U.S. Marines were deployed to help Chiang hold strategic cities, railway stations, and coal mines, and American advisers were serving in Chiang's armies.[53] All these actions, while seemingly placing Chiang in an advantageous position over his adversary, in fact greatly contributed to Chiang's bad judgment in rekindling the flames of civil war.

At the same time, Truman refused the advice of U.S. administrators who recommended balancing economic assistance with support to Communist-held areas. Truman's policies clearly biased the U.S. relationship with China at a time when the Kuomintang's survival was questionable. Although General Marshall was able to shut off the aid faucet for a short time, a new law passed in 1948 promised another $400 million in military and economic assistance.[54] Truman's support of Chiang during the civil war made reconciliation with the Communists difficult once the war ended, yet he was blamed for "losing" China and abandoning his ally by not contributing enough. His critics rejected the notion that Asian countries could follow their own course without falling prey to the schemes of either China or the Soviet Union and their quest for global domination.

A huge leap in foreign policy thinking occurred between 1944, when Roosevelt sent David Barrett and the Dixie Mission to establish official contact with the CCP, and the decision made by Truman that diplomacy was out of the question in dealing with Communists. Many years passed before that decision would unravel in the jungles and rice paddies of Vietnam.

This leap can be understood in terms of the domestic political dilemma that the Truman administration faced in fighting for the support of Congress and the general public for resources to expand U.S commitments overseas. We can never assess what the administration considered, feared, or wanted independent of the domestic political dilemma it faced. Politically, the White House could not explain to the electorate that not all Communists were equally threatening to America's security and Truman's advisers needed to contend with the assertion that any effort by the West to negotiate was a sign of weakness. The Truman administration feared that the public would not be able to grasp a policy of resisting aggression in one part of the world and not in another—that U.S. citizens would be unable to discern the differences between one Communist leader and another.

Americans accepted the notion that any cooperation with Communists anywhere was tantamount to appeasement. Opportunities to divide the Soviet bloc from within were considered too uncertain, and evidence of diversity and nationalism within the Communist camp was disregarded. This made it difficult for Americans in subsequent engagements to separate anti-colonialism from Communism.[55] After the expulsion of all the old China hands from government, the European specialists who dominated U.S. foreign policy feared that Asia's fall to Communism would jeopardize Europe. To those sitting in Washington, the danger of an emerging Communist threat to American interests and way of life seemed real, whereas strains within the Communist bloc were unverifiable and hypothetical.[56] How could any American ultimatum to insurgents in Latin America, for example, carry weight if the United States were willing to negotiate with Communists in China? A world in which a gain for the Soviet Union was a loss for the United States was easier to portray than one of fragmentation within the Communist bloc. The politician in Truman understood that depicting complexity would generate heat rather than light, but in taking the politically expedient route he inadvertently encouraged the rise of McCarthyism.[57] His rhetorical strategy exaggerated both the extent of U.S. power and the uniformity of the threats poised against it.

The United States underestimated the role that nationalism played in China's conversion to Communism and, similarly, overlooked the long legacy of European domination and Russian expansionism, the memory of which could have been a wedge to divide Chinese Communists and the Soviets. A strongly grounded, self-confident Communist leadership in China might have been disadvantageous to the Soviets, making the Communist bloc too large for the Soviets to control effectively. Planners in Washington were unwilling to hazard that Chinese nationalism might eventually fragment international Communism. By isolating Beijing, U.S. China policy strengthened initial Chinese-Soviet solidarity; it left China with Russia as its only friend.

Table 6-1. *Nationalist Party (KMT) and Chinese Communist Party (CCP) Military Strength Comparison at the Start of the Civil War*

Item	KMT	CCP
Troops	4.3 million	1.3 million
Supplies	Air force; 271 warships and $800 million surplus	Basically rifles; no planes, no tanks, a few cannons; no foreign assistance
Population under control	300 million	100 million
Regions under control	Big cities, mostly along the railway line	Small towns, villages, and backward areas

Source: Li (2003, p. 51).

The Alliance Curse and the Cold War in Asia

The American belief that the loss of China was due to passivity in Washington had little to do with reality in China. A comparison of Kuomintang and CCP military strength at the start of the civil war reveals that Chiang lost the mainland not because he did not have enough weapons or soldiers (table 6-1). He outnumbered his rival in every tangible measure of military strength, but his troops lacked morale and popular support. "Seeking *only* a military solution to the problem of Communism, he lost both his armies and the Chinese people."[58]

Nevertheless, Chiang's personal tragedy made President Truman's administration vulnerable to attack from the Republican Party. Truman countered this attack by rejecting any relationship with the new regime in China. The unrealistic notion that Chiang could have made a comeback and unified China was an illusion that distorts U.S.-Chinese relations to the present day. The refusal to recognize the winner of the Chinese civil war insulted the Chinese people, and the denial of diplomatic recognition added to their fatigue after decades of violence, leaving a legacy of anger against the United States.

Chiang's Westernized style and his Westernized wife helped him capture the affection and trust of U.S. popular opinion, just as Ferdinand Marcos and the shah of Iran were later to do. Important opinion leaders in America equated Chiang with China itself. Washington made the classic mistake of identifying with a particular regime and its leader rather than with a nation and its people. In the United States public opinion romanticized Chiang as a reliable ally in the fight against international Communism. But as an agent who had kept China weak and backward, he was the Communists' most efficient recruiter.

Ross Terrill has pinpointed the alliance curse that contributed to Chiang's failure on the mainland. "Chiang tried to be a patriot. Yet the nature of his political legitimacy made him less nationalistic than Mao. His NP [Nationalist Party] lacked roots in the peasant majority of China. As if to fill the vacuum of support, the NP sought foreign backing. In the end, Chiang turned his back entirely on the Chinese rank and file, and put himself with a self-pitying shrug into the arms of the United States."[59] Few realized at the time that U.S. policy toward China established the logic to trap America into the same mistake in a number of strategically critical theaters.

What the United States Got Wrong about China's Revolution

The United States has no national experience that corresponds to the collapse of China's political institutions. Although America has gone through periods of dramatic macroeconomic and financial crisis, and even a civil war during the nineteenth century, these shocks are small relative to the systemic breakdown of the Chinese state in 1911, which was the culmination of a process of disintegration that took place during the entire nineteenth century. Even after the American Civil War, the political system endured as southerners were reincorporated into the nation via the same political institutions they had participated in before secession.

Post-1911 China, by contrast, lacked a strong central government or a consensus on the formation of a legitimate government. It possessed several regimes that were unable to cooperate to prevent Japanese invasion or civil war or to provide national sovereignty until the post-1949 era. China's crisis lasted longer and was deeper than anything experienced in U.S. history, and its depth is one reason why China's policymakers view the role of the state differently than do their U.S. counterparts.[60] China's leaders had to establish a new basis for social and political unity while transforming their systems of production and exchange. The United States never had to self-destruct in order to reconstruct.

The goal of both sides in China's civil war was to end a century of partial sovereignty and to reassert central control over Chinese territory. Joseph W. Esherick has written, "If we understand the political demands behind the Chinese Revolution to be for fairness and order (far more than democracy or liberation), it becomes easier to understand both the crisis of 1989 and the current resilience of the authoritarian state in China."[61]

Chiang Kai-shek never returned to conquer the mainland. After losing China in 1949 he ended up losing Taiwan thirty years after his death, when the airport and the memorial hall named for him were renamed and statues of him were removed from Taiwan's military bases. The refusal of four U.S. administrations to recognize the Communist government did not lead to regime change within China. The pressure America put on the world community to isolate the Communist regime gave Chinese conservatives the excuse they needed to crush the already weak liberal factions within the Chinese Communist Party. By quarantining China the United States rendered potentially useful or sympathetic collaborators powerless. One of the architects and strongest advocates of that policy, Richard Nixon, made a presidential visit to China in 1972 to seek a remedy to the policies that he had championed throughout his career. The Chinese Communist regime survived after 1978 because its management and formulation of economic policy fundamentally differed from that of the Soviets. There is good reason to speculate that had U.S.-China reconciliation started earlier, China's path to market reform might also have begun earlier.

However, forty years ago the linkage of all Communist governments with Soviet control led the United States to support any anti-Communist regime in the region. Socially regressive leaders in Manila and Saigon were the beneficiaries of that policy, which finally embroiled America in a war in Vietnam whose main purpose was to contain China.

The United States as Master Builder in the Philippines

The problem of explaining to the American people and to friendly nations which are not sympathetic toward an authoritarian form of government why we support such governments becomes a matter of public relations, not policy.

—U.S. State Department,
Foreign Relations of the United States, 1958–1960

Perhaps the best way to understand the limits of U.S. vision for promoting adaptive social change in developing Asia is to contrast U.S. experiences in South Vietnam and the Philippines. The Philippines is where U.S. policy planners had the most time to observe, plan, and act relative to other third world interventions. Virtually no outside interference had to be contended with. Competition with forces externally funded or provisioned by China or the Soviets was minimized by the American military presence on the islands. What remains of the U.S. vision is still highly visible today, as the bilateral relationship and the character of alliance orientations has changed very little since the end of the cold war. The Philippines was America's clearest canvas on which to conceptualize and implement the U.S. view of social utility and developmental imperatives. It is here—where the population was essentially friendly, the elite was highly dependent, the common people uncritically accepted Hollywood images of the good life, and Jeffersonian ideals of political order are espoused by most political actors—that the U.S. style of campaigning has emotional resonance for the population and is imitated with little modification. Politicians kiss babies, generals think of themselves as walking in the footsteps of MacArthur. The names of American presidents and colonial administrators appear on street signs throughout the capital. Even in their self-constructed systems Filipinos use U.S. cultural antecedents. If there is anything limiting, short-sighted, or inappropriate in the application of the U.S. model of social and political gradualism and

Table 7-1. *Historical Timeline of the Philippines, 1565–Present*

Spanish colony	1565–1898
Spanish-American War	1898–1901
American colony	1901–41
World War II and Japanese occupation	1941–45
Republic of the Philippines	1946–65
Marcos presidency	1965–72
Marcos dictatorship	1972–86
Return to democracy: Republic of the Philippines	1986–present

spontaneous social regeneration, it is here, in the Philippines, that it will be most easily observable.

The United States endorsed the independence of the Philippines on July 4, 1946, as a showcase of colonial benevolence and Asian democracy, and the end of the longest sustained U.S. effort at what is now called state building. "It was in the Philippines," writes Gabriel Kolko, "that U.S. policies in the Third World, with their complex tensions and ambitions, rhetoric and interests, were revealed most clearly both in theory and practice."[1]

From the beginning of the American occupation in 1901, U.S. policymakers had more than forty years in which to erect institutions that would transform the Philippines into the first functioning democracy in the postcolonial world (see table 7-1). Planners created a civil service bureaucracy, a system of free public education, civil courts, and a supreme court. The Philippine constitution protected basic property rights and provided for constraints on power, as well as the mechanisms for electoral participation.

In a country with abundant natural resources, a relatively well-educated population, and ample foreign assistance, the devastation caused by World War II was not expected to bring development to a standstill. With the war-torn infrastructure earmarked for repair, Filipinos had reason to hope that their country would be a leader in Asia. In addition, the island nation enjoyed privileged trade access and U.S.-provided geopolitical security.

Instead of becoming a beacon to others, however, the Philippines became a warning of the mismatch between GDP growth, social reforms, and democracy. The preferred model of development in East Asia during the cold war became that of the benevolent dictator who used distortionary taxation (in the form of subsidies or tariff protection) to finance productive public expenditures, including payments and benefits to politicians. In 1972 an ambitious leader, Ferdinand Marcos, claiming that the only way to grow was to emulate the authoritarian example of its neighbors in South Korea and Taiwan and hoping to reproduce their success, trashed the constitutional model and declared martial law. Marcos announced that an enlightened autocrat was what the country needed. His immediate goal was to abort a constitutional convention that might place limits on his right to run again. His experiment magnified corruption and lowered growth, making the Philippines into the sick man of Asia by the time Marcos fled to Hawaii in 1986.

Even after the restoration of democracy by President Corazon Aquino (1986–92), political instability continued and economic growth lagged. Aquino's government was forced to suppress attempted coups from the military in 1987 and 1989. The government of Joseph Estrada (1998–2001) collapsed in the Second People Power Revolution amid charges of corruption and plunder, massive public demonstrations, and withdrawal of support from the armed forces. An Islamic insurgency in the Autonomous Region in Muslim Mindanao grew to become a major concern for Estrada's appointed successor, Vice President Gloria Macapagal-Arroyo, who won the 2004 presidential election.

In examining the nation's failure to join the ranks of East Asia's tiger economies, we will see that close strategic ties with the United States may have provided the nation's leaders with an umbrella to divert large sums, including foreign aid, to finance nonproductive government spending and transfers to elite political supporters. The nation's elites were given little encouragement to pursue useful investments in the domestic economy, and little attention was given to the basic needs of the majority. Instead of exporting goods and services, the Philippines was exporting its most talented citizens.

From Colony to Client

The social illegitimacy of the country's democracy had a legacy extending back to Spanish rule. The social institutions and oligarchy that were instruments of colonial oppression remained intact during the period of American rule.[2] They had survived during the three-year Japanese occupation, as well; many people within the Filipino elite became collaborators and wartime profiteers.[3] General MacArthur, who liberated the country and restored the government-in-exile and civil authority, overlooked that legacy of oppression and continued to depend on the oligarchy. Despite dissension in Washington, primarily from the secretary of the interior, and among Filipinos who had fought against the Japanese, MacArthur saw no point in contesting the elite regime when the country would soon receive its independence.[4] Acknowledging that the Japanese had installed a "puppet government," he nevertheless felt that the Philippine leaders had become well known to him and he refused to brand them traitors. In turn, members of the elite welcomed the U.S. liberators as heroes and became America's collaborators with hardly a blink of an eye. Most important, the elite proved to be resolutely anti-Communist.[5] As a result, the social oligarchy remained strong enough to circumvent the nation's nascent democratic institutions. Voter fraud during the first post-independence presidential election, in 1946, lent widespread rural sympathy to a guerrilla movement called "the Huk insurgency."[6]

The victor, Manuel Acuña Roxas, was accused of vote fraud and of being a collaborator (he'd served in the occupation government). Nevertheless, MacArthur shamelessly backed him. The Huk rebellion (1945–1953) prompted Truman's State Department to recommend rent reductions and land distribution, to be administered by Elpidio Quirino (1948–1953), who had assumed the presidency at Roxas's death. Quirino tried and failed to maintain a truce with the Huk insurgency and finally turned to repressive measures.

Truman's Far East advisers, who attributed Chiang Kai-shek's defeat to the Chinese Communists and to his failure to implement socioeconomic reforms, feared a similar result in the Philippines. They advocated making U.S. aid contingent on compliance with reforms to eliminate corruption. Among the priorities they identified were central government tax increases, supervision of transactions in foreign currencies, a minimum wage law, non-Communist labor unions, equitable land redistribution, rural credit, and administrative reform. Washington began to extract quid pro quo commitments, starting with the reorganization of the armed forces, whose officer ranks had grown corrupt and inefficient. Under U.S. pressure, Quirino appointed a new secretary of national defense, Ramon Magsaysay, a pro-American member of the Philippine House of Representatives, who had been instrumental in incorporating the constabulary into the armed forces. But Quirino ignored other reform measures and undermined the implementation of other measures to which he'd agreed: an integrity board created in compliance with U.S. wishes had no enforcement powers, the budget remained unbalanced, and mismanagement and corruption flourished. Still, the United States did not carry out its threats to withdraw aid, and in 1949, running against the bitterly anti-American and nationalist José P. Laurel, Quirino won the presidency with assured continued support from Washington.

In 1953 Magsaysay quit his position in government, as well as in the incumbent Liberal Party, and joined the opposition Nationalist Party as its presidential candidate. He was what U.S. policymakers needed—a champion within the elite who had nationalist and reformist credentials and who could win over the populace.[7] In addition, as defense secretary he had subdued the Huk insurgency and already undertaken major reforms of the military without alienating the support of the government. Quirino's Liberal Party denied public facilities to opposition candidates, threatened to curtail the supply of ink for opposition newspapers, restricted voter registration in provinces that supported Magsaysay, and used goon squads and massive voter fraud against him and his supporters—all to no avail. The Magsaysay victory was to be the grand day of American-led reform policy in Asia—but although Washington got its man, it did not get durable reforms.[8]

Magsaysay's accomplishments in office (1953–57) proved to be cosmetic. Large-scale socioeconomic reforms would have required the support of the wealthy landlords, who held sway in the bicameral congress, yet the defeat of the peasant-based Huk insurgency had made far-reaching reforms less urgent. Despite having campaigned on the idea that "those who have less in life should have more in law," Magsaysay did not follow through with instituting social change to address the underlying needs of the poor.[9]

In addition to opposition from elite politicians, Magsaysay faced a shifting international environment. With the election of Eisenhower in 1952 came a change in U.S.-Philippine relations. The war in Korea, the emerging nationalist insurgency in Indochina, and deteriorating security in Southeast Asia made the Philippines essential to the projection of U.S. power in the Far East. The Subic Bay naval complex and the Clark Air Force Base were again vital to U.S. military objectives in the region, and Washington could not risk losing the support of a cooperative government by harassing its leaders for land reforms or social justice. Reforming the inequitable political economy of the Philippines was not a priority, and high-level U.S. pressure for land reform disappeared altogether. Republicans in the U.S. Senate made it known that they would support any side that protected U.S. interests.

For their part, successive Philippine governments missed few opportunities to demonstrate loyalty to America. The country sent more than 7,000 troops to Korea, supported the U.S. position of blocking China's admission to the United Nations, and endorsed Washington's network of defense alliances in Southeast Asia. Even though the Philippines was represented at the 1955 Bandung Conference of Asian and African countries promoting the non-aligned movement, its participation was noteworthy for the representatives' decidedly U.S. leanings.[10]

In retrospect, the Magsaysay administration seems to have been little more than a convenient fig leaf. The president did not change laws or policies but exercised leadership by dispensing presidential largesse, depending on discretionary funds rather than on direct budgetary outlays. He had dismantled the Huk rebellion through targeted patronage to rebel regions by mediating with landlords who maintained private armies. He was unable to write legislation to legalize peasant organizations, and he left behind no legal foundation to protect the welfare of the poor. The short-term gains for the landless and dispossessed were neutralized by opposition from elites. When Magsaysay was killed in a plane crash in 1957, Philippine politics regressed to the mean, and corruption and deception again took over.

Vice President Carlos P. Garcia (1957–61) succeeded Magsaysay in the presidency and substituted bribery for reform zeal. Concerned about American approval, he banned the Communist Party and specialized in fine words such as declaring his service to the free world, and lauding, in 1958, South Vietnam's Diem as "the liberator of his people and one of the recognized leaders of democracy in Asia."[11] On a 1961 visit to the United States, Garcia affirmed his intention to lead a country "that stands for all America stands for in the way of the greatest human values—freedom, democracy and the brotherhood of men."[12] These pledges led the Kennedy administration to ignore official corruption in the Philippines, which instead focused on its Alliance for Progress program in Latin America and on its ambition to gain India's participation in the anti-Communist alliance.[13] But new aid was not forthcoming from an American president who was known to believe in economic success as the key to defeating Communism.

The Trade-Off of Growth for Security

At the end of World War II, U.S. officials advocated a multilateral trading system that, in theory, denied preferential access to particular countries. This position is frequently interpreted as a reflection of the primacy of economic interests to general U.S. foreign policy. But the United States made an exception for the Philippines, tolerating Philippine trade barriers that penalized American exporters while allowing Philippine agricultural exports into the United States.[14] These policies contributed to the domination by landlord-capitalists of Philippine industrial development. U.S. exceptions in the form of generous nontariff quotas allowed wealthy Philippine plantation owners to preserve their economic and political power over ethnic Chinese minorities and other groups that might have benefited from industrialization and urbanization. The United States justified these policies as a means to cement its strategic alliance with the Philippines and to gain broad-based support from the Philippine masses via reconstruction of the war-torn nation.[15]

The United States must share responsibility with the local leadership for the underdevelopment of the Philippine economy. Local leaders did not want to risk growth that would open the economy to competition they could not control. The exchange and import controls gave political authorities discretionary powers that could determine the fortunes of individual firms, allowing politicians to override the market and configure the creation of wealth. Keeping economic benefits among a small group of linked factions was essential to any Philippine leader who wanted to stay in office. To assert influence, government officials used insider information about import controls that consisted of restricted lists that shifted constantly. Advanced knowledge of shortages and price exchanges gave government the basis to manipulate market opportunities for political and private gain, and to remain the center of patrimonial deal making that pervaded the entire economy. "The licensing program touched off a patrimonial feeding frenzy," explains N. Cullather, "as *rentier* tycoons and officeholders sought to swap political capital for licenses."[16] Through the 1950s and 1960s, licensing of import and export quotas allowed artificial shortages and inflation to increase political leverage over the market. Licensing of foreign exchange intensified that leverage and allowed government insiders to plunder the economy.

In 1956, as the Philippine economy was deteriorating and unemployment reached 12 percent, the government made favoritism of import and exchange rates even more extreme, erecting additional tariff walls to protect an already sheltered industry. Demands for trade concessions strained the symbiotic relationship between Washington and Filipino elites, but never led to retaliatory action, despite the clamoring of U.S. investors in the Philippines, because Washington prioritized security over trade.

The Apotheosis of the Patrimonial State

In 1965 an independent and outspoken Philippine senator ran on the Nationalist Party ticket, criticizing the country's association with the U.S. war in Vietnam:

> History shows that every nation that fell to communism owed its defeat not to foreign invasion but to disintegration from within through the failure of its leadership and its institutions. . . . What South Vietnam needs is the will to fight which cannot be exported. It [Philippine-American friendship] will be served today and in the future by Filipino leaders who act with becoming dignity and maturity as well as [with] true goodwill toward America, rather than those who miss no chance to help their loyalty and display canine devotion.[17]

As a candidate Ferdinand Marcos promised that 700,000 tenant farmers would receive land and that he would streamline and purge the government of corruption. His independent streak disappeared immediately after his electoral victory, however, when he discovered that it was easier to obtain resources from the United States through promises of policy compliance than it was to gain a consensus in the Philippines for social and fiscal reform. He learned quickly how to beggar America by promising to eliminate insurgent activities. His rise to power was an example of how the war against global Communism paid handsome dividends to local autocrats. As Paul Hutchcroft, a researcher on the Philippines, has noted,

> Among postwar Philippine leaders, Marcos displayed a particularly keen insight into the nature of the neocolonial bond and knew that American strategic needs presented ample opportunity for private gain. Close relations with the United States assisted him in his efforts to cultivate closer relations with the IMF and World Bank, and for a full decade he adroitly managed to extract enormous quantities of funds from these institutions as well as from bilateral donors and commercial banks.[18]

Marcos suspended the constitution and declared martial law in September 1972: ostensibly to fight Communists he forbade political demonstrations, announced a curfew, shut down the print and electronic media, and jailed several thousand political prisoners. All this occurred without complaint from Washington, which was still embroiled in the Vietnam War and was using the military facilities at Subic Bay and Clark. In fact, U.S. aid to the Marcos regime "leapt fivefold."[19]

An end to the war in Vietnam and a change of party in the American presidency in 1976 did not shift U.S. policies. The Marcos stranglehold grew once it was clear that President Jimmy Carter's human rights policy did not apply to strategically significant allies. A visit by Carter's vice president was turned into a photo op by Marcos to convey staunch U.S. support. The visit confirmed to him that base rights came before human rights, and successive U.S. administrations continued to assist Marcos indirectly to obtain funds from multilateral sources, including the World Bank, the International Monetary Fund, and the Asian Development Bank.

The friendship between Marcos and Ronald Reagan began when Reagan was governor of California. As president, Reagan refused to see that his friend was a danger to the values he himself championed in regard to the oppressed of Eastern Europe, whose resistance to the Soviet Union he encouraged. The Kirkpatrick doctrine (named after Reagan's UN ambassador, Jeane Kirkpatrick)—that pro-American dictatorships should be supported because they could eventually be democratized—lent ideological affirmation to Marcos.[20] In June 1981, after Marcos won an election rife with fraud, Vice President George Bush traveled to Manila to praise the president for his "devotion to democracy." Reagan continued to applaud Marcos for his resistance to Communist insurgency—support that enticed an increasingly beleaguered Marcos to take new risks to hold on to power, including the assassination of the opposition leader, Benigno Aquino. Corrupt elections occurred again in February 1986, which precipitated a nationwide strike called by Aquino's widow, Corazon.

Raymond Bonner writes, "For Washington, the most bitter legacy of the Marcos era was the growth of the Communists. There weren't more than a few hundred New People's Army guerrillas in 1972, but by 1986 there were 15,000 well-armed, motivated guerrillas and a million or so supporters."[21] The crushing of Philippine democracy did not even receive notice in the voluminous memoirs of Nixon's secretary of state, Henry Kissinger. But in an article in *Newsday,* he expressed grave concern about the Reagan administration's decision to withdraw support, writing, "It is dangerous to abandon imperfect friends."[22] By the time Marcos was put on notice by Washington to step down, many Filipinos held the United States responsible for his administration's political repression and human rights violations. The tradition of anti-American election demagoguery that Marcos had silenced with martial law did not disappear. By the time the dictator finally fell, being identified with U.S. policies had shifted from being an asset to being a liability.[23]

A decade of bribery and intimidation left a legacy of social and institutional devastation. From 1972 to 1977 the real income and nutrition levels of workers and peasants declined steadily, to the point that by 1978 per capita caloric intake in the Philippines was the second lowest in East Asia; only war-torn Cambodia fared worse.[24] The decline in living standards triggered an insurgency in the countryside. Manufacturing's GDP share fell from 12 percent in 1970 to 11 percent in 1980, the lowest level of any East Asian country.[25] The nation's economic recovery after Marcos was preempted by debt repayments incurred during martial law.

American Vision of Law and Democracy in the Philippines

The absence of broad domestic support caused the Philippine leadership to depend on external influence and discouraged efforts to broaden its constituent base. Albert Celoza has observed:

Figure 7-1. *Government Revenue as Percent of GDP, 1950–2004*

Percent of GDP

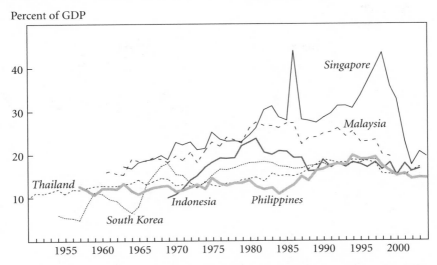

Source: International Monetary Fund, International Financial Statistics, 2007 (subscription database).

Because of the Philippines' special ties to the U.S., a symbiotic relationship developed after Philippine independence was granted. The United States became a source of economic, political, and symbolic support. A pro-American stand also served as a symbol of legitimacy for political candidates. . . . From President Roxas to President Marcos, the American government served as a source of support. To cut oneself off from the relationship with the United States was to cut off an umbilical cord of political patronage.[26]

An absence of social consensus resulted in disputes over raising revenues to provide public goods. "Powerless to tax its own wealthy constituency," writes Cullather, "the overburdened state required infusions of money from the outside."[27] Figure 7-1 shows that between 1957 and 2004 government revenue in the Philippines as a share of GDP was among the lowest in East Asia. Figure 7-2 indicates that Philippine tax revenue as a percentage of GDP was the lowest of that of six neighboring developing countries between 1979 and 1995. Since attaining independent statehood, in fact, the Philippines has experienced a severe and sustained budgetary crisis. "The government spent as though its

Figure 7-2. *Weak Performance of Philippines Tax Authorities in Comparative Perspective, 1960–95*

Percent of GDP

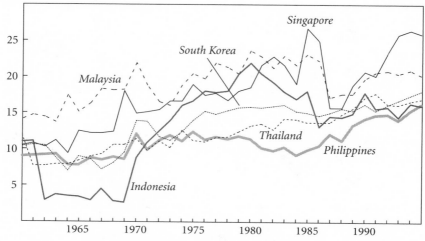

Source: World Bank, World Development Indicators, 2007 (subscription database).

revenues were limitless," wrote H. W. Brands of the governments of Roxas and Quirino, "yet taxed as though it had no expenses. At one level the consequence was an enormous and growing government deficit. . . . At another, more serious level, was widespread [public] loss of confidence in the ability of the political process to deal with [the country's economic problems]."[28]

Fifty years later, the government of Gloria Macapagal-Arroyo was unable to collect more than 10 percent of GDP in taxes. No Philippine leader has mobilized sufficient resources to eliminate the nation's underlying debts. Because citizens do not believe that the state serves the public interest, few are willing to contribute resources to maintain the status quo. Those reform-minded politicians who seek a remedy oppose the continuation of external influence over the county's political evolution. Critical of U.S. influence, they lose access to the external resources needed to purchase support at home.

During the Fidel Ramos presidency (1992–98), liberal trade reform flourished but the president was unable to gain adequate support for social expenditures from the elites in the senate. Infrastructure and social spending were often politicized, and the administration used payoffs to gain backing for trade reforms. As a result, physical infrastructure and public education continued to deteriorate, and the share of government spending on education consequently remains lower than that of other countries in the region.[29]

Although the gap in GDP between the Philippines and its neighbors was sharpest in the 1980s, it continued to widen through the early 1990s despite the reforms of the Ramos administration. Because much of the upper and mid-level bureaucracy remained political, Ramos was unable to allay investor fears that policy certainty would not last beyond his six-year term. Investors also feared that a new government would mean new personnel at key enforcement junctions, making regulatory enforcement questionable and preventing technocratic insulation of policy, in the East Asian tradition.

The hope that nourished support for liberal reform during the Ramos administration was that social cooperation could be restored by instituting fair procedures of business competition and open markets. However, deep inequality prevented competition from overcoming the historic deficit of societal cooperation. The negative intersection of injustice and corruption in the Philippines is due to the historical perception that inequality benefits a privileged minority. One reason for poor performance is that investment faces both policy and commercial risks. Social discrepancies raise doubts that reform is durable and can be protected from a new surge of populism.

Disappointment on Each Side

What security has the United States gained from its socially retrogressive, elite-based alliance with its former colony? Marcos only grudgingly joined the fight in Vietnam and mustered just 2,000 noncombatants after receiving an explicit bribe in the form of aid. He enjoyed insufficient support from his own people to sacrifice lives in the service of America, and his army was considered too politicized to be an effective fighting force.

In 2004 another Filipino president, short of legitimacy at home, found she was unable to fulfill her side of an alliance with the United States. The presence of well-organized Islamic opposition groups made the Philippines a frontline state in the war against international terrorism. Gloria Macapagal-Arroyo discovered that her administration had a powerful common interest with America in waging a war against insurrection in the Islamic regions of the South Philippines, where U.S. intelligence had reason to believe a strong al Qaeda presence existed. Her visit to Washington in 2001 produced 660 U.S. military advisers dispatched to confront the insurgency, and the White House doubled aid dollars to Mindanao, promising future military assistance. Coordination on the war against terrorism, Arroyo hoped, would also stimulate lagging commercial ties with the United States. During her U.S. trip to discuss September 11 and its aftermath she was accompanied by dozens of Filipino business leaders seeking deals in the United States.

To reciprocate U.S. counterinsurgency support in 2003, the Philippine government sent a small contingent of soldiers to help American efforts in Iraq. Their assistance was to be short-lived. In July 2004 a Filipino truck driver and father of eight, Angelo de la Cruz, was kidnapped. Arroyo struck a deal for his release by withdrawing the entire Philippine contingent of fifty-one soldiers. The Iraqi foreign minister, Hoshyar Zebari, warned that the decision would set a bad precedent by "rewarding" terrorists.[30] Arroyo rejected the humiliating criticisms from the allies—but what really hurt were the comments that appeared in the *Manila Star*: "We turned tail in the face of terror, no ifs or buts about it, and that will haunt the nation for a long time."[31]

Philippine leaders cannot govern without U.S. support, but that support constrains their ability to reach out and form a broad governing coalition at home. The question asked by the nation's poor is why they should sacrifice for a government that fails to cater to their basic needs. The distinguished journalist Harrison Salisbury has written, "Who would have been a more staunch ally of America in Asia—a dictator like Marcos or one of his constitutional opponents: a man of principle, a man honest enough to overtly disagree with the U.S. but brave enough to speak up for civil liberties and the democratic process?"[32] Marcos learned how to serve his domestic purposes by extracting material concessions from Washington, but independent leadership would have had to gain support domestically. Linking base rights with the need to prop up a dictator, the United States eventually ended up losing both.[33]

Caught between warring empires during World War II and warring ideologies during the cold war, the Philippines chose the bitter pill of continued American paternalism. This relationship has helped save the Philippines from self-destruction, but it has not produced the social consensus necessary for growth. In the twentieth-first century, the long-term viability of economic reform remains hostage to the potential for social unrest, which mars the reliability of the armed forces as an alliance partner. The residual effects of the Philippines' historical social divisions have continued to haunt the nation, and until the internal divisions are reconciled, an alliance between the Philippines and the United States provides little security to either.[34] Because its constitution is externally sustained rather than locally owned, the Filipinos have not been able to use it to prevent transgressions by political leaders or to hold them accountable, even when transgressions are publicized by the media.

Stability lags because the original inequities in the distribution of resources remain and the country wobbles from one temporary solution to another, with the legislature unable or unwilling to endorse the far-reaching reforms necessary to bring about stability and generate long-term economic growth.

The U.S. legacy of democratic institutions has not been adequate to ensure stable growth. The underlying social institutions necessary to make democracy work were undermined by deceptive elections, and the Philippine government failed to produce self-enforcing norms and rules for resolving conflict or for agreeing on how to set national priorities and to raise resources. The fledgling democracy established in 1946 was overwhelmed by patronage hiring, clientelistic lawmaking, personalized law enforcement, corrupt campaign finance, electoral malfeasance, and investor fraud.[35] Government did not provide law and order, jurisprudence, secure property rights, or adequate public goods and services. The concept of good government serving the interests of the people and a purposefully directed national will for economic and social development never materialized. Democracy did not bring prosperity, despite the rhetorical embrace it received. Instead, it became the establishment's rationalization for mismanagement and inadequate provision of health care, schools, and jobs. No Philippine government successfully overcame the political stalemate that prevented a consensus on the need for a stable and adequate revenue base. The result of this failure has made Filipinos distrustful of their government, its institutions, and its leaders.

The Philippines' constitution mimicked many institutional features of American democracy, and elections were conducted regularly between 1946 and 1973. Nevertheless, Philippine democracy is unattractive to the poor majorities of East Asia. Asia's leaders turned increasingly toward authoritarian structures, rejecting the Philippine model of development. Although Filipinos went to the polls on a regular basis, they ended up with governments that ignored the voices of those trapped in rural poverty. A democratic culture, which is needed to sustain an impartial civil service and independent courts and media, did not develop. Inequitable distribution of wealth persisted, preventing the formation of strong, transparent civil institutions that could successfully address the basic needs of the citizens.

The United States guaranteed the Philippines' external security while allowing the landed elites to control capital accumulation and industrialization—in effect modernizing the oligarchy to reinforce its political domination. This same pattern was reproduced on a large scale throughout South America. In both cases U.S. policy responded to economic crises by ignoring corruption and misdistribution of wealth, hoping that leaders would adopt political and social remedies after economic growth.

An important condition for future U.S. security may involve military interventions in other weak states, such as Afghanistan and Iraq, where establishing state capacity will be essential to meeting strategic objectives. As architects of Philippine democracy, U.S. policymakers based their beliefs on the power of the ballot box, ignoring the need to build an equitable society and a dynamic economy. Sixty years later, social exclusion turns many Filipinos into second-class citizens, despite their ability to exercise their voting franchise. The threat to democracy posed by poverty and inequality teaches that the singular act of voting is insufficient to build an inclusive polity. There is much that can be learned from this outcome to prevent its recurrence in future U.S. efforts at state building.

Spontaneous Lawfulness

Reflecting the premise that conformity with the rule of law arises spontaneously in a healthy society, the implicit U.S. foreign policy goals in the Philippines during the forties and fifties were economic, military, and political decentralization and democratization. U.S. policy advisers focused on constitutional reforms to defend the rights of assembly, speech, and property, but have always stopped short of advocating radical regime change or comprehensive redistribution that would change the coalitional structure of authority.

The American concept of freedom as spontaneous obedience to law does little to inspire those who live in societies where the rich are few, the poor are many, and where stultifying traditions perpetuate inequality. In developing nations where social inequality is deeply entrenched, the rich can capture the state and weaken constitutional reforms. Underpaid state officials can be bribed, and laws circumvented.

In the Philippines, U.S. policymakers have subscribed to the belief that "improvements in landlord-tenant relationships would have to be accomplished within the existing system and slowly, by patient administration, safeguarding the peasant rights, and by popular education."[36] Yet without radical redistribution—such as occurred in South Korea, Taiwan, China, and Japan—what could the poor, scratching out a living from two hectares of arid soil owned by a distant landlord, expect from spontaneous social action, other than exploitation? No wonder, then, that without reforms aimed at social justice, the showcase of democracy that America sought from its policies in the Philippines never materialized.

More than a patchwork of rules and regulations is necessary to ensure that social norms adapt to formal democratic institutions. According to the Philippine author and diplomat R. S. Manglapus, writing at the peak of third world disillusion with cold war models, "There is at present little enthusiasm in Asia for the American example; for it is apparent that patchwork democracy requires conditions which do not exist in the developing world." In his friendly tirade he concludes that the poor hope for an ideology that can "show the way to a sustained social revolution that will lift men to a level where they may begin to enjoy the freedom and the privilege to be spontaneous."[37]

Democracy Promotion and the Missing Middle

A definition of democracy that is largely procedural and that relies on institutions that sustain the rule of law, such as the separation of powers, frequently fails to inspire third world populations. People in developing nations are much more likely to see these institutions and procedural mechanisms as the end of a process that begins with social democracy, access to basic economic independence, and the spread of endowments such as education, health care, land, roads, sanitation, and physical security. Few third world leaders view socialism and democracy as opposites and many have espoused socialism to attain democracy. Thus, divergent views of the paths toward creating democracy existed between U.S.-backed moderates, the products of modernization theory with its notions of gradualism, and third world leaders schooled in the language of social revolution. The procedural, rule-based vision generally appeals to largely middle-class constituents whose basic household needs have already been met. But the global middle classes constitute fewer than 7 percent of the world's people.[38]

The pro-market stabilization packages for foreign nations advocated by Washington in the 1980s and 1990s have reduced budgets for education, which reduced the numbers of educated adults, shrinking the middle class. The missing middle in the global population profile reduces the coalitions for democracy. What good are courts that protect property rights to those who cannot afford to pay lawyers or bribe judges? Institutions that are not protected from influence cannot be trusted to ensure the rights of the poor.

The founders of American democracy believed that independence of social status was a prerequisite for independence in action and thought; they assumed that the prerogatives of the bureaucrats and the jealousies of the masses were the greatest threats to stability.[39] But where only the rich few have access to such endowments, putting property rights or the rule of law in place first can only ensure the entrenchment of the status quo. Explanations for why the United States was spared such entrenchment politics point in many directions. Among the most popular reasons given for the preservation of a broad base for American democracy is the existence of the frontier, which allowed many average Americans to become property owners and the fact that the agricultural endowment of the Northeast was favorable to family farming, which gave the independent farmer a secure economic foundation. These economic preconditions for U.S.-style democracy were not prevalent in the Philippines or in South Vietnam, another third world setting for a U.S. effort to create a showcase of democracy.

8 | *Illegitimate Offspring: South Vietnam*

The United States has thus far refused to face up to the fact of revolution itself, and has, therefore, failed to offer its own brand of revolution as an alternative.

—Bernard Fall, *The Two Viet-Nams* (1963)

But it is true that the U.S. administrations at the time severely underestimated the need for a legitimate government in South Vietnam and instead assumed that a shadow government and military force could win the day.

—Melvin Laird, "Iraq: Learning the Lessons of Vietnam,"
Foreign Affairs (2005)

A state exists chiefly in the hearts and minds of its people; if they do not believe it is there, no logical exercise will bring it to life.

—Joseph R. Strayer, *On the Medieval Origins of the Modern State* (1970)

South Vietnam, like the Philippines, was the object of a monumental U.S. effort at nation building. It was a U.S. foreign policy priority for nearly two decades and the largest recipient of U.S. aid from 1954 to 1973. Created by the Eisenhower administration, the country's raison d'être was to "serve as a bulwark against Communist expansion and . . . a proving ground for democracy in Asia. Originating from the exigencies of the cold war, the experiment in nation-building tapped the wellsprings of American idealism and took on many of the trappings of a crusade."[1] South Vietnam was, in the words of Senator John F. Kennedy, "our offspring."[2]

Nevertheless, neither a liberal democratic state nor an ally capable of defending America's long-term interests emerged in South Vietnam. When U.S. troops left the country in 1973, the benefits of the project, which cost the American public $150 billion, were apparent only to those who still believed in the domino theory of international relations.[3] The promise of a fair and equitable government that was responsive to the needs of the Vietnamese people remained unfulfilled. Conditions in the countryside, where the majority of the South Vietnamese lived, stagnated throughout the nineteen-year engagement. The United States' commercial import program, which inflated South Vietnam's urban standard of living, had little effect on economic development. America waged the war to bolster confidence in its promise to defend its allies against Communism. Yet the Communist victory in Vietnam had minimal effects on long-term U.S. security.

Competing Revolutions

South Vietnam was a country born of colonialism and divided by region, class, and ethnic tensions. It had great difficulty forging a symbolic, social, or historical identity, because its brief period of independence ended in 1778.[4] It reappeared as an instrument for the free world to stop the spread of Soviet and Chinese Communism. The major contenders for power in the two Vietnams of the 1950s projected themselves as nationalist revolutionaries. The National Liberation Front of South Vietnam and the Communists in Hanoi clearly were revolutionary socialists, but even the reclusive mandarin Ngo Dinh Diem, who seized power in 1954, viewed himself as a revolutionary.

In 1955 Prime Minister Diem gave the country just over two weeks' notice of a nationwide referendum in which to decide the nation's leader—himself or Emperor Bao Dai. The French had installed the latter as head of state six years earlier, but he was still living in France. Claiming to have received an overwhelming 98 percent of the vote, Diem declared victory and moved quickly to consolidate power. He proceeded to repress both the opposition and the media, and called for a national assembly election in which only three out of 123 seats went to opposition parties. He then refused to comply with the Geneva Accords, which he disputed on grounds that he had not signed them, and which called for elections in 1956 on the question of North-South reunification.[5] Excerpts of the Department of Defense report known as the Pentagon Papers, published by the *New York Times* in 1971, subsequently exposed the U.S. role behind Diem's machinations.

Determined to reduce any threat to central hegemony, Diem oversaw the enactment of a new constitution that granted the president extensive legislative power. The judiciary served at the pleasure of the executive branch, and judges did not enjoy guaranteed salaries. Disregard for rural opinion led Diem to remove the last vestiges of local self-government, the village councils set up by the French, and to personally designate officials to replace the village chiefs. Suspension of village elections prompted the observation that "at least in this one respect, there was less political freedom in Vietnam under Diem than under the ancient mandarinal and even the colonial regime."[6] Having abolished village-level authority, he did not consider establishing a province-level counterweight to balance central authority. Those he appointed to assume authority in the provinces and over the police, security, and the regular army reported directly to him. The constitution made no mention of local governments at all because Diem had dismissed them. "As time went on, Diem and his brother Ngo Dinh Nhu ignored the Constitution completely and acted by decrees or by personal—often private—orders to underlings all the way down to the village level."[7] Diem and his family exercised unchecked executive power at all levels of state activity, undermining the effectiveness of any independent action on the part of other state actors.[8]

Nothing that could be said about Diem could successfully mobilize support for his government among the U.S. electorate. Diem saw himself as a predestined leader, more akin to an absolute monarch, which made it difficult for him "to compete with Ho Chi Minh on Ho Chi Minh's own terms, as a man of the people."[9] Originally from the North, and a Catholic in a predominantly Buddhist nation, Diem relied on family solidarity to maintain control over the machinery of government. "The President's family constitutes an extra-legal elite which, with Diem, directs the destiny of Vietnam today. The family is in class, regional origin, religion, and temperament sharply set off from the population over which it rules."[10] Friends in the Eisenhower administration and the U.S. media tried to depict Diem as a democrat, but he had no inclination to govern by rule of law. Thus, Diem's regime presented the United States with a commitment trap. Without the magisterial and eccentric Diem, it would have been difficult to construct a regime that was both nationalist, anti-Communist, hostile to a continued French presence, and receptive to U.S. tutelage.

Diem's campaign of violence against political opponents, which included arbitrary arrests, confinement, and assassinations, received prime time in the American media.[11] Fearing the popularity of the Buddhists or the National Front for the Liberation of South Vietnam (NLF), both of whom enjoyed extensive organizational networks, Diem never risked an open electoral process. While several political parties existed, regime elites controlled them all.[12] "By [1963], all outspoken anti-Communist, anti-Diem leaders had left the country or were imprisoned."[13] The security forces of the government of South Vietnam (GVN) did not distinguish between Communist insurgents and non-Communist opposition.[14] Diem would not "risk diluting the power concentrated in the hands of the ruling elite in the hope of gaining more overall internal and external support," holding on to "every shred of power for fear that its dilution might bring down not only the regime, but the Republic itself."[15] An increasingly hostile population viewed his government as an authoritarian regime with little interest beyond its own survival.

A former member of the Michigan State University Advisory Group (which was contracted by Washington and Saigon in the mid-1950s to provide administrative and security training) observed while in South Vietnam, "A primary qualification for appointment to public office [is] loyalty not to the nation but rather to individual leaders . . . [This] narrow recruitment policy . . . neglects such qualities as professional competence and honesty."[16] Opportunities to extract bribes from citizens motivated administrative routines.[17] In addition, civil servants were eligible for membership in the Labor Party (it functioned as a syndicate rather than a political party), which granted members "material benefits which flow to them through the party's financial graft."[18] Diem's closest associates in the army and the bureaucracy were drawn from the 610,000 Catholic refugees who were part of a wave of an estimated 860,000 northerners who had fled to the South after partition.[19] By posting Catholics in key bureaucratic positions,[20] he constructed political obligations along religious lines.[21] An absence of local roots ensured the loyalty of the northern transplants. Commenting on the general ineffectiveness of South Vietnam's governmental institutions, Dennis J. Duncanson observed, "Uncoordinated and changeable policy, accompanied by disregard for the rule of law, made itself felt through the government machine."[22]

Diem tried to win landlord support with a 1955 government decree that returned land acquired by peasants from the Viet Minh, League for the Independence of Vietnam, who had gained control of rural areas during the group's guerrilla war against the French. But by trying to restore traditional peasant-landlord relationships,[23] he created a rural crisis that he compounded by refusing to act when his own provincial officials took the best lands from those redistributed estates.[24] Tenant farmers, now landless, learned that when grievances arose,[25] little recourse existed to enforce their claims.[26] One of the few outlets of protest available to the peasantry was to express support for Viet Cong activities.[27]

Economics distinguishes between total and marginal utility, a difference with important implications for understanding peasant movements, third world nationalism, and revolution. People rank preferences according to the costs of fulfilling them. When they stop believing they can alter their economic opportunities at a reasonable cost, they elect instead to gratify their need for self-esteem through actions that express their sense of community or loyalty to a group whose identity they share. They may gain greater marginal utility from exercising allegiance to their group, especially if measures to transform their economic well-being are out of reach. But in foreign policy circles it is often assumed that oppressed citizens of underdeveloped countries will wait to satisfy the need for self-fulfillment, self-esteem, or self-expression until after their more basic needs are met. By assuming that people fulfill their needs according to total utility rather than marginal utility, we have underestimated the appeal of nationalism in developing nations. This error led to the belief that materialism could subdue nationalist impulses in client regimes such as South Vietnam and Iran.

The South Vietnam government's deepest vulnerability was its failure to win the confidence of the peasantry, a weakness for which the United States shared responsibility.[28] Neither Diem nor his American sponsors could fathom the attraction of a "people's war" to the peasantry or grasp that semiliterate farmers had concerns beyond their daily bowls of rice. Instead, officials characterized unrest in the countryside as either a Communist or Communist-instigated movement.

Who Holds the Strings?

In key policy disputes with Washington, Diem's prerogative usually won out.[29] An early disagreement arose over the Rural Community Development Program of 1954–55, the precursor to the Strategic Hamlet Program carried out by the United States and the GVN. Washington provided $10 million to move some 300,000 northern refugees to uncultivated southern farmland, but the infrastructure needed to increase production was often diverted, causing dismay within the State Department and the economic aid mission. The program was implemented before its economic feasibility was tested, resettlement sites were chosen with little regard to soil fertility or water resources, and individual land allotments were too small to sustain the settlers. Largely uninterested in economic development, Diem became disenchanted with the program, and focused his attention on securing South Vietnam from invasion by the North.

Diem turned the 1961 Strategic Hamlet Program into a "wall of humanity" along the borders to block potential incursions. The South Vietnamese government tended to regard the strategic hamlets as a device for controlling the citizenry, while the Americans wanted inhabitants to derive social and economic benefits and have a strong voice in hamlet affairs. Although the

Rural Community Development Program diverged from U.S. government objectives, no actual penalty was imposed on GVN revenues, because "the total amount of dollar aid to Vietnam had already been fixed [for that year . . . and] unless a conflict caused Congress to appropriate less total aid the following year, attempts to impose restraints on regime elites through limiting project funding would have no effect."[30]

By 1961 or 1962, American visitors to Vietnam commonly claimed that Diem had failed to construct either an ideological rationale or an institutional apparatus for self-government. The real problem was that Americans rejected the Diem regime's ideological impulses and programs because they had little in common with American ideology. The institutional designs for reform hatched in Washington were not finding fertile soil among the South Vietnamese. Seeing that agreement on principles was becoming unlikely, the State and Defense Departments, and eventually President Kennedy, opposed conditioning U.S. aid on reforms. They chose instead to concentrate on earning Vietnamese leaders' trust in long-term U.S. support.[31] Responding to Diem's complaints, Kennedy recalled the U.S. ambassador to South Vietnam, Elbridge Durbrow, who was outspoken in his insistence on GVN reforms.[32] He was replaced by Frederick Nolting, whose instructions were to build a relationship with Diem and to try to better understand his perspective.[33] At this point Kennedy recognized that replacing Diem was a last resort, but as the rural insurgency spread, he lost patience. Diem would never let the South Vietnamese army be led by U.S. officers. Diem had to be at fault, Kennedy concluded, if the United States was not successful at counterinsurgency. A series of self-immolations by dissenting Buddhists was the last straw. Believing that Diem's policies were self-destructive, the Kennedy administration finally collaborated in his removal. That collaboration is a rare instance in which a pro-American dictator was ousted with U.S. complicity. The reasons for the U.S. move are still in dispute, but the consequences were to be a government that lacked an ideological center around which to mobilize support.[34] The best reason for keeping Diem was that he represented some kind of homegrown nationalist ideology around which the nation could rally. The United States was looking for someone who would accept the concept of a military technocracy as the alternative to Communism, but this was not Diem's view. It was precisely his nationalist credentials and his search for a homegrown consensus based on local values that caused friction with American authorities. These authorities were hoping to impose reforms for which no local constituency existed.

Diem's elimination exposed the flimsy basis on which U.S. hopes for an independent South Vietnam rested. To fill the political and social void that Diem's policies created, the United States "Americanized" the war, making the situation more dangerous and legitimacy even more illusive. A comparison of U.S. strategies in Vietnam and Korea illustrates the U.S. dilemma. Korean President Syngman Rhee shared Diem's concerns about maintaining nationalist credentials. Yet, unlike Diem, Rhee placed his military under UN command without compromising those credentials. This option did not exist in South Vietnam. Throughout the Korean War, the Republic of Korea (ROK) retained political autonomy. The task of eliminating subversion and building viable institutions was left to the ROK government. By contrast, after Diem's removal in Vietnam the United States directly engaged its forces in eliminating internal subversion. To many South Vietnamese, it meant that U.S. domination had simply replaced French domination.

Americanization of the war in Vietnam removed the thin veneer of indigenous effort and magnified the deficit of the SVG's social legitimacy. It took the United States a year and a half to find Diem's successor. The Communists used this time to demonstrate that they were the only viable alternative to foreign domination. Diem had believed that Vietnamese nationalist pride would turn public opinion against any government that seemed like an American puppet. Americanization strengthened the hand of the only viable alternative to U.S. domination—the National Front for the Liberation of South Vietnam (NLF)—and when it was destroyed, the North Vietnamese army.

Growing U.S. domination tore apart South Vietnam's social fabric. It undermined production of rice in favor of higher-value crops for urban consumers. Because toiling in the rice fields exposed farmers to combat, they joined a mass exodus to safe urban havens. Young people raised in cities were inculcated with the values of consumption for its own sake. The job of dealing with the chaos caused by the massive influx of U.S. troops and money fell to Nguyen Van Thieu (1965–75), who would lead South Vietnam to its final destruction in 1975.

Like Diem, Thieu was incapable of and uninterested in assembling a broad social constituency or establishing an institutional and ideological basis to coordinate citizen actions in support of his government. The major difference between the two leaders was that Thieu lacked ideological pretensions and had no nationalist credentials. A master opportunist, he assembled a coalition of like-minded individuals willing to share the spoils of plunder. Bureaucrats who were committed to governance to promote national welfare were stymied, and many became enemies of the regime. Expanded American involvement gave Thieu the means to be even more indiscriminate than Diem had been in using executive prerogatives to pay off supporters.

Having surrendered to an outside force the fight to build South Vietnam, Thieu was left without nationalist credibility. Two groups that Diem had spurned—the ethnic Chinese business community and the military brass—were to provide coalitional support to Thieu. These two groups and the state bureaucracy that distributed aid and controlled licenses constituted the three pillars that held up Thieu's regime. The Chinese business elites who aided Thieu's rise to power in 1967 saw their business conglomerates restored and their property, confiscated by Diem, returned. Accumulating capital by political means, the Chinese were politically nonthreatening because of their marginal stature in Vietnamese society.[35] Yet over the course of a few years, Chinese business groups were in control of South Vietnam's economy, sharing their gains with government personnel and maintaining a strong client-patron relationship with Thieu. Unfortunately, their business goals had few connections to the national interest.

Under Thieu the officer corps was packed with loyal generals, whose numbers increased from forty to seventy-three. The enlargement was intended to prevent the coordination of a coup by a few senior officers. Thieu often promoted officers to duties far beyond their abilities, and the new appointees gained shares of the state's economic resources through sanctioned venues for corruption. Eventually the most lucrative government posts were simply auctioned off, which meant that many key positions went to the officers most efficient at collecting bribes and side payments.

Thieu's strategy for political survival depended on persistent inputs of U.S. resources to sustain an economy geared to maintaining the loyalty of his officer corps and business elite. But this strategy so compromised the effectiveness of his administrative apparatus that it eliminated any prospect of implementing social policy and nullified his promises to comply with U.S. policy objectives of establishing a democratic regime. Although he reintroduced village elections and launched a land-to-tillers program,[36] the land redistribution was feeble compared to the earlier redistribution by the Viet Minh. Thieu could not overcome the rural population's loss of confidence in and support of his government.

Thieu ruled as an autocrat, using assassinations and bribery to dissuade challengers from entering the 1971 presidential election. Nguyen Cao Ky, the only viable opponent, withdrew his candidacy and left the Americans without a means of transferring power to legitimately elected national leaders.

Martial law in 1972 gave government the power to impose comprehensive censorship and imprisonment without trial for crimes as vague as supporting neutralism or jeopardizing public safety. In fall 1972, 40,000 detainees were added to the prison population, for whom no public records were kept. U.S. leaders looked the other way. Those most aware of Thieu's abuses also knew that he was their only alternative to instability. Rivalries within the opposition forces left the SVG no framework for amassing broad social support.

There was a final irony in this attempt to foster a viable democratic alternative to Communism in South Vietnam. As the war became less popular among the U.S. electorate, in 1971 and 1972 the Nixon administration tried to implement a "Vietnamization" of the conflict, replacing the U.S. army with South Vietnamese forces. This policy increased U.S. dependency on Thieu's circle just as U.S. funding was disappearing. Without arms and money from Washington Thieu lost the loyalty of the elites, whose support he needed. South Vietnam's army was taught to fight a rich man's war. But the United States then withdrew money for weapons, cutting aid to $300,000, while the North allegedly received $1 billion worth of arms from Russia. Without extensive U.S. backing, South Vietnam lacked the means to support a large, technically proficient fighting force that could withstand an invasion from the North.

Many commentaries on the cause of South Vietnam's defeat point to the regime's weak legitimacy and failing economy. The necessity of feeding the urban centers, whose economies depended on servicing the diminishing U.S. forces, proved to be another contradiction of Vietnamization that made Thieu's position untenable. Urban opposition and elite infighting were increasing in 1975, as North Vietnamese forces rolled in. According to Gabriel Kolko, defeat on the battlefield had its origin in "the ultimate dilemma of Vietnamization," which was "the absence of any real social foundation for the Republic of South Vietnam, outside of the military, whose political roles and motives made its warlike functions quite secondary."[37] Vietnamization could not succeed politically or socially, Kolko concludes, because the economic system of patronage and corruption that sustained it required massive American assistance.

How Did the United States Land in This Dilemma?

Vietnam held little independent commercial or political interest to the United States. The collapse of non-Communist China in 1949 prompted America to seek a viable non-Communist state in South Vietnam.[38] Believing that the future of Asia would be fought in Vietnam, Robert Scigliano wrote, "Diem became America's indispensable man; the United States has considered him the only alternative to Communism in Vietnam . . . the willing dependence of the United States on Diem has given him a great advantage in his dealings with his major ally. . . . [Diem] has felt safe in rejecting American demands."[39] Diem was confident that U.S. politicians would never threaten the ultimate sanction, that of abandoning South Vietnam to the Communists. Both Diem and Thieu understood that their domestic policies mattered less to the United States than did the signals other nations would read about American resolve to draw the line against Communism's advance.

Diem and Thieu assumed that the United States would stay in Vietnam until the bitter end. Like Chiang Kai-shek, both believed that an external enemy—Communism—lay at the root of their country's problems. Both refused to see the negative ways in which their respective regimes were viewed by their own people. The U.S. belief that Vietnam was crucial in the battle against Communism rendered America ineffective in its threats to link aid with policy compliance such as land reform, a wide-reaching tax system, or a socially equitable military draft. South Vietnam's two rulers staved off most attempts to impose reforms by reminding U.S. planners that total collapse and chaos in Saigon were the alternative. "Since the United States now correctly saw that its entire mission was contingent on the RVN's stability, which only Thieu was able to provide, it in turn was wholly dependent on Thieu remaining in power, a fact he perceived and exploited ruthlessly. Ironically, who was master and who was puppet was increasingly blurred with time."[40] Washington and Thieu became synonymous, but accepting Thieu's political role as the only force that could hold the country together ensured a permanent absence of legitimacy. Although few in Washington could see the parallels, it was a repeat of Chiang Kai-shek's collapse on mainland China.

Legitimacy through Consumption

Even before full-scale war with the North erupted, South Vietnam's economic development stagnated.[41] Starting from a very low base, industry in South Vietnam was virtually nonexistent before 1955, and industrial output as a share of GNP increased by only 1.2 percent from 1955 to 1963.[42] Most of North Vietnam's budget went to heavy industry rather than to agriculture, and came from Russian and Chinese investment. "Compared with the dynamic growth of industry in the North, the South was almost stagnant. For each factory built under Diem—there were fewer than two dozen—the Communist regime in the North built fifty."[43]

After the Kennedy administration, social and economic reforms came to a standstill, and the United States gave up on winning the war politically. In contrast to the insurgents, who fought a political war, South Vietnam's leaders ignored the need for political reform. With the help of U.S. aid they artificially stimulated the economy, helping South Vietnamese consumers enjoy an inflated standard of living and creating a consumer-oriented lifestyle that obscured deep-seated economic weaknesses. "One ironic aspect of the war in Vietnam is that while we profess an idealistic philosophy, our failures have been due to an excessive reliance on material factors," Henry Kissinger has observed.[44] But those material factors had a shallow base. The urban population enjoyed a lifestyle that was far beyond its means. "Saigon lived on massive transfusions of economic aid: a huge import surplus financed by the USA, bringing in a million motor bikes and scooters, 75,000 water pumps for irrigation, and large amounts of subsidized fertilizer."[45] The commercial import program and the overvalued currency that supported it caused the economic well-being of the population to depend on foreign aid rather than on entrepreneurship. By 1967 about 40 percent of South Vietnam's GNP consisted of U.S. imports, rising to 50 percent by 1970.[46] Because the countryside was essentially closed to allied forces, U.S. aid primarily consisted of maintaining the standard of living for urban Vietnamese.[47] Saigon's standard of living collapsed "once the artificial support of U.S. aid ceased."[48]

Persistent overvaluation of the currency was also partly to blame for the low level of exports during Diem's regime.[49] The United States and the GVN had agreed in 1955 to establish an official exchange rate of thirty-five piasters to the dollar, grossly overvaluing the former.[50] Importers who bought dollar credits at the official rate could profit handsomely.[51] Because one needed a license from the government of South Vietnam to purchase dollar credits, regime elites gained control over access to the market and over the elaborate apparatus of government rent seeking. South Vietnamese producers could not export their goods because of the overvalued piaster, which also made it difficult to compete with inexpensive imports that flooded the market. With exports never surpassing 10 percent of imports, the tax on the surge of imports, which "constituted the largest single source of public revenue,"[52] made it difficult for the United States to exercise supervision or control.

Domestic revenues came primarily from taxes on mass-consumption items and imports, and both declined with the retreat of U.S. funding and the loss of fiscal independence, which drove the network of government collaborators to jump ship.

Resource Mobilization and Taxation

The problem of resource mobilization emerged early during Diem's regime. Total U.S. aid to South Vietnam between 1955 and 1963 was about $3.3 billion. This represented roughly 16.7 percent of Vietnam's GNP and provided between 38 percent and 73 percent of the GVN's budget. Only 48 percent of state expenditures were financed through taxes,[53] showing the relative importance of foreign aid to domestic revenue sources. Public perception of the GVN as an illegitimate government was reflected in tax delinquency that "rose from an already alarming 44 per cent in 1960 to 47 per cent in 1961 and to 51 per cent in 1962; and it was to rise to 57 per cent in 1963."[54] GVN tax revenue was roughly 9.8 percent of GDP, which was very low compared to that of other countries in its per capita income group.[55] Public dissatisfaction caused by state institutions' general ineffectiveness to provide public goods increased the perception of illegitimacy.

Successive U.S. administrations assumed that the actions of political elites were related to their ideology and character, ignoring or simply not understanding that domestic political incentives were distorted by massive injections of U.S. aid. Most American officials never realized that their aid had facilitated the regime's unresponsiveness and illegitimacy, reducing the cost to political leaders of establishing a patron-client regime. Aid substituted for the need for effective or responsive institutions, allowing the regime to increase authoritarian control. It also resulted in weak tax compliance, as individuals refused to go along with a government that did not respond to their needs.[56] Unable to collect more than 10 percent of its estimated tax base, the government would not have been able to sustain itself without aid that essentially subsidized illegitimacy.

Vietnam faced the dilemma confronted by other polities that were based on patron-client regimes under stress. Public perceptions of government legitimacy were undermined because the general activity of the state was devoted to providing private goods to a small base of supporters. An inability to obtain enough revenue to carry out requisite state activities eroded political support for the regime and incited unrest and opposition.[57] However, to effectively collect taxes the government needed institutions that would create legitimacy among those taxed.[58] Diem and Thieu both resisted institutional reform, understanding that the transparency and accountability necessary for tax compliance would undermine the government's cut deals with its client base.[59]

Instead, these leaders' system for political survival became reform-proof. "The RVN was not simply a dependent society financially; it was systemically corrupt, and this routinized dishonesty was crucial to keeping Thieu in power. Had he attempted to redirect a significant portion of the nation's resources to meet its social needs . . . he would have lost hold of the senior officers who were major beneficiaries of his regime."[60] The South Vietnam government was reform-proof, too, because the United States was in no position to insist on change, and Washington knew this.[61]

A weak economy and inadequate state revenues contributed to South Vietnam's inability to defend itself after the American withdrawal. When the Republic of Vietnam fell in April 1975, its budget deficit exceeded one-sixth of the nation's GDP. A destructive wave of inflation, 23 percent in 1972, rose to 55 percent by 1974.[62] Of South Vietnam's urban population, 30 percent were unemployed, and real wages had decreased by 30 percent. Per capita agricultural production also declined.[63] Once a net exporter of rice in the French colonial period, South Vietnam now depended on importing rice along with other food staples. A collapsing economy left the military dangerously underfunded by the time of the invasion by the North. "South Vietnam could only secure a stock of ammunition for fifty-two days of fighting. About 35 percent of its tanks and 50 percent of its armored personnel carriers and aircraft were out of use for lack of spare parts."[64] The weak domestic economy was unable to produce even the relatively basic materials it required.[65] The U.S. Senate Foreign Relations Committee offered this assessment: "Vietnam is rich in agricultural resources but cannot feed herself. Has absorbed western technology but cannot afford the imports to operate it . . . and provides a wide range of government services but does not have the means to pay for them."[66] South Vietnam's economy could simply no longer support its people or the war.

Failure to Establish Political Legitimacy in the South

Trained to deal with domestic policy dilemmas, American policy planners take for granted a cultural legacy of shared values and national symbols that create a shared national identity. Decades of colonial domination rarely produce a similar convergence of "civic beliefs" with a national "cultural legacy."[67] Inequality and ethnic diversity often inhibit the spread of shared values or common knowledge, which prevents developing economies from Africa to Latin America from establishing deep liquid markets for their assets.[68] Peter Turchin has speculated that the primary source of variation within stateless societies is conflict between groups.[69] Vietnam historically has fit this description; its unity has been marred by continuous internal divisions among local groups.

South Vietnam was a construct of Western ambitions to stop Communism. Nothing in the cultural heritage of Vietnam linked the inalienable rights of the individual to the cultural legacy of nationhood. Social identity was grounded in loyalty to family or village rather than to some abstract state. South Vietnam's citizens shared few ideals or any unifying set of abstract values like those espoused in the French Declaration of the Rights of Man, or in the U.S. Declaration of Independence and Bill of Rights.

Vietnam's state institutions, like those of many other highly unequal third world societies, originated as instruments of colonial oppression. Believing that a shared framework for dealing with conflict is a work of social construction, Ho Chi Minh spread the germ of nationalism across historic ethnic, class, and geographic barriers, manipulating cultural markers to build loyalty to the nationalist cause. Diem also had a nationalist program. But his political philosophy was not convincing enough to overcome the fractious nature of South Vietnamese society. His philosophy failed to offer the coherent norms for sustained intergroup cooperation that were needed to defeat the North; he was overthrown by his own generals. Communism offered an equity norm to overcome the traditional divisions of status, religion, wealth, ethnicity, and gender discrimination that caused Diem's fall. By contrast, Ho Chi Minh undertook deliberate strategic manipulation to redefine the collective identity of his people to surmount traditional collective action barriers. He successfully overcame long-lived discriminatory norms. This is why, despite the failure of his economic ideas, Ho Chi Minh is admired in Vietnam for establishing a Vietnamese national identity. This identity was one in which the hope of democracy was envisioned but never implemented by his successors.

By transforming discriminatory norms into equity-based norms, Ho Chi Minh improved the state's efficiency to mobilize the use of social resources. Matching belief to behavior, he created a social dynamic that completed the work of Vietnamese unification, which had begun unsuccessfully almost a thousand years earlier. The result is that even Vietnamese who profoundly disagree with his economic policies look to Ho Chi Minh as the nation's founding father.

Equity, Mobilization, and Political Legitimacy in East Asia

South Vietnam and the Philippines were both new nations emerging from a long experience of foreign rule. In both countries, problems of state authority and national identity combined to produce one paramount political failure: both regimes were unsuccessful at establishing an inclusive formula for regime legitimacy. Despite the money and personnel the United States provided to these regimes, sustaining a system of deeply unpopular landlord rule aroused apathy and resentment in both countries. This elite-based formula for political stability was even less appropriate in South Vietnam, where the United States had fewer levers available to infuse the population with American ideals.

In the Philippines the coherent landholding elite shared a common geopolitical outlook with the United States. After World War II, America gained much goodwill there by ejecting the Japanese.[70] America lived up to its promise to prepare the Philippines for independence. In South Vietnam, however, America became the occupying power, whose promise to eliminate Communism restored Western domination. Ironically, Diem, a nationalist to the core, had feared exactly this domination. His efforts to prevent the Americanization of the conflict probably led to his elimination. It is easy to speculate that he might have sought accommodation with the North before he would have allowed a massive influx of U.S. forces.

South Vietnam followed the pattern set by the Philippines of rewarding clientelism over citizenship. To succeed at this strategy, leadership required ample resources to purchase political support.[71] The first step in both countries was the centralization of political power to expand state control over the economy and over foreign investment. Private goods were allocated through government control over licensing private industry and over state industry.[72] Production by the private sector required the approval and control of the state,[73] which would "reserve the right to participate in the ratio of over 51% in certain enterprises of vital importance to the nation's economy or affecting national security."[74] Majority GVN ownership of most industrial enterprises resulted. The growing state sector became a source of opportunities for rents that allowed the politically connected to beat out rival firms.[75] But these strategies diminished the economic performance of both nations, driving productive activities out in favor of nonproductive rent seeking.

One way to compensate for the absence of a civic culture is for political leadership to advance clients who are linked by kinship, ethnicity, or some other shared characteristic in support of the regime.[76] In this way, ethnicity or religion functions as a surrogate for ideological legitimacy. Diem did this with the northern Christians, and Marcos and Thieu provided selective benefits to ethnic Chinese business interests. Neither country's government achieved procedural fairness in delivering services or regulating behavior. The effective operation of public institutions was impaired because they were used to facilitate corruption. Land reform in both countries failed when judges in the Philippines and Diem loyalists in South Vietnam illicitly transferred peasant lands to themselves. Large numbers of provisional government employees—political hacks hired outside the civil service system—transformed core functions of government into personal fiefdoms. A clientelistic polity that required a complex network of rent-seeking venues and an absence of moral consensus made the regime in South Vietnam, like that of the Philippines, unable to mobilize adequate domestic resources. Dependency on an outside power deprived leadership in South Vietnam and the Philippines of national legitimacy.

In contrast, autocratic rulers in Singapore, South Korea, and Taiwan were state-builders. Instead of offering access to state benefits through personal clientelism, East Asia's most successful rulers acted as if they held a social compact with their constituents. They erected institutions that assured all citizens basic economic rights. They invested in agricultural research and development, irrigation, rural education, and infrastructure. These investments contributed to agricultural production and reduced rural poverty and regional inequality. Competent state bureaucracies ensured that this unwritten contract was backed by programs for primary health care and primary education. Successful leaders promoted agrarian prosperity through land reform and abundant rural credit. The non-Communist countries of the Pacific Rim—Malaysia, Japan, Singapore, South Korea, and Taiwan—found a socially inclusive form of industrialization, an equity norm that ensured their leaders' political viability. A unique form of industrial capitalism took root in response to the region's vulnerability to Communist insurrection. Instead of clientelism, these leaders forged an inclusive consensus based on sharing the dividends of future economic growth.[77] In contrast to South Vietnam or the Philippines, citizens depended on a strong state, but not on personal ties to representatives of that state.. The success of the East Asian model, blending social inclusion with private investment, has had a far greater appeal than the democratic but socially unequal examples of development associated with Washington's preferred strategy.

Was the Vietnam War a time-buying victory that protected the Pacific Rim, providing breathing space for democracy and capitalism to flourish? Walt Rostow, a national security adviser to both Presidents Kennedy and Johnson, argued that the Vietnam War allowed impressive development to take place in other parts of Southeast Asia, including Thailand, Indonesia, Taiwan, and Singapore. He assumes that an early Communist victory would have spread beyond Indochina, preventing the region's growth, and that the U.S. war effort granted these economies the time to build viable non-Communist alternatives.[78]

Rostow measures the success of the U.S. war effort by the economic growth posted by neighboring non-Communist regimes. But he overlooks the fact that the two nations that most closely followed the American model, South Vietnam and the Philippines, did less well than their neighbors precisely because the U.S. shield insulated regime elites from making concessions to popular demands for improved health and education. The nations that were to become East Asia's high performers—Japan, Singapore, South Korea, and Taiwan—gained legitimacy by investing heavily in the human development of their populations. Absent the insurgency constraint, these four nations' autocratic regimes would have been less likely to make the investments in heath, education, infrastructure, and rural credit that were the backbones of their economic takeoffs.

Another factor Rostow overlooks is that the military success of Communism in Vietnam strengthened the cohesion of alliances within the Soviet bloc and reinforced Soviet ideological influence. The hardened party dogma that resulted ultimately produced socialism's economic collapse. If not for the environment of cold war belligerence, differences within the bloc might have surfaced earlier and problems with the mismatch between ideals and economic performance might have been corrected earlier. The cold war also created collateral damage in other developing regions where America's image as a racist neocolonial power undermined support for its economic model.

Ironically, socialism led to an acceptance of private investment, market competition, and trade openness in nations where initial political support for the government was weak. When détente finally arrived it gave capitalism's most avowed enemies, China and later Vietnam, established mechanisms for social mobilization based on an equity norm that was later used to anchor broad acceptance of market allocations. Today China and Vietnam are among the most committed market-friendly reformers among developing nations. Through socialism their citizens have many of modernization's benefits, including gender equality, leisure, the flattening of entrenched elites, and laws that apply to all citizens alike. These benefits were denied the populations of countries that were more explicitly in the capitalist camp, such as Iraq, Iran, Pakistan, the Philippines, and Turkey.

Sandbox or Falling Domino?

Before Communism, Vietnam, like China, was an incoherent composite of factions incapable of mobilizing sufficient resources or strength to overcome outside invaders.[79] Communism offered an equity norm that allowed the North's leadership to overcome collective action barriers, thereby giving it the strength to defeat the French and then to form a northern government. The Geneva Accords were signed with the Communists of the North, not with representatives of the South. Southerners never found a unifying principle with which to overcome their traditional social, ethnic, and personalized fractures. Diem failed. He was undermined and eventually killed by his own generals, who for almost two years were unable to form a new government. When they did form one, it was merely a system of personalized discrimination with one strongman temporarily at the head. The polity still had no unifying principle or norm around which to coalesce. Unable to smooth over the fractures that prevented social mobilization in the past, the South was overcome by the exhausted but still unified forces of the North.[80]

The physicist Per Bak has written, "A single falling grain, containing many individual atoms, does not constitute a punctuation or avalanche in the sand pile."[81] In hindsight, Communism, which arose out of locally available particles in Russia, China, and later Vietnam, was a local manifestation of a globally critical process in which the key variable was the construction of an equity norm strong enough to overcome traditional collective action barriers and to sustain the disruptive social transition to industrialization. Now that Communism is gone, except in North Korea and Cuba, that process of mobilization continues to take new forms around the world. It seems that Vietnam was a sandbox at best, not an avalanche, as U.S. adherents of domino theory had posited.

Vietnam's fall was not the toppling event it was advertised to be for a reason that was only dimly understood at the time. Creating a one-party Leninist system was the precondition for Ho Chi Minh's success, just as it was the essence of Lenin's, Stalin's, and later Mao Zedong's strength. This precondition reflects a process of self-organization that is not easily replicated by outside intervention. Democracy, too, is a self-organizing outcome of a complex social process that is not easily engineered by foreign intervention. For reasons we will return to at the end of this book, it requires self-organization, not just transplanted institutions.

9

Mirage of Stability:
The United States and
the Shah of Iran

The evidence suggests that we are poorly equipped to deal with revolutionary societies, and when religion is added to revolution, we are paralyzed.
—Gary Sick, *All Fall Down: America's Tragic Encounter with Iran* (1985)

Iran under the great leadership of the Shah is an island of stability in one of the more troubled areas of the world. This is a great tribute to you, Your Majesty, and to your leadership, and to the respect, admiration and love which your people give to you.
—President Jimmy Carter, speaking in Tehran, December 31, 1977

A persistent oversight in U.S. reconstruction efforts around the globe has been the failure to anticipate that an externally initiated process of change may introduce greater inequality within a nation by equipping one subset of a population with better survival tools than another. This situation may polarize society and destabilize it. In Iran under Mohammad Reza Shah Pahlavi, the injection of Western economic rationality and weaponry started a cycle of inequality (see table 9-1). As in postcolonial Africa, imported skill was narrowly distributed, endowing recipients with the means to dominate less well-positioned citizens. The less well-trained fell further behind, initiating a downward spiral of recrimination and polarization that, once begun, made consensus on the future social order difficult to attain. With gains from development so unevenly distributed in Iran, the marginalized—including those operating within the economic network of the bazaar, which was Iran's traditional method for distributing goods and services—worked to destroy the system they identified with the new inequalities.

Why Such Blindness?

The fall of the shah in January 1979 was largely unforeseen in America, where the leader of Iran's revolution and the cause for which he stood were virtually

Table 9-1. *Historical Timeline of Iran, Pahlavi Dynasty to the Islamic Republic of Iran, 1926–Present*

Reza Shah	1926–41
Mohammad Reza Shah Pahlavi	1942–79
Muhammad Mossadegh (prime minister)	1941–53
Muhammad Mossadegh (ruler)	1953 (3 days)
Mohammad Reza Shah Pahlavi (dictator)	1953–78
Ayatollah Khomeini (ruler of Islamic Republic)	1979–89
Islamic Republic of Iran	1979–present

Source: Roberto Ortiz de Zárate, *Iran,* Zarate's Political Collections: 1996–2006 (www.terra.es/personal2/monolith).

unknown. The answer as to why the American foreign policy establishment was so willfully uninformed about a country it believed was critical to U.S. economic and military security highlights the limitations of U.S. cold war policies in the third world. In this chapter I divide these limitations into two categories, conceptual and strategic failures, as they pertain to Iran.[1]

Throughout the cold war America's foreign policy establishment felt secure that Islam would inoculate Middle Eastern populations against revolutionary tendencies.[2] This view was born of the belief that Communist-inspired revolution was the real world danger, and that the Islamic clergy could see this danger and could be counted on to fight it. Many Americans believed that the Russians were behind the revolutionary events that began to unfold in Iran in 1979. To think otherwise would have challenged the premises of U.S. global strategy. Few in Washington anticipated how effectively the clerics had absorbed the social critique of Iran's left and used the sanctuary of the mosque to promote leftist agendas of social change.[3] The cold war lens distorted the West's understanding of the role of Muslim clerics and their influence over Middle East populations.

The Most Strategic of Nations

The shah of Iran, Mohammad Reza Pahlavi, was a lynchpin of U.S. security in the Middle East for four U.S. administrations, beginning with Eisenhower, a cautious supporter; Kennedy was a cautious reformer; Johnson, an enthusiast; Nixon and Ford, strong and visible backers; Carter, reluctant and hypercritical. The Eisenhower administration gave the wink to covert U.S. operations to help organize the downfall of Iran's elected prime minister, Muhammad Mossadegh, in 1953. The formal mechanism that ended Mossadegh's tenure was a dismissal by decree by Mohammad Reza Shah

Pahlavi,[4] the figurehead monarch who, since taking the throne in 1941, had avoided day-to-day politics.[5] The shah's unconstitutional action was preceded by a U.S.-funded campaign to discredit and remove the elected prime minister and replace him with an appointed one, a former Nazi collaborator and general, Fazlollah Zahedi. With Mossadegh out of the way, Pahlavi began a long climb to regain the power, prestige, and wealth formerly held by his father, Reza Shah Pahlavi, the founder of the Pahlavi dynasty.

Dwight Eisenhower's use of covert action to remove a foreign leader represented a new strategy, not a new ideology. Eisenhower shared Harry Truman's fear of global Communism, but not Truman's reluctance to abet colonialists in crushing third world nationalism. What for Truman was an economic and nationalist dispute between Iran and Britain for control over Iranian oil was, in the eyes of the Eisenhower administration, part of the greater conflict to contain global Communism. The British won the new U.S. administration's active participation in Mossadegh's removal by portraying the prime minister as being closely aligned with native Communists.

For stopping the complete nationalization of the oil fields, Mossadegh's pet concern, the shah gained support from the West for dismantling Iran's nascent democracy and restoring the unlimited monarchical discretion enjoyed by his father over his subjects. The price the young Pahlavi was only too willing to pay was to share the oil revenues with a Western consortium comprising British Petroleum, Royal Dutch Shell, and nearly a dozen American companies.

Eisenhower's supporters would always view the coup in Iran as a successful covert action and one of the great triumphs of cold war diplomacy. The benefits were measured in the 24 billion barrels of crude oil that ensured that the world supply of oil would outrun demand throughout the 1960s. Furthermore, the shah offered the West a listening post for intelligence reports on Soviet activities. In turn, Western supplies bolstered Iran's national army, making it a regional military force essential to defense alliances that included Turkey, Iraq, and Pakistan.[6] The shah provided pro-Israeli votes in the UN from a major Islamic nation, while supplying Israel's oil needs for more than two decades. But scholars generally take a decidedly negative view of the coup. There is a consensus that the coup created a wound that never healed in Iran and that it served as the basis for all subsequent assertions by Iranian nationalists of U.S. betrayal. The coup became the collective grievance in the Iranian psyche that nurtured anti-Americanism. The fundamentalist faction pointed to the fall of the secular Mossadegh as the icon of U.S. imperialism, a notion that inflamed public opinion against Washington in the early days of the 1979 revolution.

Iranians forget that after World War II they were in need of protection from historic threats, both Britain and Russia. They also overlook that the fall of Mossadegh's popularity was due in part to his own intransigence, which contributed to the success of the American propaganda war against him. His single-minded focus on eliminating the British oil monopoly blinded him to the negative impact he was having on the economy, an impact that alienated the nation's elites. His disregard of inequities in landlord-tenant relations caused him to lose popular support. Today, Mossadegh enjoys a reputation for being the one Iranian leader who stood up against foreign domination. Yet his strategy for nationalization depended on U.S. economic aid. He ruled as an autocrat and indulged in many unconstitutional actions, including the temporary suppression of the Majlis (Iran's parliament). Very soon after the coup, Iranians became aware that it had been facilitated by foreigners. By contributing to Mossadegh's fall, the United States was forever linked with the shah's legacy of repression, a legacy that stands in sharp contrast to that of Mossadegh. If nothing else, Mossadegh was lenient to his opponents, forgave his enemies, and tried to apply the law evenly to all Iranians.

Like many middle-class Iranians, Mossadegh was attracted by Truman's anti-colonial, pro-democracy rhetoric. Iran had turned to the United States before for protection, aid, and ideological support. During World War II, Iran hoped that Washington would keep Britain and the Soviet Union from seizing control of the country's oil fields. In 1951 and 1952 Truman worked with Mossadegh, though unsuccessfully, to regain some of those lost oil rights for Iran.[7] By the late 1950s, however, the United States had given its full support to the shah's regime, even as the shah trampled the Majlis, crushed dissent, and systematically undermined all local institutions of self-government.[8] The shah treated dissidents harshly, and many were killed.[9] When he could not destroy opposition to his power, he co-opted it. The shah's new organ of repression, the domestic security and intelligence service known as SAVAK, was created in 1957. It was designed to ensure that the personal and material security of national elites would depend on the shah's protection.[10]

President Kennedy was the only U.S. president who was aggressive in using aid as leverage for social reform. According to some sources, in 1961 he backed the appointment of social reformer Ali Amini (whom Kennedy considered a personal friend) as Iranian prime minister, and encouraged the shah to allow Amini to carry out badly needed land reform. This same land reform, some sources say, angered the wealthy mullahs by restricting their traditional privileges. Frustrated by the lack of an administrative apparatus to deliver policy to the poorest sectors,[11] Amini resigned a year later. A student uprising took place on June 5, 1963. The United States might have seized the opportunity to distance itself from the regime's brutal response. Instead, Washington acquiesced to the repression of dissent, believing that the shah had acted to prevent Communist-inspired insurgency. Open resistance to the shah's *white revolution*—a term used by the shah to designate the program of economic and social reforms he initiated in 1963—ended for more than a decade. "The country plunged into a frenzy of construction and modernization fueled by dramatic increases in oil production and oil revenues, which climbed from $555 million in 1963 to $5 billion in 1973. Iran made striking improvement in virtually every field of human and industrial development during the late 1960s and early 1970s, though the benefits were not equally distributed."[12]

Another event little noticed by Americans in 1964[13] was the exile of an obscure cleric named Ayatollah Ruhollah Khomeini. When Khomeini reappeared on the Iranian stage nearly fourteen years later, his hostility toward the United States, displayed during the subsequent hostage crisis, seemed pathological to Americans. They did not know that "his arrest, imprisonment and fourteen years of exile were the direct result of his opposition to 'Westoxication' and, in particular, to the granting of special rights and privileges to Americans in Iran."[14]

The 1967 Arab-Israeli War further illustrated the region's instability, and Washington saw support of Iran as crucial. Still, in Iran's local elections of 1968, when 90 percent of Tehran voters abstained and "the demonstration of public indifference was not confined to the capital,"[15] the U.S. government refused to see the discontent,[16] to look beyond official explanations for answers to uncomfortable tendencies. American administrations from Kennedy onward were convinced that the threat to Iran posed by the Soviet Union warranted Iran's escalation of internal repression.

The willful blindness further increased during the Nixon and Ford years. Distracted by difficulties in Vietnam, the Nixon White House dramatically shifted U.S. foreign policy to allow regional allies access to sophisticated military technology.[17] The president directed the national security bureaucracy to defer to the shah's judgment in stocking his military.[18] The new security doctrine allowed the shah, as "gendarme of the Gulf," to purchase any non-nuclear arms on his shopping list, and by 1976, Iran was spending as much on defense as mainland China, and with less than one-tenth China's population, Iran was fielding the world's fifth-largest army.[19] In return, the shah promised to protect Western interests in the Persian Gulf.

The U.S. Department of Defense warned that Iran's military buildup was detrimental to long-term U.S. interests, but these admonitions would not alter Nixon's commitment to the shah. The officials under Nixon who doubted the shah's frantic military and industrialization expansion learned to keep their thoughts to themselves. The White House "based its entire strategic concept for the Persian Gulf region on the strength and stability of the shah and . . . was irrevocably wedded to that approach."[20]

Nixon's administration encouraged the shah's megalomania, allowing it to reach new heights. Commemorating 2,500 years of unbroken monarchy on October 15, 1971, Mohammad Reza Shah Pahlavi presented himself as God's agent with the most extravagant celebration of personal power seen anywhere during the cold war. Sensitive to the fact that his father had been a palace guard, the shah was always in search of legitimacy. The celebration at Persepolis did not alter the impression that he was the agent of a foreign god sitting in Washington.

The Carter administration, like Kennedy's, tried to shift the policy focus to reform. Carter drew attention to the shah's dismal civil rights record, his abolition of political parties in 1975, and SAVAK's use of torture against dissidents. The U.S. president threatened to shut off aid unless reforms were enacted, which prompted Pahlavi to make superficial gestures toward political liberalization. He released political prisoners in 1977, for instance, and Washington welcomed these goodwill gestures. But when the Iranian public took to the streets, overtly expressing their discontent for the first time since the arrest of Khomeini a decade earlier, the shah brutally retaliated against the clerics. The legitimacy of the shah's regime tumbled so dramatically following the government's first relaxation of repression that it never recovered. Like Nixon, for the sake of anti-Communism Carter eventually ignored human rights abuses and continued to support the shah's arms buildup. When the Senate protested the runaway arms sales, the president went head-to-head against members of his own party to procure the weaponry the shah demanded.[21]

> Throughout the summer and early fall of 1977, President Carter sent numerous signals of support to the shah. The most important example was the administration's campaign to sell the shah the technologically advanced $1.23 billion AWACS. This political battle clearly indicates a strong early commitment by the Carter administration to the shah's government—a commitment that ran against the very principles that Carter had announced from the onset of his presidency. Despite his public determination to reduce American arms sales across the board, early in 1977 Carter chose to make Iran an exception.[22]

Today, CIA analysts claim that the agency had ignored their warnings about the regime's vulnerability and that their speculation was kept from the White House. Conventional explanations for the failure to predict the shah's fall emphasize the sociology of "group think." Gary Sick, the State Department officer responsible for Iran through the Carter administration, recounts that by the time of the 1979 Iranian revolution, the U.S. foreign policy bureaucracy had essentially burned its bridges to those sectors of Iranian society not directly controlled by the shah. Even as the shah's fall became a virtual certainty, analysts withheld negative speculation. Virtually every group within the U.S. government with activities connected to Iran had a vested interest in the shah's survival. His fall would require a full-scale reconstruction of U.S. global obligations. Thus, Sick asserts that it was useless to make the call that the shah's regime was in trouble; no remedy was at hand. In State Department culture, according to Sick, it is common to view a policy that lasts for twenty-five months as successful. The department's Iranian policy had worked for twenty-five years, so there was an overriding sentiment of "let's not touch it."

The shortcoming of Sick's explanation is that inertia or group think can be used to explain virtually any case of bureaucratic conservatism without identifying the underlying reasons for the particular example of inertia. The disappointing response to the shah's doomed regime can be traced to an inadequate conceptualization of the modernization process and of long-term U.S. strategic interests, as explained below.

Conceptual Failures

The United States failed to understand the market, social, and political risks that the shah's policies and management style brought to himself and to Iran throughout his rule

Market Risks

Among Pahlavi's strongest supporters were private U.S. firms that perceived the shah as the champion of an economy based on private initiative. To gain their support the shah followed the conventional economic wisdom of his day. Heeding the advice of the World Bank and his U.S. advisers, he invested strongly in heavy industry and infrastructure. Contemporary policymakers envisioned a surge in output that would trickle down, lifting backward sectors out of poverty. Bureaucratic authoritarianism seemed to have this effect in Brazil after 1964.[23] In retrospect, we now see that the shah's economic programs violated every tenet of what is now recognized as good development management. He failed to establish low and stable inflation, he did not develop strong property rights or price-driven markets, he did not institute the rule of law; and he did not adequately provide for health and education. He conducted all aspects of economic management secretively.

Iran's economic institutions were inimical to incentives for private investment. The state controlled most investment and subsidized low-interest rates for bank loans to large industries run by loyalists. This allowed loyalists to control the economy's critical sectors. "The state used its dominance not only to promote rapid development but also to co-opt and control various societal groups."[24] Economic opportunities became barter for political loyalty, making market participation dependent on political connections rather than productivity. Opaque institutional procedures ensured the importance of personal connections. High tariffs protected preferred industries so that shah-favored producers did not have to meet international efficiency standards. The United States favored the shah's program as a showcase for capitalism that stood in contrast to the disastrous socialist experiments conducted in Egypt, Iraq, and Syria.

However, the shah created an environment of deep uncertainty. Rural society remained tradition-bound, and most of the urban population conducted business as it always had through periods of invasions, civil wars, and political instability—by remaining distrustful and self-interested. Iranian businessmen had grave misgivings about prospective partners. They generally minded their own business, mistrusting large-scale, cooperative entrepreneurial activities. Iran businessmen operated on the basis of conservatism, quick profits, and a high disregard of the future. Without the conditions for cooperative endeavor, little scope for individual initiative existed for those outside the leadership clique.

Despite their high salaries, Iranian government officials were known to use their control over regulation to extract rents from would-be private investors. Companies and investments above a certain size required licenses, creating an avenue for corruption. The costs of these corrupt practices were passed along to consumers in the form of higher prices. Consumers or businessmen who did not want to participate in a system of bribery faced violent persecution.[25]

Social Risks

The shah hoped that economic growth would be a substitute for, and ultimately a source of, social coherence. He did not anticipate the social conflicts provoked by policies that concentrated income in the handful of elite consumers who formed the basis of the home market. Planners selected projects with low value-added and low employment generation. The nation's investment program was dominated by a small number of capital-intensive projects that were insufficient to absorb the underemployed labor market.[26] The few capital-intensive plants produced inadequate linkages to an economy comprising craftsmen and artisans.[27] Domestic demand increased for high-income groups rather than for mass consumers, and labor and agricultural incomes stagnated. The shah followed standard development theory of the 1960s, which viewed infant industries as an investment in the future. He ignored short-term inefficiencies, hoping that economies of scale could be attained so that the infant industries would join the international market economy. He anticipated that backward and forward linkages would create future waves of new industries. The shah's time frame for these effects was twenty-five to thirty years. The theory was strongly advocated by U.S. policy advisers, who believed that modernization would come with the new industries, and that the new classes who propelled the modern economy would gradually absorb the traditional sectors. The shah believed it would be easier and faster to rely on new Westernized business classes and Western-trained technocrats than to modernize and educate large segments of rural society. We now see that he greatly underestimated the risks of failure, and did not see that results would not kick in fast enough to dispel the disillusion of those who felt left behind. Large sectors of the population experienced severe relative deprivation even as the economy expanded.

Between the 1960s and 1970s, GNP increased dramatically, from US$200 to $1,000 in real terms. However, social, educational, and economic conditions for the majority of Iranian citizens remained primitive, and income disparity between the rich and poor remained constant. Oil income was used to support large industries and provide high salaries to the higher administrative echelons, creating a market for upscale consumer durables, including advanced degrees from American universities. Massive consumption of arms and luxury goods contrasted with the poverty that was in evidence throughout Iran.[28] Schools and hospitals were not built quickly enough to accommodate the massive migration of the poor from the countryside to the cities in search of employment.[29] From 1960 to 1975, the availability of basic primary health and education services was far below the average of that for all underdeveloped countries.[30] The trends that modernization theorists predict are at work during economic expansion—most notably, pressures for occupational specialization, urbanization, and higher education—were suppressed.

An important source of economic discontent leading to revolution was the government's failure to develop a strategy for rural development. Agricultural production and food policy were low priorities in the shah's development planning. The agricultural sector had languished until 1960, when, with the help of economic and technical assistance, a series of land reforms created an agrarian middle class. This first phase of agrarian reform aroused expectations of equity, but 40 percent of the rural population had not benefited, and subsequent reforms were even more conservative. The government rarely provided rural credit and marketing services.[31] Villages did not have recourse to loans, and farm prices were manipulated to benefit urban consumers. The government favored private mechanized farming, despite the higher productivity per person of small and medium peasant holdings.

Large numbers of rural poor were pushed off the land to cities where they could not find jobs. The swelling migration made urban grain security a priority. Imported food further weakened the position of indigenous farmers. Nomads were deprived of their livelihood in favor of large agribusinesses managed by wealthy Iranians who could afford expensive imported equipment, cattle, and feed. The consumer-oriented price controls that increasingly favored city dwellers turned peasants into a disfavored group, while foreign grain producers gained subsidized access to Iran's urban market. Problems in agriculture can be attributed to what economists call the Dutch disease, which refers to the decline of the Netherlands' manufacturing sector after the discovery of natural gas in the 1960s. In Iran, domestic inflation and a fixed nominal exchange rate inflated the value of the riyal. Inexpensive imports of food, intended to control inflation, only made agriculture unprofitable.

Authoritarian regimes in East Asia implemented economic development that recognized the need for social reform to ensure political support. The shah's economic development was less effective, as seen by comparing the human development indicator (HDI) values for these nations during Iran's Pahlavi dynasty (see figure 9-1). The shah sought to be a model of enlightened dictatorship but his model suffers from several notable deficiencies that become more apparent when he is compared to the successful autocrats of East Asia.

Elitist policies ensured that investment opportunities in the urban sector were reserved for the shah's clients. Small shopkeepers and craftspeople had difficulty obtaining bank credit. Unable to use their enterprises as collateral for loans, they had to resort to "bazaar" rates of 25 to 100 percent. Unable to find capital to enlarge their companies, the urban core of small commodity producers—at least half a million merchants, shopkeepers, small traders, and

Figure 9-1. *Comparison of Human Development Indicators, Iran and Developed Asia, Pahlavi Dynasty to Islamic Republic of Iran, 1975–2003*

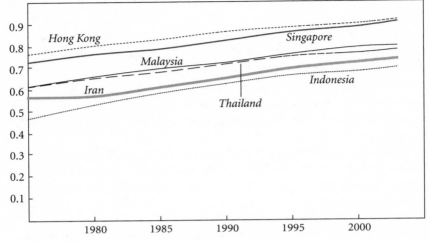

Source: World Bank, World Development Indicators.

artisans—perceived the economy's expansion to be biased against them. Their relative status was declining compared to that of groups enriched by the regime's subsidized megabusinesses. The oil workers were another group whose indignation over relative deprivation had political consequences for the shah during the 1979 crisis. A policy more favorable to small- and medium-size enterprises that diminished income inequality might also have reduced political and economic uncertainty.

Political Risks

Most scholars of the shah's regime agree that his vision of Iran's future lacked a democratic conception of social progress. Arbitrary rule and undue interference in citizens' lives engendered deep hostility toward the regime. The shah built his support on a narrow coalition of large landlords, government bureaucracy, and the military. The narrow factional support meant that policies his government offered for modernizing the economy were limited to strategies that ensured the political loyalty of beneficiaries.

Because of that narrow factional base, the government did not receive sufficient information about the failure of its development strategy. The regime was therefore unable to recognize the extent of resentment generated by inequities in wealth distribution, the feelings of relative deprivation harbored by traditional commodity producers, and the social dislocations caused by the state's economic programs. The beneficiaries of economic prosperity were dependent on the shah, who in turn depended on oil production revenues to run his government. In this sense, the shah's approach differed greatly from that of East Asia's tiger economies. In those nations, leaders depended on wealth that was created by diverse industrial sectors. These leaders therefore had incentives for inclusive policymaking. In Japan, South Korea, Malaysia, and Singapore, business-government councils were created to allow the private sector to participate in policymaking with government technocrats and sometimes the head of state.[32]

The shah's management of the economy was a projection of his politics. His administration was designed to favor an elite constituency with private goods. Consolidating real power in his own hands by undercutting effective individuals such as Prime Minister Ali Amini in favor of compliant ministers was the shah's management weakness. No major decisions such as appointments or investments were possible without Pahlavi's consent. The credibility of the political parties he introduced was undermined by the restrictions he placed on their actions. The institutions of government did not evolve to manage the conflicts that arose from his economic policies. Small farmers and small businessmen who were harmed by technical changes caused by the government's modernization program through corruption and bribery had no recourse but to go outside of the law to protect themselves.

Oil as a share of GDP went from one-tenth in 1960 to one-fifth in 1972. However, oil allowed the shah to solidify the support of a small winning coalition by granting special rights and privileges to political favorites. By reducing the shah's reliance on citizen consent for revenues, oil's political impact on Iran's development may have been greater than its economic impact. Oil revenues permitted a rigid top-down model of economic management that made Pahlavi immune to the need to consult his subjects through the parliament, business, or village councils. He did not have to tax his people in order to survive, and he did not take advice on how to govern his kingdom.[33] In the end, the shah enjoyed little social support beyond those groups that directly received government aid and privileges. This exclusionary strategy created all the elements for a revolutionary challenge.

Oil revenues helped the shah to construct a more dependent dominant class than was generally the case among comparable developing nations. It also allowed him to link opportunities for capital accumulation to a system of social exclusion. His management personnel came from political loyalists. Competency and technical proficiency were secondary criteria for recruitment and promotion. His strategy created affluence without social responsibility. Although Iran's middle class during the 1960s and 1970s was as large as that in Brazil, Mexico, and Turkey, an absence of democratic and meritocratic channels of access to the state barred meaningful policy participation and bred a sense of alienation. The new middle classes that arose with economic growth had inadequate opportunities relative to their training and expectations. Avenues for mobilization and participation were more restricted than they were in poorer emerging nations such as Egypt, India, Iraq, South Korea, Pakistan, and the Philippines. All of these countries allotted their smaller and poorer middle classes more opportunities for participation in public decisionmaking.[34] Excluded from the impressive edifice of state clientelism, Iran's growing middle class became anticapitalist and antistatist, and with the working classes formed a united front against repression. The alienation of the middle class was an important source of the social capital needed for revolutionary change.

Of the examples discussed in this book, Iran and South Vietnam simultaneously faced all three forms of potentially catastrophic risk—market risk, social risk, and political risk. Before 1949, China's level of risk was equally high, but after that year the Communist government eliminated most of the dangerous social risks to which the population was exposed. Since Marcos's fall, the various governments of the Philippines have taken some measures to protect their democracy from future economic catastrophes. In the 1970s, all three categories of risk were closest to catastrophic levels in the country on which the United States had become most dependent, Iran. Business contracts in Iran were not legally enforceable, society was deeply polarized, civil society did not function (creating a gap between state and society that only the mosque was able to fill), and rule making was at the whim of the chief executive.

The Strategic Miscalculation: Populist Rhetoric, Islamic Discourse

Many senior State Department officials underestimated the capacity of a mosque-based opposition to threaten secular authorities, believing instead that the left was behind the outbreaks of social disorder in Tehran. In an influential article,[35] Australian journalist Robert Moss wrote that the Soviets were hiding their tracks by standing behind the mosque. This conventional wisdom would eventually prove to be incorrect. Because the shah prohibited U.S. nationals from contacting opposition leaders, U.S. intelligence had no inkling of the alchemy of revolution taking place in Iran's social discourse. After the revolution succeeded in bringing Khomeini to power, U.S. intelligence attributed the clergy's success to the appeal of Islamic fundamentalism.

This reasoning missed the essence of the social transformation that had taken place. The case against the shah came from the left, but was co-opted by the clergy because the secular left had inadequate organizational capacity to take power. The shah's repression of secular reform was so effective that it ensured that labor had no power. By contrast, the shah did not have the power to eliminate the mosque, which gave the clergy an independent organizational base denied to all other sectors of Iranian society. The shah was a centralizer who did not see the advantages of pitting rival social groups against one another. Iran's history would be very different had he allowed different opposition groups to compete for reforms. Ironically, in 2008 the Marxist left has once again become a threat to the regime in Tehran. This time the Islamic Republic is seeking to shut down the extreme leftists that were allowed to speak out because of their presumed anti-Americanism, but their critique of the current regime has resulted in censure.

Historically, the political struggle against the monarchy mainly had been waged by secular nationalist forces. Iran's labor movement started in 1941, the same year the shah ascended to the throne, and the working class became highly politicized during the Second World War. It is no coincidence that he viewed this group as his greatest enemy. At that time there was little reason to fear the conservative clergy. In the 1960s the clergy had opposed the shah's land reforms, fearing cuts to its own wealth and that of village landlords who patronized the mosques.[36]

Clerics used the language of social revolution to build a case against the shah, and their audiences were the socially neglected groups. The mullahs adopted the left's populist rhetoric against imperialism and foreign capitalism, targeting U.S. interventions, the waste of natural resources on an ever-expanding army and bureaucracy, rural dispossession and the destruction of agriculture, the poverty of the working class, the shanty towns, the destruction of the bazaar economy by transnational capitalists, and the support of Zionism against Islamic brothers in Palestine and Israel. The secular left had launched these same critiques, starting in the 1960s. U.S. intelligence contained no hint at the time that the clergy could speak independently for social reform.

The fate of the secular left was sealed when a March 1979 referendum on whether Iran should be an Islamic republic resulted in 98 percent of affirmative votes. Islam alone, the only force in Iranian society that had resisted U.S.

influence, could claim to represent the nationalist cause. The religious legitimization of an essentially secular critique of the regime transformed the clergy into an effective revolutionary contender, not only against a failing regime but also against the centrifugal forces within the secular opposition.

Mingling populist themes with Islamic discourse allowed Khomeini and his followers to dominate the ideological competition against the shah's reactionary violence. Khomeini's contribution to revolutionary discourse was to meld socialist populism to radical Islamic populism (a desire for a classless society), conservative Islamic populism (a desire for utopia on earth), and liberal Islam (a desire to share power with the state). The desire to share power with the state came later. When Khomeini first returned to Iran from Paris in 1978 he advocated an Islamic republic that would be based on sharia (a set of Islamic religious laws) and whose political leaders were chosen to run for election by a council of clerics. His harmonization of these three Islamic currents made him preeminent among the opposition forces. It also allowed him to create a broad coalition of social forces and span a range of political and sociological currents, something neither the clergy nor the intelligentsia had been able to accomplish.[37] Without borrowing concepts, language, and imagery from radical social discourse, Khomeini would not have been successful in building a broad base of social support. He claimed that the Pahlavi regime had violated all elements of national identity, and his rhetoric offered the possibility of a complete cultural, nationalist, and religious revival. By promising to combine cultural and political reconstruction, he appealed to a broader population base than did the traditional left.

After the Fall

A series of U.S. miscalculations allowed Khomeini to consolidate his regime. After Iranian students stormed the American Embassy in Tehran, Washington severed diplomatic ties, exactly what Khomeini was trying to achieve. He believed that an independent Iran would not exist until all ties with the United States were broken. In November 1983, President Reagan's decision to support Iraq in a war that Baghdad instigated against Iran three years earlier had an unanticipated impact. Opposition to the U.S.-funded Iraqi forces melded the interests of the Iranian people to the Iranian Islamic Republic.

The Iraq-Iran war helped Khomeini to establish deep grassroots support for the revolution. He united the state's administrative machinery with the religious network, spreading government activities to the most remote hamlets under the auspices of the clergy. This gave the clerics a network that functioned in a similar way to the Communist Party in China. The Ministry of Reconstruction Crusade, which provided public services—roads, schools, clinics, telephones, and even communal baths—drew local populations into local resource management and won Khomeini the backing of small towns and villages. By the end of the war with Iraq in 1988, his Islamic regime had given hundreds of thousands of Iranians who were participating in revolutionary councils their first experience of national politics. These individuals became the volunteers who constituted two-thirds of the fighting forces. They also provided the public contributions that gave the regime the fiscal resources to fight. The war effort against Iraq was more effective at creating broad popular support for the national state than was the U.S.-backed effort to do the same during Mohammad Reza Shah Pahlavi's regime.

The Revolution's Record on Social Reform

By Khomeini's death in 1988, a new sociopolitical system existed, exhibiting more popular support than had the shah's white revolution. This system's accomplishments in education, public health, and opportunities for women surpassed those of the shah's regime. Female labor force participation improved noticeably despite quotas. Figure 9-2 shows that even though GDP growth is not as strong as it was under the shah, female literacy rates have increased and fertility rates have declined since the creation of the Islamic Republic. Progress in primary health care and education has contributed to a reduction in fertility and to greater life expectancy (see figures 9-3, 9-4, and 9-5). The Islamic revolution established a grassroots constituency that the shah's white revolution never enjoyed.[38] Despite growing interest among the shah's advisers in the need to address regional and sectoral income disparities, that government's sixth five-year plan to address poverty alleviation had never been implemented.

Under the Islamic Republic, human development acquired a higher place than economic growth as a priority of government investment. High government spending after 1988 improved the population's access to primary health and education. Adult literacy rose from about 57 percent in 1988 to 75 percent in 1997.[39] During that same period, life expectancy increased from 61.6 to 69.5 percent, and population growth dropped from 3.5 to 2 percent.[40]

The sharpest differences between the shah's regime and that of the Islamic Republic are reflected in the human poverty index, which declined from 31 to 18 percent between 1988 and 1997. Data are not available for the period between 1979 and 1988 on account of the Iran-Iraq War. The human

Figure 9-2. *Percentage of Females in Labor Force, Comparing Iran and Developed Asia, 1960–2004*

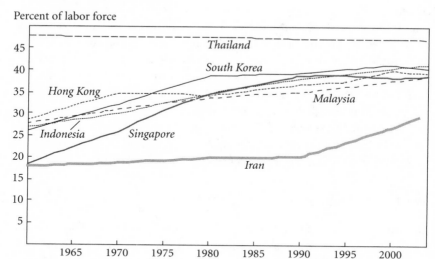

Source: World Bank, World Development Indicators.

Figure 9-3. *Comparison of Fertility, Education, and Economic Growth for the Pahlavi Dynasty and the Islamic Republic of Iran*[a]

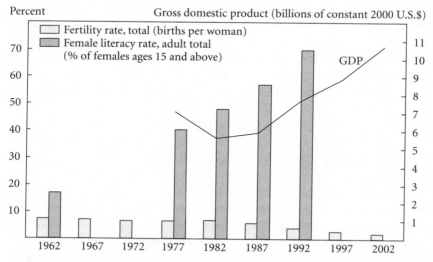

Source: United Nations Statistics, *Demographic Yearbook Special Census Topics,* vol. 12: Social Characteristics 2005 (1987–2002) (http://unstats.un.org/unsd/demographic/sconcerns/education/ed2.htm); World Bank, World Development Indicators (datapoint for 1962).

a. Data are unavailable for some years.

Figure 9-4. *Comparison of Infant Mortality Rates and Life Expectancy at Birth, Iran and Developed Asia*

Deaths per 1,000 births

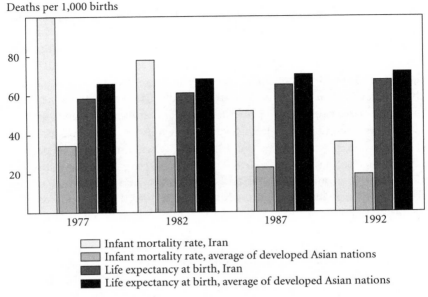

Infant mortality rate, Iran
Infant mortality rate, average of developed Asian nations
Life expectancy at birth, Iran
Life expectancy at birth, average of developed Asian nations

Source: World Bank, World Development Indicators.

Figure 9-5. *Female Literacy Rates, Comparison of Pahlavi Dynasty and Islamic Republic of Iran to Developed East Asian Economies*

Percent of females ages 15 and over

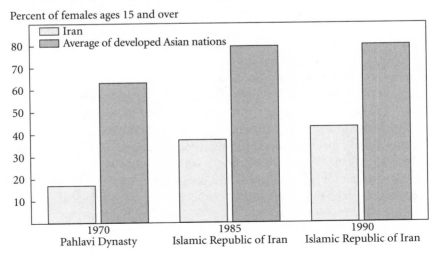

Source: World Bank, World Development Indicators.

development index, adjusted by income distribution, improved due to relatively higher gains by the poorest rather than the richest 20 percent of the population. This reversed the trend of increasing relative deprivation that occurred during economic growth under the shah. Although GDP per capita expanded from $1,985 in 1960 to $4,976 in 1976, insufficient resources were allocated to primary health and education, and Iran's human development rank was low. In the second decade of the Islamic revolution, real GDP per capita rose from $3,715 to $5,222, a smaller increase than under the monarchy. But social indicators increased dramatically.[41] Life expectancy required three decades to rise from 49.5 years to 61.6 years between 1960 and 1988; by 1997 it increased to 69.5.[42] On the eve of the revolution, adult literacy stood at 41.8 percent. It rose to 57 percent in 1988 and then jumped to 74.5 percent in 1997, reflecting a large reorientation of government expenditures.[43] Health, nutrition, and food security also saw great gains after 1988, including a significant drop in mortality for children under five. The Islamic Republic established a public health care network that offers primary health care to the entire urban population and to 85 percent of rural dwellers. Women have made progress in legally defending their rights and in participating in decisionmaking processes, though their participation in the economy lags. Much more must be accomplished in health care, life expectancy, gender equality, and education before Iran can be compared to countries with high human development. Since the revolution, however, Iran has begun to compare favorably with most medium human development countries. Compared to U.S. allies in the Middle East such as Egypt, Saudi Arabia, and Turkey, Iran has attained higher human development.[44]

Religion and democracy have worked together to form a constitution that established Islam and republicanism as the pillars of the new society. However, this combination has not expanded the population's access to economic opportunity. Elections have become a regular feature of political organization at every level from those for president and parliament to elections for an Assembly of Experts, Islamic councils, and a constitutional amendment.[45] But this has not generated high levels of accountability or transparency, because mechanisms for overseeing executive agencies are weak. Legal recourse for the exercise of citizens' rights is absent. A lack of accountability has meant that political participation has grown without contributing to economic reform or facilitating the transition to a competitive economy. Nonetheless, procedurally Iran's regime is the most democratic in the Middle East, second only to its archenemy, Israel.

If the revolutionary government had matched the energy it placed in rejuvenating the social sector into increasing per capita income through economic development, the population would have enjoyed still higher levels of human development. But the Islamic Republic places lower priority on creating a conducive environment for economic growth than it does on creating grassroots social support for the revolutionary government. An economy that stifles private enterprise and mainly serves an elite group of clerics and their followers allows critics to assert that Iran's Islamic revolution simply replaced a Westernized elite with a religious elite.

Control over the petroleum industry still furnishes the government with resources to manage the economy, and few members of the ruling elite advocate competition, decentralization, or greater international economic integration. With the international embargo in effect and alternative productive activities squeezed out, oil revenues constitute 80 percent of exports and half of the revolutionary government's revenue stream. On the quality of its regulation, Iran ranks in the bottom decile of countries rated by the World Bank. Property-rights protection, the prevalence of state-owned enterprises, and arcane Islamic banking practices all constrain competition, restricting opportunities to groups sanctioned by the ruling coalition. The government opposes rules and regulations that promote access to capital for new enterprises it does not control. It does not focus on eliminating corruption or establishing the institutional and legal capacity necessary for a market economy. The Islamic Republic government has intervened heavily in the economy, interfering with market-based price mechanisms, maintaining multiple exchange rates, and making no distinctions between fiscal and monetary policy. Competition is also constrained by a requirement in the constitution that government intervene and control most industries, factories, and enterprises. As a result, the revolutionary government's economic performance measured by per capita income growth has lagged behind that of the shah.

As part of their move to control economic competition, the mullahs even resurrected one of the shah's most criticized economic institutions—nonprofit foundations that act as conglomerates to control much of the nation's large-scale investment capital. The foundations' managers, like those of the charities devised by the shah, report directly to the nation's head of state, keeping lucrative investment opportunities under political control. Along with state-owned enterprises, the charitable foundations run at a loss, so require continuous financial support. They thereby place unsustainable demands on the government budget, already under stress from subsidies for fuel, electricity, and food. These foundations, called *bonyads*, account for an estimated 40 percent of Iran's GDP.[46] The *bonyads* weaken market competition. Their grip on the economy is another reason why Iran's productivity declined after religious rule, and has stagnated ever since.

The new regime's mediocre economic performance justifies those who claim that the revolution has changed little. However, such criticism misses the revolution's distinctive distributional impact. Beneficiaries of the revolutionary regime are not from the same social groups as those who owed political debts to the shah. The ayatollah's army of followers was recruited from among those who were dispossessed by the shah, especially uprooted rural populations who were forced by the shah's policies to move to the cities. The shah started a revolutionary process that ended with his government as the final victim.

Conclusion

By exaggerating the appeal of Communism to developing countries, Washington's cold war policymakers blinded themselves to understanding the forces that dragged America into tragedies whose costs will extend far into the future. The refusal to see the melding of religious fundamentalism with leftist social critique is an example of how mistaken U.S. doctrines and actions have been in Iran. This grand flaw in U.S. global strategy prevented an accurate diagnosis of political forces in a country where America had one of its largest embassies (which was the base for CIA operations in the Middle East), and where an extensive expatriate population mixed daily with Iranian nationals.

A number of scholars have speculated that American liberalism lacks familiarity with the requirements for social transformation that must accompany economic progress in developing regions. Reflecting the values of a predominantly middle-class society, U.S. development policy has been premised on the notion that economic growth and democracy are complements, and that abetting one strengthens the other. But economic development, measured in terms of per capita growth, has not necessarily produced political democracy. Both China and Vietnam are among the third world Communist regimes that have evolved toward market economies. Their rise has dispelled the notion that economic development and democracy come together like love and marriage. The failure of the shah's vision for Iran's development could have been another nail in the coffin of failed U.S. doctrine. But the 1980 U.S. electoral campaign ensured that this would not be so: both

Democrats and Republicans resorted to cold war truisms about Iran and the developing world in general.

It was wishful thinking to believe that liberal democracy would fulfill the aspirations of third world populations without basic social reform, or that only Communism stood in the way of global democracy. During the cold war only China, North Korea, Vietnam, and Cuba, among third world nations, sustained Communist regimes. Hunger and want have led to a wide range of political outcomes across the globe. Far more common than Communist regimes are various forms of predatory rule, neither Communist nor democratic, molded by a militaristic, hegemonic party or by monarchical leadership. It is the corrupt dictatorships of failed states—not the Communist regimes—that are the greatest dangers to global security today.

Yet after the shah's downfall, an important constituency of the U.S. policy establishment was drawn to Jeane Kirkpatrick's idea that backing friendly dictators was a prudent and long-sighted policy. Kirkpatrick was selected to represent the United States in the UN by an administration (Reagan's) that did not see that her views represented the most inaccurate refinement of U.S. cold war doctrine. Her theory that autocratic regimes were manageable evils that could be nurtured along toward democracy and markets, while Communist regimes were immobile and perpetual enemies, provided the final justification for cold war doctrine after Iran. Her deeply mistaken theory led to U.S. support of counterrevolutionary insurgencies in Grenada, El Salvador, Nicaragua, and Honduras. By supporting Iraqi forces during the Iraq-Iran war, the U.S. foreign policy establishment helped unify the people of Iran behind their government.

The cold war rationalized America's search for public goods through overseas regimes that provided private goods to narrow constituencies. This lack of discretion concerning regimes that practiced blatant social injustices is one of the most poorly understood causes of the bitter harvest that U.S. policies reaped during the cold war. U.S.-Iranian relations exemplify the role that Western democracy's large winning coalitions play in tendering ideological and material support to small winning coalitions in elite-dominated third world societies. Twenty-five years after the shah's fall, both sides continue to feel jilted and betrayed and continue to pay the price of this short-sighted policy.

The shah's fall suggests a very broad lesson that was little noticed by contemporaries who looked for conspiracies and villains. His plans for Iran followed a blueprint that was endorsed by many of the best international economists and institutions. His experiment with capitalist agriculture, like that undertaken in Pakistan and Nicaragua, followed examples of international best practice. Measured by GDP, the Iranian economy grew under the shah. Economists did not envision that ultimate bargaining caused by unequal distribution of growth would impose costs on growth. They predicted that people would accept government policies, no matter how small the personal benefits, because getting something is better than getting nothing. As noted in chapter 5, in an ultimatum game the first players, in Iran's case the Westernizers, make a take-it-or-leave-it offer about how to divide the gain from economic growth. When distribution is overly favorable to one side, the other side defies its own self-interest by taking costly actions that express its preference for fairness. This explains the support that Khomeini obtained even from the middle classes, and especially from the laborers. Even Iranians who were better off as a result of the growth that the shah's policies had produced rejected both the policies and the regime because they viewed the distribution of benefits as unfair. The shah's enemies responded to unfair behavior by harming those who treated them unfairly, bearing substantial cost to themselves. In East Asia, by contrast, leaders made systematic efforts to avoid ultimatum bargaining by distributing the rewards of greater national productivity broadly.[47]

America's Moral Dilemma in South Asia

The greatest task facing the adherents of democracy today is to discover how the ideals of democracy can be translated into realities for Asians in the face of the grim economic conditions and psychological urgencies.
    —Edwin Reischauer, in *What the United States Can Do about India* (1956)

The importance of India in the conflict between Communism and Democracy cannot be too greatly stressed.
    —Eustace Seligman, *What the United States Can Do about India* (1956)

They [U.S. officials] would rather have a stable Pakistan—albeit with some restrictive norms—than have more democracy prone to fall in the hands of extremists.
    —Tariq Azim Khan, Pakistan's minister of state for information, describing American officials' reaction to General Pervez Musharraf's suspension of the constitution, as quoted in the *New York Times,* November 5, 2007

Diplomatic relationships between the United States and the Asian subcontinent are puzzling. Although American presidents have always championed the compatibility of democracy and development, building a cooperative relationship with India has proved elusive. In contrast, India's neighbor and authoritarian rival, Pakistan, has received preference in economic and military assistance, despite a governing ethos that conflicts with U.S. ideals. The tilt toward Pakistan has been especially salient when that nation has been governed by a military junta. The U.S. bias toward Pakistan has produced a relationship of codependency that provides little satisfaction or security to either party. A $10 billion U.S. contribution to Pakistan since 2001 did not secure the loyalty of the military regime or the friendship of the population. Pakistan is neither ally nor adversary; the stability of the bilateral relationship remains uncertain.[1]

America appreciates India as an experiment in democracy and a testing ground for the idea that economic security can be achieved without sacrificing individual liberty. India demonstrates to the third world that a nation can mobilize national resources by extending governing rights to its citizens. As Senator John Kennedy stated in 1959:

> Whatever battles may be in the headlines, no struggle in the world deserves more time and attention from this administration—and the next—than that which now grips the attention of all Asia: the battle between India and China. . . . Unless India can compete equally with China, unless she can show that her way works as well as or better than dictatorship, unless she can make the transition from economic stagnation to economic growth, so that [she] can get ahead of [her] exploding population, the entire Free World will suffer a serious reverse.[2]

Yet a full decade before Kennedy uttered these words, India and America were already on the road to estrangement, in spite of a shared belief in democracy. During Kennedy's presidency in 1962, U.S. aid to Pakistan peaked, driving India into the Soviets' arms. "Is there some basic gulf dividing the two nations that cannot be bridged permanently, or is it that sincere attempts have not been made on either side in this direction?" asked India's Ambassador T. N. Kaul in 1980. "Why is it that India attaches high priority to America, whereas the U.S. attaches low priority to India? Is there any fundamental clash between their national traits or between their regional and global outlooks?"[3] These questions, which could have been asked at any time since India's emergence as an independent nation in 1947, highlight one of the great ironies of U.S. relations with third world nations over the last half century.

U.S. aid directly influenced the geopolitical loyalties of the leaders so far discussed in this book—Chiang Kai-shek in China, Ferdinand Marcos in the Philippines, Ngo Dinh Diem and Nguyen Van Thieu in Vietnam, and the shah of Iran. Yet while India historically has been the seventh-largest recipient of U.S. aid, the aid has not translated into American influence in that country (see table 13-1).[4] Even before Jawaharlal Nehru won election to lead the postindependence transitional government on May 1, 1946, he categorically rejected exchanging policy concessions for assistance, stating:

> While we welcome all help we can get from foreign countries, we have made it clear that such help must not have political strings attached to it, any conditions which are unbecoming for a self-respecting nation to accept, any pressure to change our domestic or international policy. We

would be unworthy of the high responsibilities [with] which we have been charged if we bartered away in the slightest degree our country's self-respect or freedom of action, even for something which we need so badly.[5]

With an inclusive winning coalition to court, India's leaders were not inclined to cater to U.S. geopolitical interests or to America's ideological preference for private-sector-led growth, which left the U.S. with no leverage to wrest policy concessions from India throughout the cold war. Most of the initiatives for economic aid to India came from the executive branch and encountered opposition in Congress, where legislators, disappointed by India's independent line, resisted White House aid requests.

From 1947 to 1951, India's repeated requests for bilateral aid from America were denied. When aid funds started to flow in 1951, the impact was small relative to need. And within the space of twelve months, when India refused to support the United States in a UN resolution censuring China as the aggressor in Korea and also spurned U.S. overtures for defense collaboration, the whole question of aid had become a source of intense congressional irritation. During the second House of Representatives debate on aid to India, in 1952, Congressman Howard Smith (D-Va.) denounced the administration's request. "They talk about the fact that this is to make friends; this is to help keep our friends," he said. "If there is anybody in the House who has ever seen or heard that Nehru has ever made a statement favorable to the United States, I would like him to say so now."[6] Further exasperating congressional leaders was the attitude of their counterparts in India, who acted as though they were entitled to U.S. assistance on the grounds of their nation's poverty alone, without regard to geopolitical concerns.

Meanwhile, as early as 1946 the Defense Department and Joint Chiefs of Staff had been eyeing the subcontinent's Karachi-Lahore regions as desirable sites for American air bases, naval ports, and listening posts.[7] This interest was welcomed by Pakistan's founder, Muhammad Ali Jinnah, whose approach toward the United States contrasted sharply with that of Nehru. Jinnah told the U.S. diplomat Raymond Hare in May 1947 that the United States could count on the Muslim countries of the Middle East to stand with Pakistan against possible Soviet aggression in the region, and that the region would look to the United States for assistance. Jinnah declared during a cabinet meeting on September 7, 1947: "Pakistan [is] a democracy and Communism [does] not flourish in the soil of Islam. It [is] clear therefore that our interests [lie] more with the two great democratic countries, namely, the U.K. and the

USA, rather than with Russia."[8] The remark did not initially succeed in gaining support for U.S. military aid, but it became the touchstone for U.S. policies in the Middle East and was to have significant repercussions that were unforeseen at the time. The comment also turned out to be misleading.

Not long after Pakistan's formation in 1947, U.S. military strategists began to put their plans into action, providing military support for the new nation as a means of strengthening the American presence in South Asia and protecting the region from Soviet influence. Initially, the priorities of Pakistan's military conflicted with the State Department's conception of India and Pakistan as a strategic unit. But after India rejected U.S. overtures for defense collaboration, the Eisenhower administration undertook bilateral discussions with Pakistan.

Unlike Nehru, successive Pakistani military leaders after Jinnah cultivated American friendship by endorsing U.S. policies in Korea, China, and elsewhere in Asia.[9] The Pakistani politician and eventual prime minister Zulfikar Bhutto noted that according to the *U.S. News & World Report* of January 4, 1954, Vice President Nixon "tended to favour military aid to Pakistan as a counterforce to the confirmed neutralism of Jawaharlal Nehru's India."[10] Bhutto reasoned, "Just as, after the victory of the Chinese Communists, Japan had replaced China as one of the pillars of its Asian policy, so Pakistan was to replace an India unprepared to give its allegiance to the United States' global objectives."[11]

As figure 10-1 shows, after 1952, on a per capita basis U.S. aid to Pakistan surpassed per capita aid to India. U.S. generosity also closely tracks U.S. geopolitical priorities rather than a concern for promoting third world democracy. President Kennedy, a great supporter of India, gave more aid to Pakistan than did any other American president. Aid to Pakistan shot skyward just after his election in 1960. While the United States regarded India as often neutral on the side of the Soviet Union, Pakistan was an ally. In reality, with an insecure elite, Pakistan's leadership was more malleable. It was willing to support America's geopolitical objectives in exchange for externally conferred legitimacy.

Pakistan became important to U.S. containment strategy as India became part of the nonaligned movement and took an increasingly independent attitude toward the Soviet Union and its satellite empire in Europe. India supported mainland China's admission to the UN. It expressed indifference both toward North Korea's invasion of South Korea and the Soviet Union's suppression of Hungary's revolt. India's foreign policy stance of nonalignment, expressed in its UN voting record and its domestic policies of a mixed

Figure 10-1. *Per Capita U.S. Aid to Pakistan Dwarfs Aid to India, 1948–97*

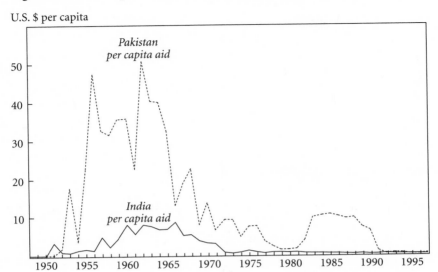

Source: U.S. Agency for International Development, *U.S. Overseas Loans and Grants.*

economy and what it called a "socialistic pattern of society," were unresponsive to U.S. economic assistance.[12]

Every time Pakistan's military regime transitioned toward democracy—between 1949 and 1950, 1972 and 1976, and 1992 and 1998—U.S. aid appropriations declined (see figure 10-2). The United States, initially lukewarm to Pervez Musharraf's regime, tried to change its policies when he established a military dictatorship in 1999 by decreasing aid. But that quickly changed in 2001. After September 11, Pakistan became strategically relevant and was showered with aid in the cause of the Bush administration's war on terror—even though Pakistan indirectly had contributed to the terrorism by supporting the Taliban in Afghanistan.

The ease with which U.S. leaders could secure the policy outcomes they preferred from Pakistan's elite governing coalition produced a great moral dilemma of cold war diplomacy. It has subsequently produced perception gaps that deeply affect the moral credibility of the United States in the eyes of South Asia's people. It has also inadvertently led to the entrenchment of Islamic opposition among a populace that resents U.S. support of repressive military governments.

Figure 10-2. *U.S. Aid Supports Autocracy in Pakistan, 1948–2002*

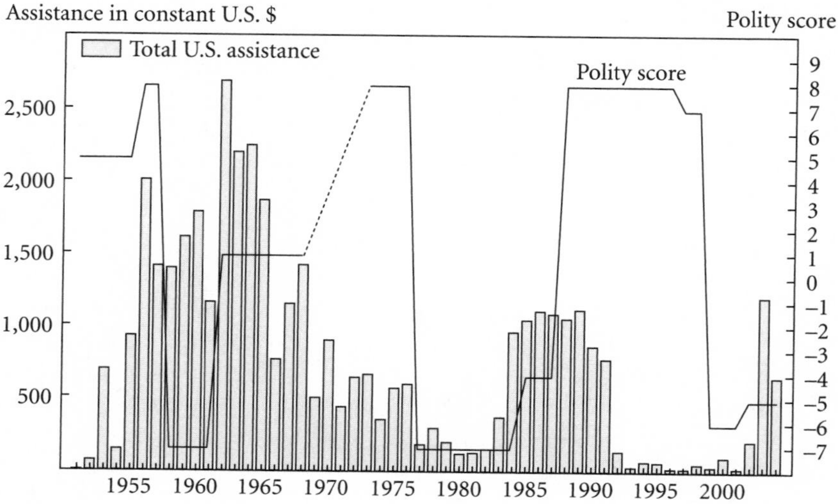

Polity score: 10 = high democracy; –10 = high autocracy.
Source: U.S. Agency for International Development, *U.S. Overseas Loans and Grants;* Polity IV.

The Unending Socialism versus Democracy Argument

Very early in the cold war, President Truman asserted that democracy and socialism were incompatible. When independent India under Nehru chose nonalignment and refused to side with the United States over such issues as quarantining Soviet actions in Eastern Europe, Washington understood only that India had chosen socialism over democracy. In the crusade against Communism, that placed India firmly on the wrong side.

What Washington failed to grasp was that for Nehru, as for other third world leaders emerging from colonial-capitalist rule, the alternative to capitalism was not Communism. It was socialism, which they viewed as compatible with democracy.[13] In fact, the Indian concept of socialism was akin to the U.S. concept of providing basic risk insurance for its population. Socialism in India implied a reduction of inequality through democratic and parliamentary processes. India never accepted the socialist doctrine that all means of production should be owned by the state; it advocated a mixed economy in which the private and public sectors would complement each other.

U.S. policymakers opposed India's publicly controlled economy and encouraged instead the adoption of American-style capitalism. Nehru and others feared that the U.S. approach would result in the control of the economy by a few family-held monopolies. He believed that state intervention was needed to establish a stable and legitimate government. Private investors were not available to supply massive funding; therefore, the state should furnish capital for industry. New Delhi's socialistic laws, which were blocking the flow of private capital, caused dismay in Washington, where policymakers believed that the socialist model was a stepping-stone to Communism.

Indian leadership also rejected the capitalist idea that GDP growth was the only measure of a country's success. Washington was expressing support for models of enlightened dictatorship committed to increasing GDP through foreign investment and aid. But India was insisting that development was not synonymous with aggregate growth, and that social and economic change that offered people a voice in the decisions affecting their lives was essential. Instead of narrowly focusing on income and consumption, India's development plans emphasized personal security and freedom. Unfortunately, these plans neglected primary education and health, further differentiating India from other socialist societies.

India took the democratic path at the same time that other Asian leaders—such as Lee Quan Yew, Park Chung-hee, Marcos, and Suharto—repudiated Western-style democracy. India's government rejected the model of the modernizing despot at a time when the idea was gaining credibility among Western development experts. (An influential U.S. report on Latin America argued that development needs stability and order, best provided by military governments.) India's Congress Party leadership did not believe that freedom and participation could come only in the wake of growth and expansion, or that democracy was a luxury that developing nations could not afford.[14]

Preoccupied with memories of colonialism, the Congress Party viewed the policies of the major Western powers with skepticism. Party leaders were sensitive to and disappointed by U.S. support for alliances with colonial powers, such as the Netherlands (which continued to maintain colonial claims in Indonesia), France (in Indochina), Britain (in Malaysia), and particularly Portugal, which had refused to give up its Indian territorial possessions, including Goa, at India's independence. Nehru often reminded Washington that the persistence of colonialism was a real blight crying out for correction, while Communist aggression was a projection of fears of actions that had not yet occurred.[15] India believed that the United States sacrificed its moral leadership in what India viewed as a greater battle—the battle to end colonialism.

Yet India doubted the peaceful intentions of Russia and China. It did not wish to incur the enmity of either, and feared that Washington's belligerent language, which dismissed these two great powers' recent emergence, would stir an aggressive response. Nehru argued that peace was more important than choosing between ideologies. India's response to America's anti-Communist crusade was to insist that third world countries needed economic growth to inoculate them against Communism, and that military defense and treaty signing with America would not prevent the real danger of Communist subversion. Security could only come by increasing the population's standard of living. Famine, not military defeat, would lead India to turn toward Communism. India's free press was critical in helping India to avoid famine.

American policymakers such as Assistant Secretary for Asian Affairs W. Walton Butterworth expressed skepticism that economic development could serve as a "general panacea" for Asia. "India should recognize the character of the Communist menace," he said, "not only to her, but to the other states of Southeast Asia . . . [and] should be moved to impress upon her neighbors the fact that the great enemy to their independence and political and economic welfare was not colonialism, but Communism."[16]

America grew skeptical not just of India's leanings, but of its intentions. Policymakers in Washington accused India of trying to become a regional power center in its own right. It is hardly surprising that in a 1949 National Security Council (NSC) paper, council staff categorically dismissed the possibility of making support for India the keystone for American policy. "India, the [NSC] report noted, refused 'to align itself with any power bloc,' seemed eager 'to form and lead a regional bloc or third force,' and did not adequately appreciate the Communist menace." The NSC staff concluded that "it would be unwise for us to regard South Asia, more particularly India, as the bulwark against the extension of Communist control in Asia."[17] To prevent Communist spread in the region and to avoid another power center, the NSC recommended supporting Pakistan and pulling away from India.

Five years later, in 1955, India still remained a low priority for American foreign aid. The projected $90 million targeted for it made up less than 3 percent of the $3.5 billion total aid budget, of which about 80 percent consisted of defense-oriented items that would benefit America's allies. Most of the economic funds went to nations that, unlike India, had showed themselves to be steadfast friends of the United States.

Ultimately it was the dispute between Pakistan and India over the status of Kashmir, not the level of aid or the different perspectives on Communism, that poisoned the U.S. relationship with India. The United States found it impossible to make progress with either India or Pakistan without antagonizing the other. India assumed that America's military assistance to Pakistan and its influence on UN Security Council decisions regarding Kashmir's accession were proof that the United States sided with Pakistan. "Thus

[America's] position on Kashmir—an issue it would have preferred to avoid—has accentuated the strong feeling in certain circles in India that on any issue concerning India and Pakistan, the United States would be likely to side with Pakistan, regardless of the merit of the issue."[18] In fact, Pakistan, not India, accepted most of the conditions and agreements made by the Security Council about Kashmir.

In India, politicians and leaders, especially Mohandas Gandhi, viewed the subcontinent's partition as a betrayal by the Muslim League, Jinnah, and the British. No wonder when the first rumors of U.S. military aid to Pakistan surfaced in 1953, huge anti-American demonstrations erupted in India. By siding with Pakistan, the United States was adding to India's sense of victimization. India's leaders suspected Pakistan of introducing the cold war into the region in order to ensure perpetual partition and to prevent India from attaining its destiny as a great power. Nehru's deep-seated aversion to the creation of Pakistan was reported by Professor Josef Korbel, a member of the first UN commission to seek a solution to the dispute over Kashmir's future.[19] Korbel, citing Nehru, writes, "We are a secular state which is not based on religion. We give to everyone freedom of conscience. Pakistan is a mediaeval state with an impossible theocratic concept. It should never have been created, and it would never have happened had the British not stood behind this foolish idea of Jinnah."[20] Korbel concedes that Nehru was willing to accept partition as a tentative solution, assuming integration would follow, but Nehru believed that the cold war offered Pakistan a mechanism to ensure that integration would never occur.

In 1954 Pakistan became one of three Asian signatories of the South East Asia Treaty Organization (SEATO), which included the United States, Britain, France, Australia, New Zealand, Thailand, and the Philippines. SEATO was designed to deter Communist aggression and to legitimize U.S. efforts to counter such threats.[21] Pakistan also joined the Baghdad Pact, or the Middle East Treaty Organization (later known as CENTO, for Central Treaty Organization), in 1955, along with Turkey, Iran, Iraq, and the United Kingdom. In March 1959, the United States and Pakistan signed a bilateral agreement of cooperation in which America assured military support against hostile actions taken against Pakistan. Pakistan was a member of the nonaligned movement and attended the Bandung Conference in 1955.

Nehru did not accept U.S. arguments that Pakistan needed arms to prevent Communist encroachments into the Muslim Middle East, or that to have a Muslim ally would buffer Central as well as South Asia. Political scientist and former State Department official Stephen Cohen writes: "The military importance of weapons transfers from the United States was historically crucial. This is quite apparent in the case of Pakistan. . . . Pakistan would not have become a serious military power without U.S. equipment."[22] Nehru believed that the United States had aimed its military power against India as much as it had against the Soviet Union.[23] He warned America that moving closer to Pakistan would force his own nation to move closer to the USSR. "In effect Pakistan becomes practically a colony of the United States," he wrote, noting too that "the United States imagines that by this policy they have completely outflanked India's so called neutralism and will thus bring India to her knees."[24] Indians blamed the United States for every Pakistani aggression. Focused on the objective of containing the Soviets, few Americans realized then that their alliance with Pakistan threatened India's security and increased the likelihood of Indian-Pakistani conflict. Nor did policymakers realize that the interpretation of political events as good or evil by John Foster Dulles, Eisenhower's secretary of state, was viewed in Delhi as a form of fanaticism.

Nehru further claimed that America's massive military aid to Pakistan had altered the political and military character of the dispute over Kashmir, increasing the confidence of Pakistan to invade Kashmir in 1965. These suspicions were confirmed when U.S. Ambassador to India John Kenneth Galbraith testified before the Senate Foreign Relations Committee on April 25, 1966, that "the arms we supplied . . . caused the war between India and Pakistan. . . . If we had not supplied arms, Pakistan would not have sought a military solution [to the Kashmir dispute]."[25] In contrast to Galbraith, however, Strobe Talbott and S. L. Poplai assert that U.S. military aid to Pakistan was designed to reduce the likelihood of war. "Nehru and other opinion leaders stated later that they did not believe that it had been the United States' intention, in giving military aid to Pakistan, to cause trouble for India, but that Pakistan's motives in requesting aid, as indicated in many public statements by Pakistan leaders, were quite different from those of the United States."[26]

The theory of power in international relations favors Galbraith's view. As rival nations approach parity, they are more likely to challenge each other and go to war. Why does the United States, using its great disparity in force, not attack Canada? One can easily imagine that U.S.-Canadian relations would be more dangerous if Canada approached parity and became a threat to the status quo and a source of dissatisfaction. From this perspective, arming Pakistan intensified the chances of armed conflict in South Asia. In the 1950s and early sixties, as Pakistan's military capability approached parity with India, the risk of conflict intensified. In the first war between the two countries, in 1947, they were closest to parity, and accordingly that war was the most intense. When the United States supplied arms to Pakistan, India realized it could not win, which triggered its approach to the Soviets.

To many observers, intensified U.S. aid to Pakistan for protecting itself against Communism did not make sense because "there was only one contingency involving external attack against Pakistan to which a reasonably high probability could be assigned: an attack by India."[27] A Chinese attack against Pakistan seemed improbable, especially since there was an intervening Indian border on East Pakistan. Negligible gains relative to costs made a Chinese attack on Pakistan highly unlikely.

The U.S. support of Pakistan's repression of Bangladesh's independence movement, its siding with Pakistan in the third Indo-Pakistani war in 1971 (even ordering a nuclear-powered aircraft carrier to the Bay of Bengal), and the 1972 release of the Shanghai Communiqué, signed after Nixon's trip to China, had dangerous repercussions in both India and Pakistan. These events intensified the security risk on India's borders. China had already won the Sino-Indian War, taking a piece of Himalayan territory.

Continuing U.S. aid to Pakistan prompted India to aggressively pursue its nuclear programs.[28] Thus, U.S. foreign policy in South Asia paved the way for another danger in the region: a nuclear arms race. The *New York Times* stated that the U.S. treaty with Pakistan strengthened Soviet influence in the second most populous nation in Asia—and the world—at the expense of the United States.[29] Selig S. Harrison (1981) wrote:

> It is becoming increasingly clear that the combined impact of the Administration's overtures to Islamabad and Peking has produced the most dangerous crisis in relations between New Delhi and Washington since India won its independence in 1947. . . . America should not exacerbate tensions and stimulate an arms race between India and Pakistan. . . . For America, it would be the ultimate folly to become embroiled in this struggle. . . . Indian anxieties concerning the Soviet presence in Kabul are giving way to renewed preoccupation with the Chinese-Pakistani-American challenge.

The U.S.-Pakistani Partnership against Evil

To Americans like John Foster Dulles, the Soviet Union was dangerous because of its atheism and its bombs, and during the cold war, the United States shared a pious affinity with those countries allied with it in the battle against a godless enemy. Religion played an important role in unifying the Americans and Pakistanis. Although Pakistan came under military rule for decades at a time, the United States still saw it as a religious ally, ignoring the fact that the dictatorship's weak social roots caused it to seek allies among religious leaders of the rural hinterland at the expense of supporting the more secular urban middle classes.

The strong religious sensibilities of John Foster Dulles and other policymakers such as Secretary of State Dean Acheson and Secretary of State Dean Rusk were offended by Communism's atheistic orientation. They were also offended by the perceived ethical ambiguity of the Hindu Indians, who insisted on nonalignment but seemed morally compromised and unable to distinguish between good and evil. The Hindus were polytheistic, as well, and believed in a religiously ordained social hierarchy, the caste system, which Americans found objectionable.

Dulles and others convinced themselves that the monotheistic people of the Middle East, believing in a single truth, saw the Communist bloc as evil. (America's capitalist agenda has since revealed social components that are anathema to conservative Islamic clergy.) Pakistani leaders emphasized their belief in the supreme sovereignty of God and in the equality of men, and Dulles, "immensely impressed by the martial and religious characteristics of the Pakistanis,"[30] also showered praise on such countries as Turkey, Iraq, and Syria, claiming that their leaders realized the Communist danger. Dulles envisioned these nations as a "northern tier" of defense that together could form an effective ring to encircle the Soviet bloc.

But Dulles and his colleagues overlooked the fact that India's leaders represented the democratically voiced concerns of most of the electorate. The countries Dulles admired were authoritarian. The irony of a democratic America fighting autocratic Communism by aligning with other autocrats was not lost on the Indians. Dulles did not live to see it, but Pakistan took atheistic China's side in the 1962 war against India, and did not refuse offers from the godless Communists to assist in its nuclear ambitions.

While the United States criticized India's state-oriented development plan for suppressing private-sector initiatives, it praised Pakistan's economy as a model of good management. Yet Pakistan's Convention Muslim League—the political party of Field Marshal Mohammad Ayub Khan, who had seized power in 1958 in a bloodless coup—became to Pakistanis a symbol of favoritism and nepotism. Bureaucrats issued permits and licenses to Ayub's favorites; those who were not part of the ruling clique had to buy their permits from regime insiders. Rent seeking was legitimized throughout the economy, creating a class of industrialists who enjoyed government-protected monopolies for their subsidized products, creating huge pockets of private wealth even as the tax base narrowed.

Pakistan's evolution toward oligarchy is a classic model of the political economy of national failure. Elites played a positive role in early economic development by keeping the wheels of commerce moving before efficient, decentralized markets were possible. Because the governing coalition was small, the mix of subsidies, restrictive licenses, and inefficient government procurement contracts did not initially undermine the economy. In fact, under Ayub's leadership in the 1960s, the country's 6 percent growth rate was the envy of the developing world.

Yet Pakistan's brief era of rapid growth exacerbated social inequalities. Little in the way of education, health care, or housing trickled down to the poor or rural populations. This pattern contrasts sharply with East Asia, where the fastest-growing countries experienced growing equality. Robert Looney, an economist at the Naval Postgraduate School in Monterey, California, estimates that under Ayub just twenty-two Pakistani families owned 66 percent of industry, 97 percent of the insurance sector, and 80 percent of banking. Only one landlord in a thousand owned more than 500 acres, yet these large holders possessed 15 percent of the country's land.[31]

Zulfikar Bhutto writes that Pakistani policies

> brought the country to the brink of economic catastrophe. A new class of capitalist baron, as rapacious as any in Latin America, was created to control the national wealth. The system adopted was anything but *laissez faire*. Businessmen under government patronage were given licenses that converted the collective resources of the nation into personal fortunes. Predatory capitalism ran riot with all the inevitable political consequences, and the country became more rather than less dependent on foreign assistance.[32]

Islamabad and the Road to the Middle East

Although Washington expressed verbal support for the rise of democracy in Pakistan, it provided Pakistan's democratically elected leaders with virtually no financial assistance. As figure 10-3 illustrates, in 1994, during a brief period of democratic governance, Pakistan was not among the top ten recipients of U.S. aid. In 2004, however, it is prominently on the list. After the attack on the World Trade Center of September 11, 2001, a Pakistani dictatorship

Figure 10-3. *Total Foreign Aid from the United States, 1994 and 2004*

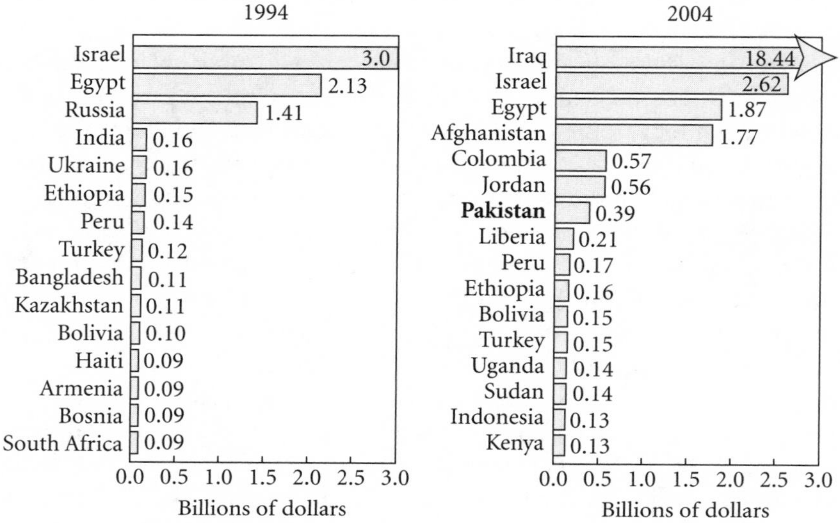

1994

	Billions of dollars
Israel	3.0
Egypt	2.13
Russia	1.41
India	0.16
Ukraine	0.16
Ethiopia	0.15
Peru	0.14
Turkey	0.12
Bangladesh	0.11
Kazakhstan	0.11
Bolivia	0.10
Haiti	0.09
Armenia	0.09
Bosnia	0.09
South Africa	0.09

2004

	Billions of dollars
Iraq	18.44
Israel	2.62
Egypt	1.87
Afghanistan	1.77
Colombia	0.57
Jordan	0.56
Pakistan	0.39
Liberia	0.21
Peru	0.17
Ethiopia	0.16
Bolivia	0.15
Turkey	0.15
Uganda	0.14
Sudan	0.14
Indonesia	0.13
Kenya	0.13

Source: Tarnoff and Nowels (2004), derived from USAID and Department of State.

once again became a vital strategic ally, and again U.S. aid resumed. As of 2007 Pakistan has received $10 billion in U.S. assistance and loan write-offs, given by the United States to win Pakistan's support in the global war on terrorism.[33]

The rise of Islamic fundamentalism makes Pakistan a soft Islamic state that is essential to U.S. security. The *9/11 Commission Report*, released in July 2004 by the independent bipartisan National Commission on Terrorist Attacks upon the United States, confirmed the importance of Pakistan as a strategic ally.[34] Yet the hope that Pakistan can be a counterterrorist hub in Central Asia conflicts with the reality that Western Pakistan is a haven for terrorists, and that Islamist sympathizers operating within Pakistan provide nuclear know-how to terrorist groups. For decades, Islamist fundamentalist parties in Pakistan provided people and ideas to support military penetration into Afghanistan and Indian Kashmir. Musharraf's government has openly admitted that its army helped militants from Pakistan attack Afghanistan and supported Taliban training camps in Pakistan. In the 1990s the army provided arms and manpower to support the Taliban regime in Afghanistan. Yet after the U.S. invasion of Iraq, Pakistan was calm. Musharraf was able to convince his nation's religious leadership that Pakistan, a nuclear state that supports terrorism, could be next. But five years later he acts as if he cannot prevent the militants from gaining control of entire regions within Pakistan's tribal belt. This suggests that when necessary the Pakistani military has more potential control than Musharraf likes to indicate. The larger strategy of the Pakistan military, which is anti-Indian, is that extremism is a weapon to be used opportunistically. The army views Afghanistan as part of its Indian policy and of its efforts to foil India's moves to foment rebellion in the Pashtun tribal areas that Pakistan's Punjabi elite has never wholly controlled. Pakistan's primary focus on India is highlighted by the fact that most of the U.S. military aid that Pakistan has received since 2001 has been used to purchase sophisticated hardware such as antimissile systems that are of little use against tribal insurgents.

Pakistan's Intractable Extremism and U.S. Policy

On November 3, 2007, President Pervez Musharraf shredded Pakistan's constitution by declaring emergency rule.[35] By so doing he shattered several illusions on the part of the United States about its policy in Pakistan since 9/11. The first illusion was that economic aid would produce a cooperative leader committed to spreading democracy in the Muslim world. Musharraf ignored U.S. appeals to avoid martial law.[36] A second illusion was that supporting a dictator would buy stability. But stability became more elusive than ever as Islamic militancy was joined by middle-class unrest. Despite massive direct payments to the Pakistani military, cooperation with the United States on confronting extremists in the tribal belt has been disappointing. A final illusion was that twisting Musharraf's arm to cut a deal with the pro-Western former prime minister, Benazir Bhutto, could sustain and legitimate his presidency and build moderate support for U.S. objectives in the region.

Before her tragic assassination, Benazir Bhutto promoted herself as the force of modernity against backward-looking extremism. The subsequent ascension of her son as the titular head of her party put to rest such illusions. Bhutto never had a broader vision for how she would eliminate Pakistan's endemic extremism. She never outlined the steps she was prepared to take to change the feudalistic political structure from which she emerged. She ran her party by patronage, without debate or competition, acting as if it were the natural right of her family to govern. Why would she have acted any differently if elected to run the country?

Convinced that the destiny of Pakistan is being shaped outside of Pakistan, moderate Pakistanis today distrust the United States more than ever.[37] Despite the storm over Musharraf's declaration of emergency rule in 2007 and his battle for power, first with Benazir Bhutto, now with her heirs and with the former prime minister Nawaz Sharif, a transfer of power at the top will not stop the appeal of extremism to the average Pakistani. Nor will elections erase memories that Pakistan's democratic aspirations were stunted because of Western security strategies that began during the cold war and were reaffirmed with new urgency in the war against terror.[38] A poll found that in fall 2007, only 19 percent of Pakistanis viewed the United States favorably.[39] Western support has helped Pakistani dictators stay in power far longer than their democratic counterparts (Musharraf has held power for eight years, his elected predecessor for not more than three). The Western media generally assume that the restoration of democracy will ensure that Pakistan is controlled by the moderate, secular center that will be pro-American and antiterrorist; terrorist experts do not agree. Specialists maintain that elections are likely to make the war on terror even more tenuous, because a democratically elected government is likely to reflect the view, widely shared among the population, that terrorism is a U.S. rather than a Pakistani problem.

Restoring democracy will not eradicate extremism's appeal because democracy will not be effective against the two most entrenched causes of discontent. First, control over Pakistan's parties and provinces by powerful elites ensures that people at the bottom are not heard. Second, Pakistan's political institutions lack basic checks and balances such as budgetary and procedural transparency that might put restraints on the ruling party, further exacerbating resentment among the disenfranchised. Real democracy may be the only path to stability, but it will not be built until a constitutional and administrative structure exists that can protect the rights of all sectors of the population.

Sympathy for extremism in the tribal regions reflects a history of social and ethnic discrimination. The winners who formed the governing elite of the new Pakistani nation—mostly transplanted, anglicized, urban Islamic Indians—had few connections to Baluchistan and the Northwest Frontier Province (NWFP), which make up the Pashtun tribal belt bordering Afghanistan. The Punjabi elite, expecting to dominate the country because of ties to its largest and richest province, made inadequate efforts to share wealth or power with the tribal regions. The constitutional convention that began with independence in 1947 lasted for ten years, but was inconclusive. Tribal warlords, feudal landlords, and urban elites could not reconcile their differences. Instead, separatist aspirations arose among the Pashtuns and the Baluchs, both of whom sought to carve homelands out of the new nation.

To his credit, Musharraf did try to build an alternative power base that could shift Pakistan politics away from elite control. Between 2000 and

2002, his government promulgated a series of laws to promote decentralization. The aim was to take power away from the provincial seats, where the traditional political parties were well organized, and devolve authority to lower levels of government. Provincial leaders responded with deliberate but quiet resistance. In their view the laws did not divide power, they only took it away.

Musharraf's efforts were further stymied by his inadequate attention to breakdowns in bureaucratic process such as the absence of bottom-up administrative communication and coordination. His plan tried to remedy this problem by devolving decisionmaking authority for local security, education, and health to local authorities, but financial or managerial capacity never reached the bottom. The failure of Musharraf's devolution plan means that today the poor still lack mechanisms to make their needs known and are still unable to hold anyone accountable to meet those needs. Leaders at the top of the governmental hierarchy have no one to familiarize them with the complexity at the hierarchy's bottom.

Social reform agendas stagnated during the 1990s, further constrained by the need to comply with International Monetary Fund requests for fiscal restraint. In Baluchistan and the NWFP, especially, the regions most in need, public services foundered. One result of the breakdown is Pakistan's low literacy rates. For both males and females they are among the lowest in all developing countries, and the discrepancy between male and female literacy is among the world's greatest. Persistent inequality means that large pockets of the population, even in the better-off regions, harbor resentments that make them susceptible to the appeal of extremism. Religion is not the core of that appeal, because the tribal belt's religious beliefs vary greatly from those of the Punjab. The mosque has captured the cause of fundamental social reform in Pakistan just as it did in Iran during the shah's dictatorship.

Sixty years after independence from Britain, Pakistanis still suffer from the absence of a constitutional framework for inclusive government. Basic requirements for accountable governance such as protected budgetary scrutiny are not guaranteed by the constitution. This opacity in financial management allows incumbent politicians to hide fund transfers to loyal coalitions. As a result, the country's political parties have never attempted to create broad-based support for national policies. When the central leadership is Punjabi, public spending is lavished on Punjab; when it is Sindhi, then Sindh prospers. Baluchistan and the NWFP remain underdeveloped.

The military budget is characterized by the same opacity. The government's defense budget is published as a one-line item, far short of the NATO criteria for defense budgets, and there are so many off-budget items that the military has become a huge commercial holding company. The military is Pakistan's largest real estate owner and the owner of many large companies that often crowd out private-sector initiatives. Military business acquisitions range from cement to breakfast cereal. The $20 billion empire controls 30 percent of heavy industry and manages 12 million acres of land.[40] Pakistan, once described as an army looking for a state, has found its state and is now a state within a state.

Foremost among the reasons that poor Pakistani communities turn to alleged terrorist organizations for protection is their suspicion of the state police force. To reduce police venality, in 2001 before 9/11 Musharraf's government issued the first major reform since the Police Act of 1861, which was designed to control the population for purposes of British imperial domination. Musharraf's reforms stipulated the establishment of federal, provincial, and district public safety commissions to increase public oversight and police accountability, yet the government put off limits technical assistance to provinces where the population was most vulnerable and the arm of the state was weakest. The Asian Development Bank has documented that poor populations perceived that "a brutal police force and a corrupt judiciary" were more insurmountable causes of poverty than were inadequate access to health or education and concluded that "weak social cohesion, declining confidence in the police, and inadequate police accountability severely undermine social regulation and public safety in Pakistan."[41] Consistent with the bank's assessment, resistance from local elites has thwarted Pakistan's government from fulfilling legislated mandates to reform police institutions. The management training needed to overcome the deficit of local capacity has not been delivered to the regions most in need, Baluchistan and the NWFP. With such an obvious gap in the provision of public safety and justice, how can Pakistan play a role in the frontline defense against global terrorism?

If police reform and, with it, devolution, were to succeed, they needed the chance to endure, regardless of whether Musharraf stood or fell. But after the 9/11 attacks, instead of rallying to support Musharraf's police reform initiative, the international donors prioritized short-term measures to subdue global terrorism. To help Pakistan live up to this strategic mission, Western donor nations contributed large amounts of aid but exercised limited supervision over how it was spent. They simply looked the other way when funds for foreign assistance went into weapons procurement,[42] leaving Musharraf's devolution efforts with a tiny fraction of total donor assistance.[43] A historic opportunity to reverse the politics of feudal dependency requires a democracy that enables people at the bottom to have the means to manage their own lives.

The impulse driving Musharraf's decentralization was to improve efficiency by separating the functions of provincial and district governance: provincial governments carry out policy and legislative functions; district governments implement policies and laws. This principle of good administration, separating steering and rowing, was circumvented by the national assembly and provincial assemblies. Musharraf filled both with supporters to ensure his electoral success. National Assembly members had budgets to undertake development projects in the districts. These budgets, essentially slush funds disbursed without constituent oversight, allowed the assembly members to construct their own patronage networks to serve as a parallel bureaucracy, weakening any attempt to make local governments accountable to local constituents for the provision of local services.

As opposition to his rule grew, Musharraf became less capable of combating resistance from local elites who thwarted the government's reform efforts. And his inadequate efforts at devolution cost him support in the districts, where he failed to secure local-level alternatives to entrenched party elites. Nor did he anticipate that deficient local-level capacity gave the provinces a platform on which to stage a bid to regain their lost powers. Pakistan's president was weakened by the backlash from provincial ministers, who turned against his allies in the battle for devolution. As traditional elite families enjoyed a comeback in the provinces in the name of democracy, the reformers who joined Musharraf early in his tenure fought for their political survival. On November 15, 2007, Musharraf dismissed Daniyal Azziz, head of the National Bureau of Reconstruction and a champion of devolution, to allay hostile opinion among elites in Azziz's native Punjab. In short, for all of his pretenses Musharraf was no Napoleon, who broke France's aristocratically controlled provinces into equally divided districts to be governed bureaucratically. By weakening traditional support systems without offering effective alternatives, Musharraf found he had only superficial support from the populace still locked into the traditional flow of obligations to local leaders. The coping devices of the past based on patronage and centralism are still the only ones that work.

After Musharraf's big losses in the parliamentary election of February 19, 2008, U.S. officials reasoned that if the president's days were numbered, so, too, are opportunities for cooperation on geopolitical objectives. Fearing that Pakistan's newly elected democratic parliament and prime minister would be difficult to influence, U.S. warheads struck sites in Pakistan's tribal areas the next month. The day after the missiles were launched the *Washington Post* confirmed: "The United States has escalated its unilateral strikes against al Qaeda members and fighters operating in Pakistan's tribal areas, partly because of anxieties that Pakistan's new leaders will insist on scaling back military operations in that country, according to U.S. officials."

Pakistan is once again on the path to democracy and the expectation among American policy planners is that another cycle of mistrust and non-cooperation will come between U.S. geopolitical aims and Pakistani affinities.

Democracy Will Not Be Enough

To contain the threat of extremism by diminishing the expected utility from a revolution, Pakistan's leaders have two options. They can expand public goods provision, especially those suitable for civic coordination such as a free press and the right to assemble. More civic goods improve the utility for everyone outside the coalition, and could also improve welfare inside the coalition. Leaders can also reduce the provision of civic goods, hoping to reduce the probability of a revolution. This path can improve coalition welfare while diminishing the welfare of those outside the coalition. However, neither option offers a viable way to contain extremism in Pakistan. Because the tribal extremists will not be part of any future governing coalition, they are unlikely to receive greater civic goods from which they can obtain access to national resources. Repression in the tribal belt will not work either, because the army is not equipped to carry it out, nor is it committed to doing so.

Democracy advocates in Pakistan like to point out that if elections are held in Pakistan, the Islamist fundamentalist parties will receive no more than 12 percent of the vote, not enough to form a government or to keep the provincial elites of Punjab and Sindh from exerting control over national decisionmaking. Even if elections bring a change at the top, this will not be enough to stop public support for terrorism, because Pakistan's elected leaders have a tradition of collaborating with an elitist bureaucracy and an ambitious military against the people. Throughout Pakistan's history, instead of organizing a legitimate opposition focused on policy alternatives, the ruling elements have supported any leader who would protect their privileges. Weak public institutions have allowed powerful personalities or families to operate outside of the law while their assets are protected from the risks of market competition, ensuring fossilization of enterprise. In a textbook written for Pakistani educators, the authors explain the sources of resentment that keep extremism smoldering:

The same powerful families appear to be the leaders of any government in power because each branch of a family is a member of another political party and most families are related to each other through marriages. They also constitute a fair portion of the senior bureaucracy, the higher judiciary and the military, as the youngest are "encouraged" to seek a career, implicitly to protect their elders from the ravages of law. Thus they control the economy, deny access to social services to the disadvantaged segments of society, and the benefits of growth have accrued to them disproportionately.[44]

Because previous elected civilian governments in Pakistan left them with fewer endowments of safety, literacy, health, wealth, or access to justice than those enjoyed by their Asian neighbors, Pakistanis have no reason to believe in the revival of a democratic system. Radical separatists flourish in the tribal belt because the population has not been encouraged to believe that basic economic aspirations can be satisfied within a democratic framework. These radicals are gaining allies among dispossessed groups throughout the nation.

The notion that an elected government in Pakistan could offer better intelligence and logistical support for the global war on terrorism is wishful thinking. Unbalanced economic development continues to discriminate against the tribal regions that need it most, favoring instead the populous and powerful eastern regions. To prevent the misuse of another opportunity at democracy, fundamental institutional reforms are needed to meet the social and political injustices that have existed in Pakistan since independence.

Long-term indirect efforts are necessary to regain the trust of the tribal regions. The surge in U.S. popularity after the effective earthquake relief America provided in 2005 is an example of how important it is for the United States to seem concerned with the needs of average Pakistanis. A substantial U.S. aid package should be offered to Pakistan's people, but not until Pakistanis have debated viable policy alternatives, repaired public finance system leakages, instituted workable public oversight, and put in place a revenue system to meet future public spending—and not until the courts have fully reviewed charges of corruption against all candidates for prime minister. All contentious issues must be placed on the table, including the largesse shown toward Punjab's interests within Pakistan's national decisionmaking institutions. Jurisdictional reconfiguration and administrative reform that distribute power more evenly among the various population groups are needed. Baluchistan's claims to revenues from its natural gas deposits must be resolved. Most important, national and provincial assembly members must limit their role to legislating and policymaking. They must stay way from managing developmental spending, a situation that has created a parallel bureaucracy in the districts.

After the September 11 attacks, President Bush announced to the world, "You are either with us or against us." Pakistanis ask, "How long will the United States remain interested and keep the money flowing?" Pakistani-U.S. relations are the subject of an alliance curse captured in Zulfikar Bhutto's question, posed in 1965, "Friend or master?" With Pakistan once again recruited to aid the United States in its fight against global jihadism, the incumbent leader who enjoys weak legitimacy at home cajoles external support by reminding the West that the terrorist threats as well as the democratic alternatives—the Muslim League led by Nawaz Sharif and the People's Party led by the Bhutto dynasty, remnants of a corrupt past—are potentially more dangerous or, at the least, less promising, than the status quo. Keeping the threat alive, Musharraf gains a basis to demand continued loyalty by making himself indispensable, while the United States fails to acknowledge that the source of instability in Pakistan is not global jihadism, but long-standing local grievances.[45]

Neither Americans nor Pakistanis see the present relationship as a suitable basis for long-term cooperation. Relying on alliance rents, the American-backed dictator neglects to strengthen citizen engagement in delivering basic services and security. Local champions of reform who are seeking an alternative to dictatorship end up mistrusting the United States; democratic sentiment becomes anti-American sentiment. The United States responds by mistrusting democratic forces and by distancing itself from its own democratic rhetoric. This boosts anti-Americanism, leaving the United States with little leverage to promote internal reforms in Pakistan. A relationship so deeply marred by mutual mistrust on both sides will require a generation to correct. A first step is to stop referring to Pakistani extremism in terms of global jihadism, and to start focusing on the long-simmering local grievances that nurture extremism. We will only begin to take necessary corrective actions when we recognize the underlying source of Pakistan's domestic problems: failed economic development, discrimination, and exclusion.

A balanced democracy requires balanced growth free of the distortions caused by top-down collusion and rent seeking by entrenched elites. The perpetuation of alliance rents from the West frees incumbent politicians from the need to impose proper checks and balances on the use of power. Alliance rents also prevent these politicians from decentralizing access to power so that disenfranchised regions receive a balanced share of future growth. Going from an alliance-cursed autocracy to an alliance-cursed democracy will not reduce extremism. A democracy in Pakistan that strengthens regional stability is of great interest to America. But holding elections will not reverse the negative impact on U.S. security resulting from decades of misguided support to regimes of impunity and privilege. Trust and cooperation will not be restored as long as U.S. assistance is seen as mainly concerned with preventing the use of Pakistan as a safe haven for anti-American terrorism. To play a constructive role in regional security, Pakistan must first overcome its internal fragility. This would require U.S. aid to shift focus from short-term antiterrorism to long-term development. A Pakistani leader who hopes to be successful against extremism ultimately must undertake fundamental institutional reform. Until meaningful constitutional changes are enacted, domestic mass movements will seek to revolutionize the political system by replacing it with new governance institutions.

Neither Ally Nor Adversary: Managing the Contradictions

The U.S. policy tilt toward Pakistan since 9/11 has created tension in America's bilateral relationship with India, even as it has not succeeded in reforming domestic governance within Pakistan itself. U.S. support of friendly authoritarian regimes in Pakistan overlooks the absence of shared values and disregards evidence that Pakistan does not widely accept U.S. policy goals. The United States has been reluctant to encourage democratic reform due to fears of a possible outcome—the election of an unfriendly and anti-American regime undermining U.S. security interests. As a result, America coddles Pakistan's autocratic rulers, even as the current regime clashes with powerful internal social forces. These forces include a growing middle class that seeks a greater political voice, and a rural population that suffers from dislocation and tension caused by uneven economic growth and religious extremism. Corruption and large inequalities in living standards nurture resentments against the government that are exacerbated by the failure to hold elections.

By conceding too much to Western pressures to contain terrorism, General Pervez Musharraf further incites fundamentalist leaders who seek to overthrow the government. Yet as the military's credibility weakens under revelations of past collaborations with radical Islamists, Musharraf is finding it harder to ride two horses—to placate the West and to eliminate extremism. If the general's support narrows, the West will be in a greater quandary than ever. Codependency between the Islamists and the military has resulted in collaboration on the regional battlefields of the jihad movement.

The slow meltdown of the Pakistani polity reflects the failure of Western support for regimes that deny self-governance to their people. Homegrown Islamist parties modeled after Hamas and Hezbollah are learning that by providing public goods, they can advance their own political ambitions. The military regime that enjoys only superficial support among the Western-leaning middle classes has been playing a dangerous game by supporting Islamist extremists. Domestically the army's goal is to weaken mainstream parties and make itself indispensable. Internationally it seeks a way to garner Western support on grounds that it alone has the capacity to contain extremism. This strategy offers political Islam an opportunity to define the state and to become a collaborator with anti-Western forces in the countryside.[46] The military is continuing a pattern that began earlier in Pakistan's brief history when the bureaucracy was in charge and it, too, used Islam to reject mass politics and to foil the demands of the secular left. The persistence of military rule results in the erosion of secular political powers, a process helped by the constant harassment of secular party workers. By preventing new secular leadership from emerging, Pakistan's military rule creates a political vacuum that religious extremists would like to fill.

Nowhere are the moral contradictions and shortsightedness of U.S. cold war policy more apparent than in this region, as the United States tries to strengthen its alliance with India as a foil to China's power. Cold war policy linked Pakistan with U.S. security interests while India, despite U.S. neglect, has become essential to long-term U.S. post–cold war security interests. Trade, technology, and political affinity are combining to bring the United States and India, the world's two largest democratic nations, toward greater cooperation. Distrust remains, even as interests converge. Ties are complicated by past U.S.–Indian relations, and by the U.S. view of India as a second-rate power that was denied markets, technology, or strategic partnership as punishment for not toeing Washington's geopolitical line. The United States was seeking a compliant ally willing to place its own development struggles on a lower rung so that East-West battles could be played out in its backyard. This was something that the leaders of an old and proud civilization would not accept.

Today, India is being asked to play in great-power politics, but it still resists being a pawn in the hands of a single power and it is no more eager to contain China than it was once willing to stop Soviet Communism. It has eschewed great-power alliances to strengthen its bonds with peers, and does not view developing close ties with China and being a counterweight as mutually exclusive. India seeks closer commercial ties with China, but it must balance that interest with its security interests and the need to avoid aggression. If India and the United States are to build an enduring alliance, America must learn one key lesson: though eager to join the boardroom of executive nations, India will not embrace a subordinate role in an alliance. India has responded to U.S. arms sales to Pakistan by building up its own arsenals, diverting money away from development. India's acquisition of arms measured in dollars between 2003 and 2006 has surpassed that of all other developing nations, but its people feel no safer, making them deeply resentful of U.S policies.

The U.S. relationship with the subcontinent illustrates several seemingly insurmountable obstacles for U.S. foreign policy. First, it is difficult for America to reconcile its short-term security dilemmas with its wish to see the norms of democracy take root around the world. This difficulty compromises the moral foundations of America's global leadership. Second, the United States is unable to draw the relevant lessons for establishing democracy in a third world environment. Third, and most ominous, Jinnah's promise that Communism would not flourish on Islamic soil has turned out to be one of the cold war's failed prophesies. The belief that Islam would inoculate the region from Communism blinded the United States to another danger: Islam could itself become a radical force, once secular reformers were eliminated. It is in Iran where this certainty first collapsed. But Pakistan could be the place where the consequences of misapprehending Islam's social and political influence might be even more lethal to Western interests. Applying a double standard by renouncing its own values, the West alienates Pakistan's urban middle classes as well as those of India, serving neither Western nor South Asian security.

There will be a huge price to pay for the mistaken policies of the past. The status quo—Pakistan as the last rampart against extremism—is not secure. But believing that flawed cooperation is better than none at all, the West seems unwilling to exchange today's risks, which it believes can be managed, for the hope of a better tomorrow that it may be unable to manage.

*U.S. Security Risks from
Failures of Global
Economic Development*

11

Walking with the Devil: The Commitment Trap in U.S. Foreign Policy

"My children, it is permitted you in time of grave danger to walk with the devil until you have crossed the bridge."

—Old Balkan proverb used by Franklin Roosevelt

By the standards the George W. Bush administration set for itself, a successful conclusion to the Iraq invasion was well within reach by the time the president declared victory on May 1, 2003. A constitution was ratified on October 15, 2005, and a general election took place on December 15, 2005, to elect a permanent 275-member Iraqi council. A government, headed by Prime Minister Nuri al-Maliki, took office on May 20, 2006. Yet this government—as of early 2008— had not met one of Washington's benchmarks for national reconciliation, security, or governance. Maliki's government refused to distance itself from radical clerics or curb their private militias. Non-sectarian technocrats were not invited to join the cabinet. Police units that practiced sectarian partisanship were not suspended, Government ministries stacked with loyalists bred corruption.[1] Even the surge of additional American troops in the winter of 2007–08 has failed to provide the breathing space to pass the 18 legislative benchmarks the Bush administration called vital to political reconciliation.

How could a government so utterly dependent on American collaboration defy U.S. wishes, yet hope for U.S. forces to remain in Baghdad? With ample evidence of Iraq's failure to meet the public security and civil service criteria of a secular state, why had the Bush administration not tied aid to policy performance? Why has it not made continued support contingent on achieving explicit milestones?

The trap the United States faces in Iraq exemplifies a recurring dilemma in U.S. foreign policy. Presidents have continuously coddled client regimes that are unwilling to make the political trade-offs necessary for national legitimacy. Despite American rhetoric about overseas reform and ambivalence about backing dictators, throughout the cold war many U.S. political leaders relied on one authoritarian regime to help defeat another more odious authoritarian regime. And there were the proxy wars, too, when the United States armed Iraq against Iran and the mujahedin against the Soviet Union in Afghanistan. Such myopic policies consequently impaired America's ability to forcefully advocate domestic reforms within those regimes. Once engaged, U.S. support weakened American demands for pro-reform quid pro quo terms.

This is the U.S. commitment trap. Committed to the survival of allies but lacking the leverage to discipline recalcitrant regime leaders, America creates a strategic vulnerability that even weak client states can exploit. The commitment trap reduces America's credibility as a reform advocate. It binds the United States so that America cannot walk away from allies without eroding its credibility.[2] Curiously, this trap isn't sealed abroad but at home—by the fears that have driven the U.S. electorate since the cold war.

Supporting Reform in Cold War Client Regimes

Client regime reform is within the U.S. ideological tradition, and attempts at such efforts have been an important component of American security policy since the cold war. In 1946 General George Marshall attempted, without success, to form a coalition government in China and to persuade Chiang Kai-shek's ruling Kuomintang Party to accept Communist Party participation in elections.[3]

In another example of U.S. efforts to change the behavior of a client regime, Secretary of State Dean Acheson suggested to the shah of Iran in 1949 that the best way to deter war and achieve security "was not by military preparations but by so developing free economic and social structures as to protect them from foreign aggression and upheaval."[4] Presidents Kennedy, Eisenhower, and Carter gave similar advice to the shah. In early 1950 President Truman warned South Korea's strongman, Syngman Rhee, that he would receive no more U.S. aid if he canceled elections. His successor, Park Chung-hee, was put on similar notice by Kennedy in 1961 and again in 1963.

However, under stress of civil war or external aggression, even U.S. presidents who entered office advocating overseas reform eventually reinforced the very regimes they once condemned. Regardless of their political philosophies, every American president has put democracy on hold when larger security issues arose. As keen observers of U.S. policies, autocrats such as Chiang Kai-shek, Shah Pahlavi, Ferdinand Marcos, and Park Chung-hee used security threats of insurgency or invasion to serve their private ambitions.

When Chiang Kai-shek defied a cease-fire and attacked Manchuria, he was convinced that resumption of hostilities against the Communists would leave the United States with no choice but to support him. Decades apart, both Presidents Kennedy and Carter looked the other way when the shah of Iran used violence to suppress leftists. The shah's excuse was the need to prevent Communist infiltration. South Vietnam's Ngo Dinh Diem defied American reform entreaties in 1962 even as his regime became increasingly precarious, remarking to his brother that the United States was too deeply committed to halt aid.[5] Nor did the United States act in 1972, when both Park Chung-hee and Ferdinand Marcos declared martial law. The United States was distracted by the need for Southeast Asia's support for the Vietnam War.

Why are we not surprised, then, that Iraq's Maliki wagers that Bush will hold extremists responsible for his government's failures and will admonish the prime minister's detractors for underestimating the difficulties of implementing reform? In the past, a client regime obtained commitments from America by painting dire scenarios, implying, "It's either me or the possibility of something far worse."[6] And in each case America lost its bargaining leverage. In fact, it was the implicit strength of the U.S. commitment that allowed these client regimes to ignore external requests for accommodation and reform—notions that often enjoyed strong support among client regime populations. Thus, the commitment trap can turn a great power into a creature of a smaller power.[7] The tail wags the dog. The client can gain leverage because adversaries, other clients, and domestic political opposition within the United States will interpret the failure to defend an ally in need as the erosion of U.S. credibility. Such reasoning by Washington is exactly what Maliki has counted on.

Given such an uneven record, it may be easy to overlook the many U.S. efforts on behalf of reform in client regimes. The United States has three ways to approach the problem of reform: work with the incumbent to implement reform, buttress the incumbent by suppressing oppression, or withdraw support and abandon the incumbent. In a 1961 address delivered in the Dominican Republic soon after the assassination of the dictator Rafael Leónidas Trujillo Molina, President Kennedy explicitly referred to all of these options. The United States, he said, "had three options, in descending order of preference: a decent democratic regime, a continuation of the Trujillo regime, or a Castro regime. . . . We ought to aim at the first, but we really can't renounce the second until we are sure that we can avoid the third."[8] Should we be surprised that an engagement rationalized by cold war logic should mire the United States in a cold war–type commitment trap?

The third option has, with few exceptions, remained unthinkable. No matter how repugnant a regime, its loss as an ally has invariably damaged the U.S. president's domestic political credibility. Republicans excoriated the Truman administration over the loss of China, asserting that U.S. resources should have been committed earlier and more intensively. The president's dilemma is that the U.S. incumbent administration, not some developing country, is always the final domino to fall. The loss of China helped precipitate the Democrats' loss of the White House in 1952, and the loss of Iran led to Carter's fall in 1980. The domestic political debate over the inability to win in Vietnam similarly doomed Lyndon Johnson's administration. Throughout the cold war, any administration that exercised the withdrawal option would have faced charges of ignoring the spread of third world Communism. A prisoner of his own rhetoric, President Bush now fears being attacked from within his own party for not having done enough to prevent the spread of terrorism throughout the Middle East and beyond.

Moreover, changing a government's policy generally requires changing the government itself, along with its major institutions. In cold war America it was impossible to argue publicly that a radical leftist regime was preferable to a repressive rightist regime. Both political parties feared the rise of an anti-American alternative to previous regime elites. Unpredictable behavior is far worse than the status quo. "Sure, he's a son of a bitch, but he's our son of a bitch," a phrase of disputed origin, is said to refer to America's attitude about either Spain's Franco or Nicaragua's Somoza. If insurgents even appear ascendant, a client regime can strengthen its position in Washington by arguing that it represents the only alternative to chaos and uncertainty. Again, the more power a regime gains over the U.S. foreign policy process and the more assurances of U.S. support it receives, the fewer incentives it faces for greater accountability—to the United States or to its own citizens. The real issue is not so much one of inconsistency in confronting those governments. The underlying problem is a flaw in cold war strategy, which narrows the band of policy options for client regime reform.

Falling Dominoes and Commitment Traps

By invading Iraq, the United States has created a new commitment trap for itself. The logic for getting to this point mimics the logic that got America into Vietnam: if Communism was not stopped there, all of Southeast Asia, and then the rest of the third world, would be at risk. Similarly, supporters of the Iraq War argue that abandoning the Shi'a-dominated government would allow the jihadists to win. Having beaten the Russians in Afghanistan and the Americans in Iraq, the jihadists will seek hegemony over the entire region. Thomas Sowell, a Hoover Institution fellow, offered a particularly compelling example of this logic in an opinion piece for the *Wall Street Journal:*

> Whether we want to or not, we cannot unilaterally end the war with international terrorists. Giving the terrorists an epoch making victory in Iraq would only shift the location where we must face them or succumb to them. Abandoning Iraqi allies to their fate would ensure that other nations would think twice before becoming or remaining our allies. With a nuclear Iran looming on the horizon, we are going to need all the allies we can get.[9]

In a similar vein Max Boot writes in the *Los Angeles Times,* "Bad as the situation is today, it could get a lot worse if we simply pull out. . . . The resulting backlash could produce an Islamist dictatorship that would threaten American interests. We would also be hurt by the perception that we are a weak horse (to quote Osama bin Laden) that can be driven out of a country by a few suicide bombers—a perception sure to embolden terrorists."[10] Thus, trapped into supporting regimes such as those in Libya, Kazakhstan, Pakistan, Saudi Arabia, Tunisia, and Uzbekistan, all regimes that make insufficient efforts to build an inclusive understanding of citizen rights, the United States sacrifices its moral authority as an honest promoter of global democracy.

Let us consider a possible scenario resulting from the Iraq War, one that is consistent with entrapment. The Shi'a ascendancy in Iraq, which includes sectarian allegiances that penetrate the army and the police, is widening the gulf between the Shi'a and the Sunnis. Policies of extreme de-Ba'athification, including limiting Sunni access to Iraq's oil revenues, will only continue to feed insurgency support among the Sunnis. A winner-take-all outcome means that Saddam Hussein's Ba'ath dictatorship would be replaced with a Shi'a dictatorship, and under the banner of democracy Shi'a ascendancy would plunge the country into civil war.

Unable to take a neutral role, the United States would again be caught in a commitment trap, this time backing the Shi'a. This trap will be just like those that led to the unfortunate estrangement with China, the support of successive dictators in Vietnam, the rise of Marcos, and blind commitment to the shah of Iran. If the base of the Sunni insurgency widens, a secure secular state will not be possible. If the United States is trapped into supporting a Shi'a government that eschews a compromise, a regionwide insurgency could lead to even broader U.S. military involvement in the area. Having acquired deep roots among the civilian population, the insurgency would poison relations with America for years to come. As it did in Vietnam, the United States will extract political defeat from military victory. As doubts about the wisdom of intervening in Iraq spread, the U.S. debate will veer toward the question of who lost Iraq. Such a debate may restrain future interventions in the short run. But a comprehensive assessment of cold war lessons might offer a variety of perspectives from which to frame future decisions about overseas interventions. A shared set of convictions about social change and the value of democracy led supporters all along the political spectrum to be enthusiastic about the U.S. invasion of Iraq. But the failure of Iraq's democracy to improve quality of life, provide security, or induce cooperation has debased democracy's value for Iraqi citizens.

Let us consider one final historical analogy. Despite the victories of U.S.-backed forces in the Vietnam War, both sides understood that America had a short time horizon and that the warring forces in the North could wait out the external actors. For this reason, the institutions created by the United States in Vietnam had little credibility. Both southerners and northerners understood that institutions of power not born of internal consensus had doubtful durability.

There is only one definitive way for the United States to extricate itself from future commitment traps. That is for the White House and the overseas incumbent administration to break ranks with the military view of conflict and accept that such a view mischaracterizes the complexity of social change in emerging nations. Throughout the cold war the U.S. military and the civilian bureaucracy fought over supporting the status quo. The fear of failure led both parties to do too much, never too little. "Too much" meant that American administrations put too much effort into buttressing regimes. This latest chapter of U.S. military involvement, in Iraq, resembles the other failures in that military advisers conclude that training and assistance for the nascent army are the key missing ingredients for victory. It took four years before the U.S. military realized it was a mistake to close Iraqi government-owned factories, which were that nation's second largest employer after the army. Procuring goods from those factories would have created desperately needed employment for Iraqis and might have lowered costs for U.S. armed services. Such gaps in military reasoning had a huge negative impact on building support among the Iraqi population.

A more plausible assessment of the situation in Iraq must combine military with political, social, and economic analysis and fully engage other centers of expertise. Such a change would require reconfiguring the entire structure of policymaking that currently informs the president's decisions.

Unconditional U.S. support of the Maliki government only fanned sectarian violence and pushed the Sunnis into greater collaboration with al Qaeda. By helping Maliki to crush the Sunni insurgency without insisting on federalism, higher employment rates, a revenue-sharing compromise, a moderation of de-Ba'athification, and curtailment of Shi'a militia abuses, the Bush administration was suckered into a commitment trap, just like its cold war predecessors. Inadvertently fueling Sunni resistance, the Bush administration pushed Iraq closer to all-out civil war and set the stage for the winning moves to occur politically—not on the battlefield, where U.S. forces have overwhelming superiority. Hoodwinked by their own rhetoric into not crediting the opponent with anticipatory skill, U.S policy planners have again ceded political victory to an insurgency.

12

Redeeming Democracy through the Market: Do Open Markets Produce Open Politics?

> No country can afford to have its prosperity originated by a small
> controlling class. The treasury of America does not lie in the brains of a
> small body of men now in control of great enterprises. . . . It depends on
> the inventions of unknown men, upon the originations of unknown men.
> Every country is renewed out of the ranks of the unknown, not out of the
> ranks of the already famous and powerful in control.
>
> —Woodrow Wilson (1912)

The idea that the free market is the best school for the spread of democracy enjoys the status of a truism. Milton Friedman helped to popularize the view by stating that democracy requires private centers of economic power to counterbalance central state authority. The corollary is that commercial ties between nations nurture a freedom-loving, commercial middle class that will eventually rise up to demand democratic reform.[1] U.S. forbearance toward the rise of crony privatization during Russia's transition attests to the force of this conviction.[2] The concept still underpins the mission statements of U.S. intervention around the world and shapes plans to rebuild Afghanistan and Iraq, mollify Arab radicalism, and transform Chinese society.

The political scientist Michael Mandelbaum attributes the surge of democracy during the last quarter of the twentieth century to the rise of the free market, writing that the market has become the most influential and universal school of democratic politics and liberty, providing the skills, habits, and values that democratic practice requires. Those skills and attitudes are then transferred from the economy to the polity, fostering democracy, because in the market people form "the habit, and the expectation, of exercising, through individual choice, a measure of control over the larger economic system. . . . It is natural for them to carry over into the larger political system in which participants in the market also reside: and this habit, and this expectation, encourages the practice, essential to democracy, of popular sovereignty."[3]

Mandelbaum also attests that free markets create the wealth that underwrites democratic political participation by creating and sustaining organizations and groups such as businesses, trade unions, and professional associations that are independent of government.

Globalization's contribution to the spread of democracy has many enthusiasts. Robert Pastor, a political scientist, expounds:

> Citizens would choose their leaders in a free political market within their state, and consumers would choose their products in a free economic market that would expand as technology shrank the world. . . . In the new epoch, leaders would be compelled to respond to popular preferences or lose elections. Citizens would be shareholders in the state, just as they might own stock in a business. To stay in business, firms would need to respond to their shareholders' demand for profits and to the changing preferences of their consumers. The world of empires and monopolies would be replaced by one of democratic governments and private markets.[4]

Yet the rapid pace of globalization has altered the balance between the market and the ballot, exposing a deep flaw in the assumption that global economic freedom will be the path to global democracy. The behavior of key international agents is not consistent with this belief.[5] The free market system has made organizations such as multinational corporations so powerful that they compromise the capacity of democratic institutions to constrain them.

The frictionless accommodation of capitalism to democracy is an illusion that is difficult to maintain, even among the most developed market democracies. In Anglo-American democracies, global business is eroding the power of people to constrain powerful business organizations—the same kind of organizations that free markets have created. If the triumph of global capitalism threatens democracy and civic life even among industrialized democracies, what can be expected in developing countries that provide few safeguards against the economic power of local business elites? Should we be surprised to learn that among developing world populations multinational corporations have a reputation for being a danger to the poor?

Democracy and the Market

The optimism that links democracy with open markets and the private sector to enhanced political competition stems from idealized notions of how markets function, notions that are taught in economics textbooks. The promise of a convergence between global capitalism and global democracy assumes the presence of effective public institutions that motivate self-interested actors to gather and process information, monitor corporate managers, and disclose information.[6] That model of market efficiency ignores barriers to trade caused by information gaps that distort resource allocation in developing regions. Some information gaps are intrinsic to the process of underdevelopment; others are deliberately crafted to protect the endowments of incumbents.[7]

Information asymmetries intrinsic to the process of economic development create the danger of entrenchment by incumbent interests that resist market competition. In many countries, trade openness gives entrenched interests increased opportunities to collaborate with transnational capital to extract monopoly profits from advantageous positions they already enjoy. International traders maximize their positions in the global economy by gaining access to excessive returns earned by alliances with informed local traders. Regulatory distortion or political influence in the local market is often the currency of such trade.

Many of the business deals that benefit from a combination of foreign policy and government power involve insider trading between government officials and closely connected domestic and transnational capital. This tendency toward global-scale collusion challenges the viability of globalization. As global markets become more competitive to meet shareholders' demands, an emphasis on corporate governance and accountability often places firm managers in conflict with citizens' interests (in both home and overseas markets), often producing suspicion abroad about multinational corporations' motives, as recent work by Robert Reich and Joseph Stiglitz indicates.[8]

The expectation that market capitalism will create social foundations for the spread of Western-style democracy fails to anticipate this reality: in emerging states, wealthy minorities capture weak institutions by collectively organizing to exploit local market imperfections. The young democracies of the developing world do not have the resources or the institutions to resist the enormous lobbying power of global business. They have few mechanisms to prevent large corporate contributions from influencing political outcomes.

In developing countries, inequality, ethnic polarization, and political actors' discretion create uncertainty that prevents traders from realizing their optimal plans. Institutional devices to signal trust are inadequate but do not cause a complete breakdown of trade. Many developing countries have seen significant growth because local traders adapt, learning to create informal social organizations that internalize the missing structures of formal markets.[9] Three critical adaptations to information gaps include family ownership of large firms, pyramids, and investments in political connections.[10] These three strategies are not mutually exclusive; in many emerging markets they are seamlessly interwoven.

Family Control of Markets

Distortions of resource allocation that both reflect and reproduce declining rates of innovation can be mitigated by family control.[11] In many countries, family firms report higher-than-average returns because poor institutions produce incomplete markets in which traders unrelated to the handful of powerful families find it difficult to enforce contracts.[12] Since external financing for long-term investments is feeble, family firms typically depend on self-financing or on financial organizations owned by family members.[13] Family control can have a beneficial effect on company performance but rarely produces companies that achieve sufficient size or managerial sophistication to be players beyond their own national borders. One reason is that senior management is limited to the competency of family members—inadequate institutional trust makes engaging outsiders at senior levels difficult. Hence, family-owned firms are likely to lobby for protection from global markets. Most of Latin America's private sector and the private sector in China and in much of East Asia's Chinese diaspora (excluding Singapore) fit this pattern. Ownership of large firms by a single family or network of families does not correct the underlying cause of an economy's bottlenecks; they are merely an adaptation that helps individual firms succeed without correcting the systemic sources of underdevelopment.

Pyramids

A particularly effective way for private traders to overcome incomplete risk markets and to grow bigger than family-owned firms is to form pyramid control structures, whereby traders gain control by owning special company shares.[14] Pyramids arise to overcome intrinsic problems of resource allocation as economies scale up. Pyramids increase traders' access to advanced technology. However, this setup has many downsides.

The East Asian financial crisis of 1997 exposed the dangers of special company shares that are held by a small number of families and that grant these families control over company decisionmaking. The owners extract excessive private benefits from the firms they control without risking their own wealth. They also stifle competition by using multiple voting shares and cross-shareholdings so that firms in the same sector can be owned by the same families. Pyramids provide sources of capital that allow firms owned by insiders to outperform independent firms. They direct trade and investment away from producers outside the group, make credit available mostly to members, and stymie independent firms that seek to compete without political connections on the basis of managerial competence. Such constraints on competition, common before the Great Depression in North America, seem to be characteristic of the first stage of industrialization in almost all countries.[15] These constraints are often widely considered to have caused the financial distress that East Asian economies experienced in the late 1990s.[16]

Today, pyramids gain opportunities from globalization because most capital that sloshes around in the international economy is concentrated in a small number of global funds that invest in a small number of industries controlled by a small number of families. The pyramids are often the first to drink deeply from these international wells of global investment capital. American pro-market policies during the cold war overlooked the risk of allowing oligarchic capitalism to be protected under a liberal umbrella.[17]

Large controlling shares in the corporate sector easily transfer to political influence in countries where rules prohibiting conflicts of interest between public and private spheres are weakly defined and poorly enforced. Pyramids have repercussions for national productivity, stifling innovators who by definition lack political clout and who typically operate on a scale too small to attract overseas capital. With greatly amplified political influence, the incumbents use political access to protect their positions in the market, manipulating public policy to protect their property rights and their access to capital.

The Premium on Connectivity

Although pyramids frequently lobby to prevent competition, political connectivity presents a more general and widespread challenge to effective competition than the formation of pyramids. A strong tendency to become politically connected is typical among successful firms in developing countries. Preferential treatment may facilitate access to government-controlled financial institutions, government-controlled raw materials, government-owned industrial enterprises, and government agencies such as the army or the police that contract for services and equipment. Along with procurement contracts, government connections can offer tax advantages and lax regulatory oversight, which allows political agencies to determine how stringently to enforce conflict-of-interest laws.

Many firms invest heavily in political connections by contributing to electoral campaigns and by making direct payments, sometimes offering political allies shares in private enterprises. As political sponsorship increases among firms, risk insurance and hedging through market forces are restrained. The effects of purposefully created opacity may offset the informational utility of prices in the marketplace.

In the most corrupt nations, such as Myanmar, political connections facilitate the restriction of foreign investments. In democratic countries, economic nationalism becomes a rationale to protect the power of incumbency, which can inadvertently amplify the effects of connectivity. In both scenarios, once an economy opens, already established firms have the resources and the information channels to monopolize access to new investments and new partners. This pattern of collusion is another reason why globalization and inequality are frequently linked.

Enter the Foreign Investor

In theory, multinational corporations can help to counterbalance the power of crony local capitalists, but in practice they are often in cahoots with these very groups. This occurs because in virtually all countries, high-level political connections are almost always important sources of asset value. The larger firms, which are most likely to be attractive to foreign investors, are generally the most connected. In Suharto's Indonesia, where political connections contributed greatly to company value, opening the economy to private foreign investment enhanced the value of connections to regime officials.[18] Trade liberalism attracted new investors to Indonesia who protected their investments by establishing connections with members of Suharto's family. Among the firms that formed partnerships with the president's relatives are Japan's NEC and Sumitomo; America's Hughes Aircraft, Ford, and Union Carbide; France's Alcatel; Germany's Deutsche Telekom; and Switzerland's Nestlé. Similarly, as developing world economies open to foreign investment, transparently managed publicly owned Western firms seeking risk-adjusted returns for their shareholders seek out partners with ties to top officials. The retinues of business leaders that accompany U.S. presidents overseas exemplify the link between high-level political connections and investment in emerging markets.

When Anglo and American firms expand their operations overseas, the rhetoric of liberalism asserts that they would project the values and habits of their home-market governance standards.[19] However, the quandary of the American investor seeking overseas partners in underinstitutionalized markets is solved by selecting well-connected partners. Such partners are often firms owned by entrenched elites with insider connections to political officeholders. These officeholders offer impunity from public scrutiny and from the supervisory standards of competitive capitalism, such as sanctions against mismanagement or seizure of collateral in bankruptcy cases. Firms that lack the protection of connected elites are easy prey to possible expropriation, which reduces their investment appeal.

Should we be surprised that democratically governed Western firms are behaving just the way democratically governed states do—seeking alliances with small winning coalitions overseas? In markets where the courts cannot be counted on to protect property rights or where tax collection is discriminatory, investors will seek out politically convenient partnerships. If managers of international capital were to act otherwise, they would disregard their fiduciary responsibility to their shareholders. In fact, in markets like China, firms that disclose information about abusive practices can invite reprisal by powerful local actors.

As promoters of global public goods, Western firms find that their power is constrained by their responsibility to make good for their investors at home. Should it be any surprise, then, that U.S. democracy activism is viewed by many people outside the United States as a form of guiltless imperialism? Collusion in the entrenchment of wealthy family cliques is the unintended consequence of making the right decisions for shareholders, but such collusion creates enemies of global capitalism. Enmity toward global capitalism is a negative global good that weakens systemwide legitimacy, but it is out of the purview of firm management. As Robert Reich has pointed out, improved corporate governance makes companies less likely to be socially responsible.[20] If company executives maximize returns to their investors, as they are supposed to do, their role as agents of constructive social change will be secondary.

U.S. firms' investments in political connections can increase the value of asymmetric information to a developing country's insiders. Such investment can strengthen the influence of controlling families over poorly funded legal systems and political parties. Domestically owned private sector firms in China often dispute the privileged access to public resources that foreign investors obtain through political channels. Complicity occurs with the very constituencies that retard the development of capital markets, hobble entry of innovators, hinder growth, and foster inequality during the process of economic globalization. The policy distortions that result are not only a cause of underdevelopment; they ensure its perpetuation.

Capitalism without Democracy, Liberty without Competition

Democratic convergence has yet to result from pro-market reforms in China, where the Communist Party is welcoming wealthy business leaders into its ranks.[21] A compliant middle class is a cornerstone of a repressive centralizing regime in Russia. In China, Russia, Kazakhstan, and Singapore, to name but a few examples, citizens will forgo venues for free expression and coordination in exchange for opportunities to consume.[22] Leadership cynically averts the danger of being overthrown by eliminating channels for opposition groups to recruit, organize, and disseminate information while permitting citizens opportunities to acquire items that boost their economic status. A larger middle class has not been translated into strong sentiment for democratic reforms because as the marginal cost of political expression becomes unattainable, citizens accept consumerism as a substitute, trading the right to assemble and to speak out for access to the latest designer kitchen and luxury sports sedan. Thus, capitalism and democracy need not go hand in hand. The goods and services that Americans receive from the expansion of global free markets can often come from the erosion of citizen rights in other countries.

Academics have been busy testing the correlation between market reforms and liberalized political expression. One study shows that trade openness does not make a dynamic contribution to institutional reform in non-democracies, and it correlates negatively with democratic institutions in a wide cross-sample of regimes. As the Chinese and Russian cases cited above suggest, the level of democracy decreases as trade openness increases.[23] Other studies have argued that the increased inequality often associated with foreign direct investment disrupts democratic stability.[24]

For democratic regimes to succeed at trade liberalization, their citizens must enjoy protection from volatility that occurs when economies, especially small economies, open to global forces. The implication of such findings is that the development of effective government taxation and the administrative capacity to offer equitable risk insurance to vulnerable sectors of the population may be a prerequisite for stability in democratizing regimes that are opening to international trade.[25] Without effective mechanisms for collecting and spending revenues, democratic regimes that open their economies are vulnerable to failure because they will lack resources to provide risk insurance to exposed sectors of the population.

The theories that attribute political pluralism to the influence of markets or to the commercial classes fail to provide a realistic explanation for the behavior of individual traders. Such theories also fail to identify how activism for a purely public good such as democracy is consistent with the interests of private agents. Policy goals that typically include political stability, the rule of law, balanced budgets, and broad employment are public goods that are available to all traders, even if the traders do not commit private resources to obtain them. The commercial classes are more likely to engage their private resources to lobby for private goods that are firm- or sector-specific rather than economywide.

The vision that links open markets to global democracy has not given us the tools to produce winning forecasts. We must first adjust our lenses to better understand the links between the rational expectations of individual actors and the systemwide incentives that define their actions. The principles of the international regime and the incentives of individual actors are out of alignment and do not produce the outcomes that our theories would predict or our values find acceptable. We must be prepared to acknowledge that seeking better deals for shareholders will not make corporate managers into better global citizens. Many of the benefits that we gain from being consumers or investors in global capitalism, as Robert Reich argues, come at the cost of social benefits that we value as citizens. We should not expect corporations to be the purveyors of liberal political values or to act as bulwarks of democratic institutions overseas. Their duties to their shareholders will circumscribe their support of democratic political activities in the countries where they do business.

Since the end of the twentieth century, U.S. defense and foreign policies have been shaped by the assumption that liberal markets are a precondition to liberal politics, but what is needed to ensure sustainable democracy in the developing world is principles to cope with the social bifurcation that results from complex, irreducible, irreversible, and asymmetrical global change. One of these changes, the emergence of a hypercompetitive global supply chain, will place global consumers and investors in conflict with the ideals of global citizenship and democracy promotion. The great deals that we obtain as consumers of new products and services may add to the influence of well-organized corporate insiders. We receive these great deals at the expense of nascent democratic institutions overseas.

During the cold war, virtually every American president declared that economic growth and democracy were so closely intertwined that more of one would inevitably produce more of the other. The political scientist and historian William Williams has observed that America's economic expansion unfolded as if economic opportunity and political liberty were joined at the hip: "Expanding the marketplace enlarged the area of freedom. Expanding freedom expanded the marketplace."[26] During the war on terror, these links continue to define U.S. ideas about stability and security. But the pursuit of these two great principles has linked the United States with antirevolutionary internationalism and the bolstering of domestic political hierarchies in client regimes. To be what Clinton's Secretary of State Madeleine Albright calls "the indispensable nation" at the center of a new world order, we must acknowledge that liberal trade agreements can reinforce the social networks that connect elites to each other unless deliberate corrective actions are taken to protect competition and diversity. As Woodrow Wilson so well understood, a commitment to the preservation of existing local hierarchies is hardly a legacy that the United States should seek.

Linking U.S. Security to Third World Development

The safety of the nation is the supreme law.

—Thomas Jefferson (1807)

Is there an alternative to militarizing the battle against terrorism in the image of the cold war? In 2002 Clare Short, secretary of Britain's Department for International Development, proposed a shift away from military solutions and toward sustainable development. Such an alternative would open the policy arena to an array of interest groups, organizations, and institutions, closely mirroring the reality of a diverse and interdependent world. Yet such an approach would also dilute U.S. presidential control and would not be hospitable to presidential leadership, as the Clinton administration discovered. The forces of policy diffusion that unfolded during Clinton's presidency offered a glimpse of the future that the Bush administration did not like or want to replicate. In this chapter we consider the long-term implications of making sustainable global development the template for U.S. foreign relations.

Since the cold war, U.S. national security has remained distinct from all other policy areas. This separation has created a clique of national security elites whose opinions carry weight on topics that go far beyond their areas of expertise. It is common, for example, for these national security elites—in the CIA, the State and Defense Departments, and the Joint Chiefs of Staff—to discuss topics such as the political uses of military power. Yet after examining the record of U.S. engagement with key third world, allies we find that the primacy given to military expertise has often produced consequences that these cliques failed to anticipate.[1]

In European history, wars occurred between nations that shared the same general level of development, so that battle outcomes translated easily into peace terms. The victors did not have to install new political systems. Typically, leadership remained with the same privileged groups that held domestic sway before the war. However, a war that unleashes forces for social change is much harder for outsiders to control; military intervention is likely to set into motion unforeseen events beyond the stated goals of intervention.

The Unintended Effects of U.S. Military Interventions

Consider the major U.S. military interventions in East Asia, the outcomes of which were as unforeseen as the social changes they precipitated. In World War II, one U.S military aim was to protect a pro-American China from Japanese aggression. Yet during the cold war years a defeated Japan gained U.S. backing as the principal bulwark against Chinese regional expansion. After World War II and the defeat of the conservative Kuomintang Party, the success of Chinese Communism made social reforms incumbent on leaders in neighboring countries (Indonesia, Malaysia, South Korea, Singapore, Thailand, and ultimately Taiwan) who wanted to mitigate potential sources of Communist insurrection. These leaders met the imminent threat of Communist expansion by introducing policies and programs to bolster social cohesiveness.

Although the United States fought the war in Vietnam to constrain Chinese influence in Asia, Vietnamese reunification produced one of the most stable regimes in the region and contained the spread of Chinese influence. In fact, having won the war, Vietnam's Communist Party ultimately became a champion for pro-market reform; in 2006 the party gave its officials formal approval to engage in commercial activities.

Meanwhile, the Philippines remains among the least developed economies in Southeast Asia, despite massive U.S. naval and air protection against the threat of domestic Communist insurgency and Chinese expansion. The primacy that America gave to military alignment and the United States' unspoken alliance[2] with traditional landed elites led to support of anti-Communist leaders whose interests were antithetical to their country's stability and development.

Like the Philippines, Latin America—a region that benefits directly from the U.S. security umbrella—has fallen behind East Asia, the area most threatened by U.S. cold war–era enemies. However, the social elites in the Philippines, Pakistan, and most of Latin America have formed governments that were comfortable under the U.S. military umbrella; American support substituted for internal social reform and, ultimately, the capacity to implement social programs. The social imbalances in Latin America that have resulted from America's strengthening of the region's military elites have produced chronic political instability.

In Central Asia, too, massive U.S. military intervention has failed to produce the desired consequences. The U.S. tilt toward Pakistan pushed Afghanistan and India into dependence on the Soviet Union. Subsequent aid to the freedom fighters in Afghanistan gave rise to the most virulent anti-American regime in the world.

The lessons here are simple: economic and social change may create new coalitions that completely transform the foreign policies of a given nation.[3] There is little military action can do to arrest such forces once unleashed. Military strength can only prevail over social forces in the short term. Memories of past oppression, however, influence the prospects for future cooperation by making it politically costly for popularly elected leaders to stand with the United States.

Can Development Policy Lead Foreign Policy?

National security forms the basis for American cooperation with foreign governments. Because alliances exist to provide security and are cemented by the perceived urgencies of external threats, preserving those alliances receives priority over commerce or concerns with economic growth and sound economic policy. "The National Security Act of 1947, as amended, specifies three primary missions: defend the American homeland from external attack; safeguard our internal security; and uphold and advance the national policies and interests of the United States, including insuring the security of areas vital to those interests."[4] When American lives are at stake and an administration's fate depends on events occurring beyond U.S. borders, the distinction between foreign and domestic policy evaporates. When the body count rises, security always trumps economics; politicians know that American casualties, more than economic costs, affect public support for military intervention.

During the war in Vietnam, it was the number of U.S. casualties, not economic assessments of the $150 billion spent or the war's considerable impact on the domestic economy, that dominated the news. During the war with Iraq, the number most often cited in the U.S. media was the American casualty count, not the war's costs or the consequences to Iraq's economy. Visitors to the D-Day memorial in Normandy see the names of the troops who died in the invasion, not the cost or the quantity of materiel used in the conflict.

Yet economics often determines the outcome of military encounters and the durability of alliances. World War II was precipitated by the harsh economic terms of peace imposed on Germany at the end of World War I. The demise of South Vietnam was sealed by economic policies that stressed consumption and consumerism over the stimulation of production, savings, and investment. Flawed economic policies contributed to the inability of U.S. forces to form a viable government in Vietnam. Similarly, unsustainable consumption caused the economic failure of Iran under the shah and the Philippines under Marcos—both U.S. client regimes. The failure to revive Iraq's economy during the post-Saddam U.S. occupation exacerbated grievances that led to insurgency.

"Political leaders normally see investment in Third World nations as a means to an end (economic development and stability), rather than an end in itself. Self-interested economic gain has played a relatively small role in American policies, and decisionmaking is a much more complex process" than simply overseas investment opportunities for large corporations.[5] Business finds provisioning American troops to be more lucrative than investing in former battlefield nations.[6] Trade concessions and foreign aid policies are made on the basis of strengthening alliances like those America made with Japan, Taiwan, and South Korea during the cold war. Loans and foreign aid were offered to preserve alliance cooperation against a perceived shared enemy. Yet again, in the war on terror the United States faces some of its greatest security threats from countries with which it attempted unsuccessful security alliances. The security menace now emanating from these regimes can be linked to U.S. support of their leaders' failed economic, social, and political policies. Security threats do not originate from former battlefield enemies such as Great Britain, Mexico, Spain, Germany, Japan, or Vietnam.

As argued in chapter 2, securing geopolitical consent for stationing U.S. troops to protect pipelines can be easier from a regime that is unpopular at home than from one that enjoys broad-based political support. Small winning coalitions that depend on foreign assistance for political survival are more likely to trade foreign policy concessions for aid. However, risk accrues from lending support and legitimacy to narrowly based authoritarian regimes. Although such regimes are likely to accede to donor demands for geopolitical alignment, they are unlikely to carry out domestic policy reforms that jeopardize their grip on market opportunities. The failure to link security and development undermines the ability of the United States to see the dangers of making short-term concessions to autocratic regimes that impoverish their people.

Although security and development aid are generally considered to be independent of each other, in reality they are linked. The United States gains little strategic leverage from aid-dependent regimes such as Iraq, Egypt, or Pakistan when these governments' policy concessions to the United States alienate domestic support. Generous military assistance toward the Congo, Egypt, Iraq, Iran, Pakistan, and the Philippines did not prevent these nations from becoming weak links in the current chain of alliances, while former enemies China and Vietnam are bulwarks of stability in the war against terrorism. Vietnam, once viewed as the domino whose fall would bring down the region, is stable and making social progress, while the Philippines continues to be threatened by civil unrest. Nixon tolerated Ferdinand Marcos's martial law, thinking it would provide breathing space for America to concentrate on Vietnam. But a legacy of social and institutional devastation has made the Philippines less stable than Vietnam. U.S. affiliation with the Marcos dictatorship strengthened nationalist opposition to the American military presence on Philippine soil.

Gaining U.S. support for aid requires presidential support, and linking aid to America's security interests is the best way for a foreign regime to get a U.S. president's attention. According to scholars who have studied the aid-security link, "The defense-security goal is predominant, developmental needs least important."[7] U.S. overseas development assistance has been subsumed under a broader security orientation. Aid programs that disregard recipient countries' welfare needs produce "results that are often inconsistent with U.S. foreign policy interests and the development needs of its intended beneficiaries."[8] Linking U.S. security interests with foreign development can result in assistance that is diverted to elite survival and regime longevity. As a result, alliances initiated to make America safer often contribute to the long-term weakness of the other party, as regimes that are illegitimate in the eyes of their own people eventually succumb to a cycle of self-destruction.

The distribution of overseas assistance has not changed since the cold war. Only one of the top ten recipients of U.S. aid between 1946 and 2003, India, is on the list because of economic needs alone (see table 13-1). In figure 13-1, we see a strong security bias in U.S. government aid, with security aid representing almost 50 percent of the total aid budget between 1946 and 2004. Table 13-2 illustrates the misalignment between the distribution of aid and global poverty. The Middle East, which received 38.4 percent of total aid dollars in 2004, has only 2 percent of the world's poor. Most of the world's poverty lies in Asia and Africa (see figure 13-2).

During the cold war, the U.S. government divided the civilian and military functions of its core agencies, producing a sharp divergence in the perception of tasks and responsibilities. Military officers, for example, were ordered to avoid political, economic, and social questions, and to focus on defending the peace to protect American lives and interests. The civilian bureaucracies

Table 13-1. *Top Ten U.S. Aid Recipients, 1946–2003*

Constant 2003 U.S. dollars (in million of dollars)

Rank	Country	Total loans and grants
1	Israel	140,142.80
2	Vietnam, South	96,514.70
3	Egypt	85,419.70
4	Korea, South	62,793.20
5	United Kingdom	58,296.10
6	Turkey	56,151.30
7	India	52,301.50
8	France	52,147.70
9	Greece	38,255.10
10	Pakistan	36,676.90

Source: Tarnoff and Nowels (2004).

Figure 13-1. *Composition of U.S. Foreign Aid, 2004*

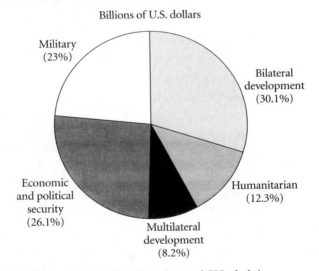

Billions of U.S. dollars

Military (23%)

Bilateral development (30.1%)

Humanitarian (12.3%)

Multilateral development (8.2%)

Economic and political security (26.1%)

Source: House and Senate Appropriations Committees and CRS calculations.

were instructed to stay out of military affairs. The result was entrenched, divergent views about strategy and policy, attributable to very different interpretations of adversarial behavior. During the Vietnam War, civilian advisers emphasized counterinsurgency against domestic insurgents, while the military wanted to wage wholesale war against North Vietnam, seeing victory in

Table 13-2. *U.S. Foreign Aid Goes Where It Is Least Needed, 2004*

Region	Percentage of total
Middle East	38.4
Africa	18.3
South Asia	17.3
Latin America, Europe, and Eurasia	11.4

Source: U.S. Agency for International Development, *U.S. Overseas Grants and Loans.*

Figure 13-2. *Proportion of Population Living on Less than One Dollar a Day, 1987–2000*

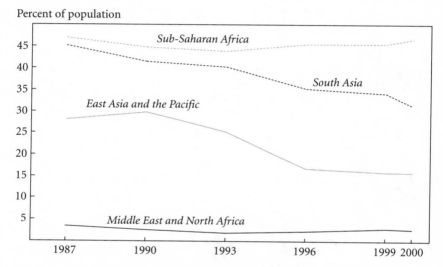

Source: World Bank, World Development Indicators (various years, subscription database).

the destruction of an enemy state. The National Security Council was created to increase dialogue between the two groups, but its efforts were insufficient. Military officers focus on immediate causes, while political officers are likely to be more sensitive to underlying social forces. The asymmetry of these two concerns favors the military view, and development tends to recede into the background.

Nonetheless, military and social issues are inseparable, and downplaying one can result in unanticipated social consequences that will determine the course of war. Civilian and military differences of perspective undermined policy effectiveness and deeply affected the outcome of U.S. programs in

China in the 1940s, Vietnam in the 1960s, Iran in the 1970s, and Latin America and the Philippines throughout the cold war.

The Folly of Prizing Security over Development

In the past, American foreign policy elites underplayed the idea that well-developed countries benefit America's long-term security interests. The dominant notion was that the United States could more easily buy, manipulate, or control weak states. Investing in development had a "feel good" aspect but lacked underlying value. Preserving national security was traditionally defined in terms of geopolitical strategy; the realpolitik was that development must wait. But when the United States ignores the link between development and security, it often counts as allies regimes whose internal weaknesses will become liabilities. Nicaragua's Somoza regime and that of Iran's shah, both solidly on the U.S. side, disintegrated into a legacy of bitterness directed against America. Social forces within their own countries more often than not undermine third world military leaders to whom America had turned for stable authority and loyalty.[9] Internal, institutional patterns of political and social inequality cause countries like Pakistan to become weak links in the ally chain.

In developing regions, domestic security is most threatened by internal sources of corruption, poverty, and insufficient services—not by external aggression. Regimes that overlook basic human needs only exacerbate the forces of civil disorder, insurrection, or civil war. During the cold war, U.S. foreign policy often made it even harder for third world populations to build effective self-governance. Perverse incentives have existed for the United States to keep small winning coalitions in power, thus contributing to failures of self-governance in strategically important states.

Today's greatest security threats originate in the political and institutional failures of regions where development took a back seat to U.S. military imperatives and alliance building. Yet the United States continues to give military operations the dominant role in foreign affairs, and the Department of Defense is expanding into public diplomacy, emergency relief, and democracy promotion. To some extent, this is understandable. America bears the greatest burden of global military security. But in the long term, dependence on military solutions undermines the moral authority of U.S. claims for global leadership.

At a time when U.S. security increasingly depends on global solutions for nuclear deterrence, environmental degradation, pandemics, and terrorism, concern for citizen access to economic and social opportunities is crucial for cementing stable alliances.

Meanwhile, Western allies are creating well-funded agencies to formulate and implement development policies that are integrated into the broader frameworks of their foreign policy. In the United Kingdom, for example, the Department for International Development enjoys cabinet-level status. In contrast, development programs in the United States lack unity of purpose and are managed by overlapping agencies with conflicting objectives. Thus, the United States makes its diplomacy depend largely on its defensive capabilities, instead of building a similar capacity for development management. Many of the problems developing countries face can only be overcome by encouraging alliance partners to empower institutions, expand accountability, and promote civil society and models of local self-governance. People living in nations (like Iraq and Pakistan) whose boundaries were drawn by others must be given tools to agree on the prerequisites necessary for a functioning state.

We have thus far argued that victory in a U.S. election is what guides the strategies of U.S. presidents in overseas engagements. Political survival is also the goal of adversaries and friends in developing country conflicts. Preventing the economic frailties of developing nations from damaging U.S. security interests will require a new foreign policy tool kit, a reexamination of the links between security and development. To this end, the United States will need an institutional framework or agency structure that can collect and dispense the expertise of various parts of government. Rethinking counterinsurgency operations is an excellent starting place to consider what a new agency might look like. Conventional military forces have rarely succeeded in defeating third world insurgency. Insurgents cannot be defeated by military force alone because they organize to ensure political success. Alongside military operations, the United States must coordinate a range of political, economic, and social activities. Insurgent forces must be outgoverned. Creating a government that offers a better hope for the future than the insurgents can provide is the most effective way to defeat a third world insurgency. The military approach to the reconstruction of failing polities tends to overlook the long-term macro-political feedback effects of a particular intervention in favor of direct consequences.[10]

Politicians of various persuasions can easily agree that institutional obstacles (discussed in chapter 4) prevent creative and cross-disciplinary problem solving. However, reforming the institutions responsible for planning and implementing U.S. foreign policy requires a consensus on a new set of foreign policy priorities that bridges the security-development divide.

Throughout the cold war, the greatest economic challenge posed by the third world was a teeming population, which translated into global poverty on a massive scale. In the twenty-first century newly industrialized countries such as Brazil, China, and India will exert more influence over global resource flows, and the demands and preferences of their populations will determine global resource scarcity and prices. These industrialized newcomers' cooperation and scientific capabilities will be needed to contain weapons proliferation, train human capital, preserve the value of the U.S. dollar, keep global financial channels open, arrest the spread of new strains of deadly microbes, and prevent environmental destruction. Thus, future security will depend on relationships with partners that lack equal standing in the international system. A test of our wisdom and leadership will be to ensure a stable environment for these shifts in global power. By advocating global trade and commerce without erecting appropriate governing institutions, we create a deficit of global legitimacy that is easily exploited by incumbent powers.

The basis for seeking new analytical frameworks and organizations to manage foreign aid, conflict, reconstruction, and international diplomacy is that the same principles that govern complexity in social development also govern the evolution of conflict. Most conflicts do not begin on the day that violence erupts. To strengthen U.S. security, we must discover the thread or common principles that run from state failure to the outbreak of civil and regional conflict. The present organization of knowledge and decisionmaking freezes into permanent patterns assumptions that are inaccurate and that lead to ineffective policies. A critical insight from our case studies is that how various social building blocks interact may be more important than their composition. Conflict is part of a larger process that includes economics and society more generally. We cannot optimize our own fitness without considering its effect on the larger system or ecology of which we are a part. Thinking of the world in an "us versus them" framework, we downplay the necessity of co-adaptation. What is optimal for us ultimately must be systemically optimal.

14

Reframing the Purpose of U.S. Globalism: Strategies, Institutions, and Beliefs

> How much freedom does evolution allow for giving purpose to the game?
> —John Archibald Wheeler, *At Home in the Universe* (1994)

In the twenty-first century, prosperity in the United States will hinge on the growth of developing economies. As this book goes to press, more than half of global economic growth occurs in the third world. American security will be closely linked to developing a better relationship with emerging economies. Here are twelve key lessons that the United States should bear in mind.

Learn from Soviet Experience Not to Overestimate the Universality of Our Institutions

During the cold war the Soviets acted as universalistic imperialists and, like the Americans, tried to impose their ideal of a just and equitable society on their sphere of influence. Yet after withdrawing from Afghanistan in 1989, the Russians altered their strategy, realizing that the benefits of third world interventions rarely exceeded the costs.[1] The leaders whom the Soviets presumed to be fellow travelers failed to build Leninist-style one-party states and remained interested in little more than their own aggrandizement. The Soviets ultimately recognized that third world conflicts were more about identity and ethnicity than about class. Today many third world leaders are similarly unresponsive to another Western blueprint for social change—the U.S. crusade to spread multiparty democracy.

Washington's cold war fear of a domino collapse of non-Communist regimes in Southeast Asia overlooked a prerequisite for the spread of Communism: the creation of a one-party state. North Vietnam had managed to build such an apparatus, but the achievement was difficult to replicate in patronage-based third world cultures. Because it bans political rivals, an autocratic regime could be the perfect arena for a one-party state to mature, but this rarely happens. The strength of domestic patron-client loyalties confounded efforts by both the Soviet Union and the United States to foster political order based on their respective principles. Assessing the costs and benefits of intervention led Mikhail Gorbachev to place human rights and self-determination above the realization of socialism, allowing the Soviet empire, which had taken hundreds of years to assemble, to disappear without a shot being fired.[2]

According to O. A. Westad, U.S. leadership has never experienced the kind of basic introspection that changed Soviet perceptions of third world development. American policymakers have never questioned their belief that U.S. history represents the privileged vanguard of an evolutionary process that is applicable to all nations. U.S. triumphalist rhetoric often misconstrues the attributes of development—industrialization, occupational specialization, social mobility, urbanization, mass literacy, and public health—as the triumph of Western liberal values.[3] But being literate and enjoying wealth and a clean government do not necessarily make one "Western." Other nations also seek to enjoy modernization's benefits as projections of their own cultural values and historical experience. Seeking to impose liberal values where basic social endowments are absent, the United States and its allies have alienated large majorities in Iran, China, Russia, and elsewhere.

Before the decline of the Soviet Union, the U.S. intelligentsia and its global counterparts shared many perspectives on U.S. interventionist adventures in the third world. Since the West won the cold war, a gap has widened that separates American thinking from that of other nations.[4] America must stop using its own history and triumphalist beliefs as the universal template for transforming others.[5] Third world nations must be able to blend their own social systems and values with the demands of their particular industrial and bureaucratic processes. That blending will provide the framework for integrating into the global economy.

Future U.S. contributions to third world reconstruction can benefit from two lessons of computational science: a set of simple rules such as those implied in a decentralized market environment can generate enormous diversity, and all complex systems show increasing diversity rather than convergence to an optimal standard.[6]

The Marshall Plan Does Not Apply

Calls abound for a new Marshall Plan for African development, for the battle against AIDS, for South America; the list goes on. Yet the Marshall Plan, the basis of all blueprints for U.S. interventionism, is one of history's most misrepresented reconstruction paradigms. When American troops arrived in Germany and Japan at the end of World War II, they contributed to a reconstruction that had begun several generations earlier. The introduction of protocols for industrialization and public administration based on a process of bureaucratic universalism was under way in Japan with the Meiji restoration in the second half of the nineteenth century, and in Germany with unification under Bismarck in 1871.[7] In these two cases, change already in progress was expedited by the military defeat of belligerent preindustrial elites.

Introduce a New Deal for Global Development

After World War II, the leaders of East Asia's newly industrializing countries ensured growth with equity by establishing effective management to keep basic public goods—health, education, physical infrastructure, public security, and credit—within the reach of the common man. They campaigned against nepotism and favoritism, and made public service remuneration commensurate with that of the private sector.[8] In Japan, Taiwan, and South Korea, land reform was also necessary.

Taiwan's population endured Chiang Kai-shek's institution of martial law in 1949 because of his successful land reform, industrialization, education, and health care development. His political party, the Kuomintang, is credited with establishing income equality—the poverty rate was reduced to 1 percent by 1968—while initiating an annual GDP growth of 6 percent from 1953 to 1968.[9] Chiang Kai-shek targeted land distribution before focusing on industrialization. He expanded Taiwan's proportion of cultivated land from 53 percent to 93 percent from 1949 to 1973. Rent payments decreased from 70 to 37.5 percent of total crops, and the number of landowner peasants increased from 30 to 77 percent.[10] Taiwan's reforms catered to the economic needs of the majority rural population and drastically reduced income inequality. Although the Kuomintang was highly oppressive, its ability to recognize and serve the economic needs of the country's poor perpetuated its power and, more important, allowed Taiwan to develop into the massive democratic and economic force it is today.[11] Taiwan's development program, like that of Korea and Japan, was designed with technical assistance from policy planners who shared the goals of Franklin D. Roosevelt's New Deal for America's workers.[12] Roosevelt's successors did not elevate social justice to the level sought by allies and adversaries.[13] U.S. presidents after Roosevelt put equity on hold until Communism could be defeated. For example, in the Philippines, in a dramatic departure from the promises of Roosevelt's New Deal, military objectives—using the islands to bolster the defense of Japan—took precedence over social justice.

Within a nation's asymmetrical social order, the poor accept the status quo because their ability to manage household risk—unemployment, injury, or a breadwinner's death—will generally increase only through the patronage of a stronger party. The New Deal offered American workers the promise of liberation from Tammany Hall, protecting the risk-averse urban poor against dependency on informal loyalty networks.[14] Only when developing nations' poor populations enjoy such security will notions that appeal to U.S. policymakers such as spontaneous lawfulness and adherence to rule of law become meaningful objectives of social mobilization in the third world.

It is widely recognized that Communism and the ideals of homogeneity that it embodies promoted stasis. But the antithetical policy—heterogeneity and indifference to degrees of inequality—strains social order and can result in a backlash against Western notions of transition. In post-Communist Russia, a small vanguard of local capitalists acquired former socialist assets. Today, the average income of the top 10 percent of Russians is forty-nine times greater than that of the bottom 10 percent; 83 percent of the population is poor; and male life expectancy is fifty-eight years. Instead of being a potential ally to the United States, Russia is neither stable nor friendly and it flaunts anti-Western policies to gain Western attention.[15] China's mad quest for private wealth produces many more beneficiaries than does Russian oligarchs' seizure of Russia's national assets. Heterogeneity in China is framed within a set of shared values and social conditions still defined by socialist ideology. Because they provide broad-based access to the benefits of economic growth, China's leaders are able to find socially optimal support for open trade policies. Too much heterogeneity narrows the consensus on opening the economy in South Asia, where caste-based divisions foment sectarian conflicts.

Even if a society's average level of discontent (defined by drug use, failure to vote, and suicide rates, for example) is high, as it is in developed regions like Europe, the United States, or Japan, such discontent is not disruptive. On the other hand, angry people at the extremes in Latin America, South Asia, the Middle East, or Africa can cause system breakdowns. In highly unequal societies like Africa and Latin America, the tail of the distributional bell curve ends up wagging the dog. Policies to foster inclusive societies must be encouraged for no other reason than to protect the objectives that America seeks to promote as the basis of global prosperity.

Drop the Analytical Dichotomies of the Cold War

We must distinguish among differences in autocratic regimes, where a wide disparity of policies and practices exists. Some governments are selected by a subset of the population that is relatively inclusive like those in China and Vietnam. Others are tin pot personalized fiefdoms where policy is conducted entirely to benefit a ruling elite. Autocracies also differ in the amount of repression they use and the level of popular support they receive.[16] Totalitarian regimes may enjoy considerable support from some segments of the population. Not so with most personalized tin pot autocracies, which rarely leave behind a framework of institutions and competencies, and offer little hope that aid or natural resources will be used to build a stable, prosperous, or participatory polity. The differences among so-called authoritarian states can be as wide as the gulf that separates them from democratic alternatives.[17]

During the cold war many East Asian dictators built the scaffolding for future democratic transitions by strengthening the interface between government and business. Endowments of primary education and health services helped average citizens benefit from future growth. Meritocratic, rule-abiding bureaucracies created the foundations for eventual democratic transitions by protecting policymaking from elitist capture.[18] One commonality among East Asia's democratic transitions is that the prior introduction of democratic social conditions made democratic political institutions durable.[19]

If a general definition of democracy is government that facilitates compromise among conflicting political, material, and ideological interests, then the institutional variations that meet this requirement are virtually unlimited and require adaptability to a particular environment. Most important, democratic stability reflects self-organization, complex adaptations to rules and administrative patterns, and relationships with various interest groups that cannot be repeated or copied.

We need sharper analytical tools to identify the preconditions of democratic stability. We cannot make progress without acknowledging that the appositions used by policymakers to explain development—markets versus states, authoritarianism versus democracy, and socialism versus capitalism—have proved to be weak tools for understanding complexity during economic transition.[20]

Depoliticize the U.S. Foreign Policymaking Process

How do we improve the quality of political analysis? Foreign policymaking has become highly politicized. Presidents circumvent State Department expertise by means of executive branch appointees who make foreign policy in conjunction with electoral cycles through the politically dependent National Security Council. Just as a politicized monetary policy is opportunistic and short-sighted, so too is politicized treatment of national security.

One way to reduce opportunism is to create a career bureaucracy that functions as a brain trust with cabinet-level authority to lead international policymaking. Like the Federal Reserve Board, such a trust must be protected from the vagaries of the electoral cycle and from special interest groups. Its director and top officers must be appointed for terms that do not overlap with electoral cycles. If Congress and the White House were to make appointments to senior positions in the middle of an administration, they would follow mechanisms to promote bipartisan cooperation on the selection.[21] The appointees must meet the highest professional and academic standards, and salaries and other remuneration must compete with private sector standards.

Foreign aid programs have failed because of the inability to base distribution on consistent, verifiable economic criteria. These programs are diverted by peripheral military and political considerations. A trust could help integrate foreign policy, economic development, and long-term security by insulating aid programs from domestic and international fluctuations of opinion and influence. Currently, the ad hoc and inconsistent manner by which congressional mandates control aid appropriations and priorities undermines long-term effectiveness.

An independent agency would also strengthen U.S. negotiations with multilateral organizations. Bilateral programs between the United States and individual borrowers have limited impact compared to the possibility of leveraging larger, multilateral flows. Speaking with many voices weakens aid effectiveness in multilateral arenas. A unified, coherent, and consistent agency designed to coordinate security and developmental activities could have much greater impact.[22]

Inadequate coordination between security and developmental agencies is exemplified by inadequate attention to civilian policing in crisis environments. Neither defense nor development agencies have capabilities or expertise in local policing, which ensures the failure to implement key developmental objectives.[23] No wonder that providers and potential aid recipients cite insufficient public safety and friction with security forces as key obstacles to disseminating essential social, political, and environmental assets. Powerful incentives for the military and development sectors to collaborate will only arise once joint sector training and decisionmaking have been institutionalized.

In 2007, reports coming back from the field in Afghanistan five years after the U.S. intervention there concur that the institutional capacity to create policy that coordinates development and security is inadequate. Priorities are ultimately determined by those who have the vehicles and the weapons. As a last resort, many development agencies hire private security to carry out developmental objectives such as building roads or keeping schools open. In the absence of procedural cooperation between sectors, interagency policy coordination in conflict zones depends on personalities. Because U.S. interventions in transitional and unstable regions are likely to increase in the years ahead, better institutional coordination is needed to ensure that the lessons of reconstruction in Afghanistan and Iraq are applied effectively.

Third World Battles Must Be Won Politically

General David Petraeus, the senior U.S. military commander in Iraq in 2007, wrote his 1987 Princeton Ph.D. thesis on applying the lessons of Vietnam to the use of force in the post-Vietnam era. Force should be used sufficiently at the outset, he noted, to ensure a quick and decisive resolution of the conflict. To avoid another Vietnam, before committing American troops be sure that "you have established clear-cut, attainable military objectives for American military forces (that is, more than just some fuzzy political goals)."[24] The problem with this sensible advice is that third world crises rarely present clear-cut military objectives. Issues such as national and ethnic identity inevitably defy simple homilies on the decisive use of force. General Douglas MacArthur's dictum for the total annihilation of Communism in Asia— "There is no substitute for victory"—has done incalculable harm, because military victory does not always mean winning the political war. Raised in the same school, General William C. Westmoreland never understood that he could win all the battles in Vietnam and still lose the war.

Social discrimination often disrupts the creation of mechanisms that would support postconflict cooperation. Putting the Shi'a in control of Iraq exemplifies how the fuzzy details can foil the easy path to state reconstruction. General Petraeus's misreading of history and the miscalculations of his predecessors reflect a short-sighted vision that, as in Vietnam, led a mighty military into political defeat by an economically and technologically weaker adversary.

Vietnam and Iraq present the same conclusion. Once the forces of social change are unleashed—for example, by removing an unrepresentative elite from power—the outcome will be determined politically, no matter how favorable the balance of forces is to the U.S. side. Even after all the battles have been fought, regime stability will remain elusive until an enduring bridge is built between formal institutions and informal social norms.[25] Rebuilding Japan or Germany, U.S. administrators and their local agents did not have to face interference from ethnocentric favoritism or the patron-clientelism that is typical of social order in the third world.

Mutual Interests Are Insufficient to Ensure Cooperation

The greater the common interests between a stronger and a weaker party, the less leverage the stronger party is able to wield. This proved to be the case when the U.S. Congress voted on March 27, 2007, to link its support for the war in Iraq to specific timetables for reform. Those conditions were set in vain; six months later the Iraqi parliament enjoyed insufficient attendance to enact legislation to share oil revenues or to remove rules that bar Sunnis from middle-class employment. Desperation in Washington translates into Baghdad's recalcitrance to contain sectarian violence. Without Washington's backing, the political future of Prime Minister Nuri Kamal al-Maliki would be much more vulnerable. He has held on to power without winning support from large sections of the population. The support he receives from Washington provides him with the latitude to turn his government's security forces into an instrument of revenge and domination that provides little protection for the Sunni minority.

The U.S. predicament in Iraq succumbs to the logic of a commitment trap: the client sees clearly that the Bush administration fears losing Iraq to Iran. As David Baldwin has reasoned, "Other things being equal, the greater the donor's gain from the aid relationship, the more dependent he is on maintaining the relationship and the less able he is to make credible threats to forgo it."[26] Thomas Shelling has argued that an analogy exists "between a parent's threats to a child and the threat that a wealthy paternalistic nation makes to the weak ... government of a poor nation in, say, extending foreign aid and in demanding 'sound' economic policies or cooperative military policies in return."[27]

Throughout the cold war, realists like John Foster Dulles and Henry Kissinger argued that it was essential to maintain commitment credibility on the world stage through steadfast support of client regimes, no matter how much their behavior diverged from our standards or interests. But the dictum "support any friend at any cost" weakens the United States as a reform agent in the eyes of client regimes. It weakens American credibility by allowing regime incumbents to pursue private agendas that threaten their own nations' well being. The threat of cutting aid to recalcitrant friends must be added to America's diplomatic arsenal.

Divorce Neoconservatives from Their Classical Liberal Allies

The policies of the George W. Bush administration have revealed a hitherto unexposed conflict within American conservatism. Neoconservative advocates of massive regime change are usually clustered in the same think tanks (the Hoover Institution, the American Enterprise Institute, and the Heritage Foundation) that preach the virtues of decentralized coordination.[28] Yet neoconservative doctrine diverges from the classical liberal principles to which it claims affinity. Classical liberalism stresses the emergence of order from the bottom up through self-organization brought about by the actions of countless unsophisticated agents; it does not dictate order from the top down through regime change.[29]

One hope of neoconservatives is that transplanting enlightened U.S. institutions to foreign soil can lead to predictable wealth-enhancing changes. However, institutional transplants are sensitive to prior conditions that help determine whether a particular reform is stabilizing or destabilizing. Two sets of institutions that look entirely alike on paper—for example, the constitution of Nigeria and that of the United States, or the civil service code of the Philippines and the Pendleton Act that governs U.S. civil service recruitment—yield different results in practice. It is unreasonable to assume that developing nations can adopt the same institutions as those in fully industrialized nations. They cannot do so unless they start from similar conditions and then develop institutions through a process similar to that followed by developed nations. The future state of a society depends on its earlier state. How can a grand strategy for promoting democracy and human rights abroad through top-down interventions be reconciled with the classical liberal belief that durable institutions must emerge from the collectively expressed will of the people they serve?

How is it that Americans who accept as a matter of faith that efforts at large-scale social engineering are doomed to failure can believe that they will spearhead democracy throughout the world by using massive prescriptive interventions?

Market Liberalism Requires Formal and Informal Transformations

During the 1950s, U.S. policymakers consistently emphasized the difficulty of linking economic growth with the goal of political and economic liberalism[30] and suspended the latter goal. But since the fall of the Soviet bloc, finding the right strategy to transform political and economic institutions overseas is a top policy item for both Republicans and Democrats. The operational challenge is to help governments gain the capacity through taxation to address social welfare issues whose arrangements are currently mediated through informal channels.

Formal institutions in many third world societies are burdened by the expectation that the individual has obligations to a large number of people. Extended families and other social obligations intrude into business and professional decisionmaking. These obligations are a form of social capital because they help individuals to survive in a difficult environment. However, such social bonds encumber formal institutions in developing countries by preventing highly capable people from putting the interests of the public, or of the enterprise they serve, before duty to a family member in need.

The unequal patron-client relationship is another form of traditional social capital; it offers the weaker party insurance against household calamities. But this relationship interferes with political development by making the vote of individual citizens beholden to the patronage system. A successful transition to full-fledged market democracy requires substituting abstract formal obligations for informal social capital. Whether they are advancing political or economic policies, the advocates for global democracy have no theory on how to fairly allocate the social costs involved, no metric that determines how quickly formal market or political institutions can be mobilized without causing disintegration of older, informal norms.

Pakistan's Devolution Trust for Community Empowerment, an initiative backed by the UN Development Program, is a noteworthy effort to synthesize market principles with informal practices. In this pilot project launched in the Punjab region in 2004, selected police precincts were asked to list all forms of remuneration, including those stemming from bribes and other informal fees. Once the entire sum was calculated, the precinct chief received a lump-sum payment equal to the amount of income forgone—on the condition that his employees desisted from further exactions. The chief then apportioned the funds among all stakeholders. The idea is to make incentives for individual officers conform to formal rules. The program covers the entire management hierarchy within a given precinct.

A similar process using market incentives is needed to eliminate patron-client ties that pervade the newly emerging urban sectors and the entire agrarian sector of most developing societies. Market liberalism must address the codependency of market and nonmarket relationships with a comprehensive risk-mitigation settlement, shifting risk management from the informal to the public or market sphere. This cannot be done without transparent, rule-bound systems of public finance.

Markets for all kinds of risks make industrial societies socially cohesive.[31] In theory, market liberalism gives individuals more opportunities to hedge against economic risks. In practice, this promise is complemented by public sources of risk mitigation such as social security or worker's compensation, which eliminate dependency on informal power brokers. Transitioning societies rarely offer a universal or public source of risk mitigation.

Market liberalism assumes that losses or gains to social capital are secondary and can be paid for out of the surplus generated by growth. Yet most market-liberalizing policies are incomplete, protecting the interests of operators in the sectors most exposed to external investment without ensuring that the surplus is equitably distributed.

Informal risk contacts pervade premodern societies, suggesting that informal customs of social reciprocity must be replaced with public safety nets, not simply eliminated. By itself, more trade and regional economic integration will not be enough to address the new risks of dependency that the rise of market democracies inadvertently causes. High-speed growth is inevitably a cause of social bifurcation. When social capital is destroyed in the rush to build market capital, polarization increases and cohesiveness weakens. Economic growth that exposes one sector of the population to greater risks will be contested politically or by passive noncompliance.[32] Political development requires progress in strengthening the risk management regimes of emerging societies so that the inevitable bifurcations do not cause system-wide destabilization.

Apply to Foreign Policy the Principles That Unify East Asia's High-Performing Development Model

Some of America's biggest foreign policy disasters have occurred in East Asia: the collapse of the U.S.-backed Nationalists in China, the wars in Vietnam and Korea. But the greatest foreign policy successes also seem to be clustered there. Autocratic Singapore seems like a model of enlightened despotism, having already acquired first world status. South Korea and Taiwan are now both democracies on the verge of acquiring first world status, and Thailand is not too far behind. Technology in the region is no longer mere replication; innovation is starting to drive productivity growth, and political decision-making is becoming more democratic and decentralized. Yet East Asia's powerhouse economies traveled most of the path to middle-income status as autocracies that enjoyed strong U.S. support.

The region's success seems to embody theory that this book has tried to refute. The area's vibrant economies prospered under dictatorships that eventually transitioned into full-fledged democracies. These countries seem to be Jeane Kirkpatrick success stories that illustrate the wisdom of supporting procapitalist autocratic regimes.

But there is an important difference between the path these nations pursued—growth with equity—and the model of market liberalism espoused by U.S. foreign policy, especially after 1980, when China ceased to be an exporter of socialist revolution. East Asia has done more to reduce income disparities over time than any other region, and it has done so without increasing total government spending. The most important contributors to sustained growth were not the forward-looking, high-tech, and engineering-intensive sectors, but the backward and refractory agricultural sectors. Asian leaders have provided public good interventions in primary health and education and expanded the scope of credit markets to enable the poor to acquire assets, giving the poor property rights where they once had only customary-use rights. Broad-based social endowments—public security, bureaucratic universalism, accessible finance, and nationwide banking—explain why East Asia reduced income inequality while growing faster than other regions.[33] Without these tools, contract enforcement can disenfranchise the poor, exacerbating longstanding inequality and ethnic bifurcation. Latin American or Middle Eastern big government cannot redress the distributional consequences of insufficient institutional capacity.

East Asia's high-performing regimes put their entire society's knowledge to work, building capacity at the bottom and linking that capacity to the center in a rule-bound manner. Rural credit and banking, rural roads, rural markets, rural education, and basic rural health and sanitation all made reconstruction a nationwide process.[34]

A message about the importance of governance innovations that improves equity stands out. Development is a process in which all members and sectors of society must possess basic endowments and skills such as access to credit. Information must be shared among many interacting elements. Even the humblest members of the population must be involved, as critical information moves in all possible directions. If, as in Pakistan or Iran, one group is going nowhere while others are on a superhighway, collisions causing social disorder will occur. The stability that results from lower inequality improves investors' perceptions of long-term risks.

Relative to earlier examples of economic history, East Asia's rise is notable for its rapidity. Japan industrialized four times faster than the United States and England, and twice as quickly as Germany. Korea's rise was faster than

Japan's, and China's rise seems faster still. The answer to how these regimes industrialized so quickly also solves the puzzle of their relatively stable democratic transitions. Inclusive policies that made industrialization a broad-based reality strengthened the region's democracy. The pooling of information among diverse social strata and from one production sector and region to another was facilitated by a large number of governance reforms that occurred before the introduction of electoral democracy.[35] An essential lesson of the East Asian model is that network properties that are essential to development emerge from a society's micro-architecture. Homogeneity and symmetry of behavior across social networks propelled the rapid equilibrium-breaking transition, which spread from economic to political goal setting.

Does economic change drive political change or does governance come before democracy? The answer from East Asia seems to be that the same principles of social networking that stimulate economic transformation will also stimulate polity transformation. The laws that govern democratic transitions may not be very different from those that govern economic transitions. Diverse social processes may share a unifying principle that is broader and more common than U.S. thinking and policies, which assume separate political and economic realms. Social processes such as the economy and the polity may share a common driver. Dynamic systems are those in which information moves symmetrically across society. Both economic and political development originates in social complexity that builds on network effects from the bottom up. Development requires a huge number of interacting elements that are systemwide; it occurs when everything happens to everyone.

Finally, we must recognize the external environment in which East Asian polities thrived after World War II. Four exogenous variables played a critical role in East Asia's rise: the legacy of Japanese imperialism; the security provided by U.S. regional hegemony, which reduced the likelihood of regional wars; access to U.S. consumers; and the revolution constraint posed by the threat of Chinese-style peasant insurgency. Combined, these factors produced the dynamic outcome that has yet to be replicated anywhere in the developing world during this period since the end of World War II.

Beware of Developing Country Growth That Alters Social Status

Growth changes the relative prosperity of rival groups in developing countries, thereby unleashing conflicts over social dominance. One group may prefer a poor economy to a stronger economy in which rivals gain advantage. The winners and losers of industrial transitions typically come from different locations and social strata. Yesterday's poor and tomorrow's poor are not

necessarily the same. New technological development implies a correspon-
ding loss of value in traditional skills. New patterns of wealth distribution
often generate costly depreciation of existing stocks of social capital.[36] Even as
some people gain greater income, they may, in turn, lose status relative to
that of newer groups. For example, Brahmins benefit from economic growth
in India but may lose status in relation to so-called untouchables, who have
the chance to become wealthy when the economy is liberalized. Fears of relative deprivation will motivate opposition to market-building activities and
can matter as much as increases in absolute prosperity. As the effects of economic reform spill into other sectors of social organization, major transformations such as industrialization require the simultaneous remapping of
social and political organization.

Growth that inspires ethnocentric polarization is particularly threatening.
The resentment of wealthy Chinese minorities in Southeast Asia is one example of such a danger.[37] Such conflicts resemble an ultimatum game, a concept
explained earlier in this book. The game has been played with remarkably
consistent results in diverse cultural settings. Most people will reject offers
that are perceived as unfair even if doing so means rejecting a sure financial
gain; they are even willing to give up resources to punish the winners. People
care not only about what they gain and lose. They notice the results for other
people, which is why rapid Westernization programs like that launched by the
shah of Iran risk violent rejection.

The dangers of alliance-driven growth and the polarization it can produce
have prominently emerged in the reconstruction of Afghanistan. Western
governments have been unable to deliver developmental services or economic
opportunity to the rural regions. In sharp contrast, Western donor projects
that employ English-speaking actors in select sectors of the urban economy
provide inflated salaries. For example, UN taxi drivers receive $1,200 a month,
while regional police who are fighting drug traffickers receive $70 a month.
Such glaring gaps in well-being and access to basic services among the rural
population and among traditional merchants and crafts people exacerbate
existing divisions. These discrepancies provoke hostility toward foreign-paid
local workers and toward highly paid westernized Afghanis who have
returned home to enjoy top positions in the government. Social polarization
undermines military efforts to pacify the population; instead, the resentment
it provokes nourishes a growing Taliban-based insurgency.

The French ethnologist François Bizot, observing the Khmer Rouge's rise
in Cambodia in 1971, wrote about the cultural consequences that occurred
when massive U.S. aid disrupted an "age-old way of life":

Unfortunately, the arrival of the Americans did nothing but arouse greed and feed corruption. The new employee heard himself called "brother" and, with a great slap on the back, received a sum of dollars equivalent to what an American in the United States would have earned for the same work, ten to twenty times the salary of a local provincial governor. With wages like this, clerks, laborers and artisans hurriedly gave up their jobs and beat a path to the American Embassy.[38]

The disruption to the local sense of proportion and status fostered resentment toward the recipients of foreign salaries. But an even more corrosive effect resulted when terms of the agreement with the American contractors could not be fulfilled:

> Believing sincerely in the brotherhood of man, the employer demanded in return American-style efficiency, which few Khmers could deliver. The relationship of the hierarchy with its employees then deteriorated quickly, creating strain and humiliation and forever dashing the extraordinary hopes of trust and friendship that everyone had nurtured. These circumstances soon led to duplicity and a total absence of mutual respect at every level, creating a climate of bitterness and irreparable suspicion.[39]

Paternalism turned into mutual animosity that intensified as the leadership's dependence on U.S. aid increased. What Bizot observed about social dislocation in Cambodia was also found in South Vietnam, in Iran under the shah, and in Pakistan under Pervez Musharraf, causing irreparable damage to the incumbent's credibility.

Preventing donor-induced wealth disparities from undermining durable market-friendly environments requires better cooperation between military and development efforts and, most of all, the creation of multilateral frameworks so that if polarization does result, it does not carry the signature of Uncle Sam. When a revolutionary movement's struggle against its own tyrants becomes a struggle against American imperialism, the outcome is tragic for all sides.

Prepare for the Global Power Transition

In this period of power transition, the United States still has the opportunity to be instrumental in making changes that will secure the institutional arrangements for global security.[40] To redefine our relationship with the developing world, we must redefine the intellectual foundations of American foreign policy.

Earlier chapters suggest that it is essential to generate metaphors and archetypes that capture current policy dilemmas in order to increase public understanding of foreign policy. Central to the metaphors that Americans have adopted thus far is the notion that we have control over global processes. It is comforting to believe that, with the proper leadership, we have the tools to affect outcomes beyond our borders. But we are part of the history that we create. Even if we are more powerful than friends or foes, we often act without knowing how others will react. Even our most astute statesmen have insufficient foresight to predict the web of interactions between multiple agents that will define the future.

Despite a preponderance of force in our favor, eliminating cold war rivals made us a target for international terrorism. Many unforeseen risks have arisen as a result of America's post–cold war polarity, as issues such as non-proliferation become primary U.S. burdens although the outcome affects other developed countries equally. The Internet and other tools that make global economics easier to manage are exploited by criminals and extremists. Polarity did not produce a simple, inert outcome of U.S. global dominance; rather it produced complex responses and unanticipated opportunities for allies and adversaries alike, all based on heterogeneity, adaptation capabilities, externalities, and different learning rules that ensured continuous bifurcations within emerging systems. Our actions in one arena are the building blocks for responses in other arenas. A tendency to see ourselves and the third world as something different, casting ourselves as the history makers, ignores that fact that we are but one part of the system that will change us. Strength does not insulate us from co-evolutionary change and feedback from other actors. Yet accepting the constraints of growing interconnectedness does not diminish the importance of allowing our moral compass and our values to give meaning and shape to the future.

U.S. foreign policy must be an instrument with which we can seize control over our future in an indifferent and often hostile world. If we do not set the goals for the kind of world we want to live in, someone else will set them for us. The purpose of our foreign policy must be to ensure that America's fate is determined collectively by what Americans want. Foreign policy is a commitment to our own survival but its purposefulness comes from the survival of the values and morals that define our nationhood.

Just as we understand that we must take control over our fate, so we must help our allies to do the same. Just as we seek power over the future for ourselves, so we must grant it to others. Our most enduring contribution to the well-being of our allies will be to allow education to provide the motivation for cooperation. When we raise the flag it must be to signal our idealism. Supporting tyrants for our own short-term gain, we lose our sense of purposefulness.

As the traditional goal of achieving dominance in the world economy becomes obsolete, perhaps the greatest risk America faces is this: as other nations specialize to reduce their exposure to the increasingly complex global marketplace, the United States will find itself without a niche. It will try to address all possible realities, and it will incorrectly assume that its institutions are suited to addressing them all. No final or definitive form of society exists that optimizes human potential. The possibilities are too great for one group to ever fully imagine or control. While other nations adapt decision-making strategies to carrying out tasks of specific relevance to the emerging global economy, the United States may find itself unable to identify those tasks for which its talents are best suited.

We are the minority in a world that was not built for our special benefit. Our current preeminent role is in part accident and in part comes from the suicidal conflicts between our industrial and colonial predecessors. Our relative decline is unavoidable. Unless we work toward a larger unity, we may face isolation like so many minorities before us. We must consider that we will cease to occupy a central position on the playing field if the field itself ceases to exist, and we must learn to cooperate with our competitors to attain objectives beyond our own capacity. The greatest opportunity the United States enjoys today is the possibility of shaping a future in which it will not enjoy the privilege of preeminence.

Notes

Chapter One

1. Gilman (2003).

2. Fighting the cold war required inculcating norms for continued social and personal sacrifices, coming on the heels of an entire decade of hardship and separation caused by war. We constructed a cultural space insulated from random currents that might trigger new cultural and ideological recombination and selection. The imperative of consistency was needed to protect America's once open intellectual heritage from challenges to the central claims of containment. Evidence to the contrary was abandoned as not critical to the central hypothesis about the dangers of international Communism. Once institutionalized, hypotheses central to the conceptual web of containment became irrefutable. We made cultural investments in the model, named heroes and villains, and memorialized sacrifices made by our ancestors as we learned to attribute our security to their efforts. Then just as we were ready to declare victory, jihads against America surfaced in countries considered to be bastions of pro–United States sentiment, stable pillars of our alliance system.

3. Unfortunately, the rebels who challenge long-standing autocratic rulers may not necessarily seek to expand the size of the winning coalition, but to seize control of the state.

4. Generally in long-standing autocratic regimes the leadership—and not the people—captures most of the gains the alliance provides.

5. Bueno de Mesquita and Root (2000, pp. 404–08).

6. The connection between political survival and good governance is discussed in Bueno de Mesquita and Root (2000) and Bueno de Mesquita and others (2003).

7. That foreign aid serves as bribes from rich to poor countries was stressed by Morgenthau (1962, pp. 301–09). Bueno de Mesquita and Smith (2007) provide an analytical model that links the appeal of such deals to the size of a regime's winning coalition. They concluded that "the US was most likely to give aid to its friends

during the Cold War. Alternatively, as our theory suggests, the US buys alignment through aid."

8. *Economic rent* refers to the difference between what a factor of production is paid and how much it would need to be paid to remain in its current use. In perfect competition economic rents do not exist—they would be eliminated by competition when new firms enter a market. *Rent seeking* refers to activities that consume resources to achieve a pure transfer of wealth from one sector, group, or individual to another. These activities are wasteful because they use up resources without creating additional value for society at large. Lobbying for a monopoly is a good example of one such wasteful activity.

9. An example is the takeover of many privately owned firms and the expansion of state ownership during the U.S.-backed Marcos regime. When democracy was reestablished in the Philippines, the weakness of mechanisms to prevent the misuse of government allowed the new leaders to continue the looting of the public treasury that Marcos had begun.

10. *Internal conflict* measures the level of political violence in the country and its actual or potential impact on governance. Countries without armed opposition to the government and in which the government does not indulge in arbitrary violence, direct or indirect, against its own people receive the highest rating. The lowest rating reflects an ongoing civil war.

11. Bueno de Mesquita and Root (2000).

12. The resource curse is sometimes referred to as the *Dutch disease* (Sachs and Warner 1995, 2001; Sala-i-Martin and Subramanian 2003; "The Dutch Disease," *Economist*, November 26, 1977, pp. 82–83). The original formulation of the resource curse focused on the economic consequences of resource exports, causing the country's currency to rise in value against other currencies and crowding out nonresource export activities. Ross (2001) found that between 1971and 1997 reliance on mineral wealth eroded democratic tendencies in a sample of 113 states. The discovery that resource rents are likely to induce autocracy has expanded the scope of discussion about the resource curse to include questions of governance. See also Ross (1999) and Auty (1993) on how mineral wealth stunts political development.

13. Cohen and Chollet (2007).

14. The return on investment is impaired by projects that yield an inflated rate of return to the beneficiaries, who are generally regime loyalists. White elephants and cost overruns are among the commonplace reasons that the resource surplus does not translate into sustained income increases.

15. "Other things being equal, the stronger the donor's interest in creating an asymmetrical dependency relationship, the harder it is to do, since it is precisely the strength of the donor's interest that creates his own dependency and thereby tends to equalize the dependency relationship" (Baldwin 1985, p. 308).

16. Stohl (2007). A country was selected if there was a policy statement identifying it as a participant in the antiterrorist coalition, if the country was in close proximity to terrorist sites, or if it had engaged in a quid pro quo exchange of compliance for

arms. In 2006 the State Department listed twenty-eight countries that had joined the coalition of the willing.

17. Sudan receives funding from the International Military Education and Training program.

18. Center for Defense Information, "U.S. Arms Exports and Military Assistance in the 'Global War on Terror,'" Press release, September 27, 2007.

19. Many Iraqis have cautioned the United States that the police and paramilitary being trained today will turn against this country tomorrow. The GAO reports that 200,000 weapons are unaccounted for. Weapons have already landed in the hands of insurgents and criminals, yet, as of 2003, $2 billion more in arms deliveries is on the way (United States Government Accountability Office 2007).

20. The new accounts are under Defense Department funds.

21. Grimmett (2007). Between 2003 and 2006 the United States and Russia dominated arms sales to the developing world. The United States ranked first for three of four years, Russia second for three of these same four years. From 2003 to 2006, U.S transfer agreements with developing nations totaled $34.1 billion in constant 2006 dollars, 32.4 percent of all such agreements. Russia's total was $25.8 billion, or 24.5 percent.

22. Destler (1998, pp. 89–107). Destler argues that the Clinton administration was far more interested in economic issues than strategic issues.

23. Hook (2005, pp. 12–15). The massive level of aid that was supplied to industrial allies in Europe had no equivalent in the third world, where aid flows were much smaller as a percentage of the recipient nations' GDP.

24. Edwards and others (2000, p. 645).

25. The military strategies that prevented the Soviet Union from spreading can be considered separately from the reasons for its eventual decline.

26. Spulber (1997 and 2003).

27. Page and Bouton (2006); Holsti (1998); Rielly (1995).

28. With its feudalistic traditions repressed by socialism, Vietnam's population has been inculcated with the belief that the path to education and self-betterment is open to everyone. Enthusiasm for economic improvement has spread through the population, which provides strong support for the government to open the economy. Reformers inside the Communist Party have started to make demands for pluralism that are as strong as the demands being made from the outside. The Philippines, by contrast, still struggles to implement economic reforms while its middle class dwindles.

Chapter Two

1. On November 15, 1977, the visit of the shah and Empress Farah to the White House sparked protests from thousands of Iranian students studying in the United States. Former American hostages in Iran recall that the Islamic leaders who condemned America were the very same ones requesting special favors and visas for friends and families. The long lines of Iranians seeking U.S. visas often included family members of the radicals who had seized power.

2. Blum (2000, p. 29).

3. Ibid.

4. Manglapus (1976, p. 60).

5. Pew Global Attitudes Project, "2007 Survey" (www.pewglobal.org/reports/pdf/256.pdf [June 27, 2007]).

6. Root (2006). Comprehensive constitutional or institutional reforms require long gestation periods. The progressive movement that created the meritocratic civil service in America required two generations to build up the public trust in government before the population was willing to allow it to directly tax incomes. Managing social security required an additional fifteen years after the introduction of the personal income tax.

7. Kuziemko and Werker (2006) confirmed the link between foreign aid payments and vote buying. They observed that aid to rotating members of the UN Security Council increased 59 percent and aid received from the United Nations, especially from UNICEF (an organization over which the United States exercises considerable influence), increased 8 percent. The Security Council can invoke sanctions and military action and it recommends the appointment of the organization's secretary general. A rapid return to the aid baseline level after service on the council is ended suggests that aid was not extended as a consequence of a country's becoming more globally integrated or by acquiring greater skill in manipulating media coverage. The conclusion was that rotating members trade votes for favors by promoting the interests of members that can influence aid allocations. Alesina and Dollar (2000) also observed that foreign aid flows are heavily influenced by strategic variables.

8. Since the end of the cold war, preventing "the spread of nuclear weapons" and "combating international terrorism" are number one; during the cold war an additional concern was "world wide arms control" (Page and Bouton 2006, p. 228).

9. We will see, in fact, that a strong humanitarian and altruistic thread runs through Americans' foreign policy preferences, producing strong support for humanitarian foreign aid, protection of threatened peoples, and participation in peacekeeping forces (Page and Bouton 2006, p. 43). Promoting healthy economies overseas enjoys much weaker support. The same finding is reported in Rielly (1995, p. 6) and Holsti (1998, pp. 144–45).

10. Results reported in Bueno de Mesquita and Root (2000) and Bueno de Mesquita and others (2003).

11. Between 1947 and 1960 U.S. strategists concluded eight mutual defense pacts with forty-two countries, plus executive agreements and other formal pledges with some thirty others (Collins 1998): "Nearly 1,700 U.S. installations large and small eventually circled the Northern Hemisphere in locations selected especially to monitor military activities inside the Soviet Union, ensure early warning if Soviet Armed Forces attacked, and block the most likely land, sea, and air avenues of Soviet advance" (p. 247); "The United States maintained no cold war military bases in Africa, save two communication stations on Morocco's coast. U.S. installations in other Arab

lands were limited to berthing privileges in Bahrain for a minuscule Middle East Force that consisted of a flagship and two (later four) elderly destroyers" (p. 254).

12. Those who fear China's self-proclaimed peaceful rise often argue that a peaceful and cooperative China can only be ensured once "China embraces openness and pluralism at home" (see "China's Great Game in Asia—The Great Game in Asia; China and Its Region," *Economist,* March 31, 2007, p. 14). The arguments made here suggest that if China embraces democracy at home, its elected leaders may have to be even more responsive to a resurgent nationalism than were its unelected leaders.

13. For analysis of policies that contributed to a potentially revolutionary process in the Middle East, see Berman (2003).

14. The World Bank has been more active in comparison to other donors in governance-related initiatives, but like bilateral U.S. programs it is less active in governance-related assistance than in other parts of the world. The World Bank has concentrated on fiscal management, procurement, and civil service reform. USAID has been active in agriculture, health, education, and public works. Overall U.S. engagement focuses on security, the Europeans on fiscal reforms. The U.S. displayed limited interest in reform before 2002.

15. Kalantari (2005).

16. Aid was an ineffective way to gain voting concessions from third world countries in the United Nations (Kegley and Hook 1991).

17. Asia Foundation (2004, p. 11).

18. Kerry (1990, pp. 87–99).

19. One misperception of Americans is the presumption that foreign visitors, once exposed to civic-minded U.S. domestic politics, will cease to be resentful and will return to their homes as friends. But the opposite often occurs. Visitors exposed to democratic values up close want to bring these values back with them, and will be doubly frustrated to find American foreign policy obstructing the realization of the very democratic aspirations their contact with the United States has nurtured.

20. Axelrod (1984, pp. 169–91).

21. Vogel and Witte (2005, p. 8).

22. Kinzer (2006).

23. For more on this subject see Bueno de Mesquita and Root (2000).

Chapter Three

1. Odom and Dujarric (2004, pp. 8–9).

2. Mann (2004).

3. Summers (1982).

4. Powell (1995, p. 149).

5. Odom and Dujarric (2004, pp. 8–9).

6. George W. Bush, speech given at the National Endowment for Democracy, Washington, D.C., October 6, 2005.

7. Fewer than 25 percent of Jordanians and fewer than 10 percent of the populations of Morocco, Egypt, Saudi Arabia, or the United Emirates believe that the United States invaded Iraq to promote democracy (Gause 2005).

8. In the Middle East, where U.S. allies received the means to deal crippling defeats to leftist opposition leaders, a more virulent strain of anti-Americanism resulted. The violent repression of the indigenous leftists allowed the Islamic opposition to become the sole bearer of reform. The success of religious fundamentalism is largely a response to the failure of nationalism and Communism resulting from the earlier U.S. intervention in the region's domestic politics. The U.S. inadvertently created a political vacuum that is being filled by a far more dangerous opposition than the eliminated secular reformers.

9. Pollack (2004, p. 18).

10. Sick (1985, p. 165).

11. Kennan's argument was based on political and social as well as economic weaknesses (Kennan 1947, p. 580).

12. Wintrobe (1998).

13. Dickson (2003).

14. They look only at the last step, creating an indigenous business class, and do not realize that this is not the first but the *final* step to economic growth and prosperity. What keeps the market open and free from devastating social contestation are the social contributions made by previous policies of social regeneration and integration.

15. Root (2006).

16. United Nations Development Program (2001).

17. The breakup of the Soviet Union is frequently misconstrued as a victory of capitalism over Communism. Yet a number of former Communist countries have successfully transitioned into market economies, and some have evolved into flourishing democracies without shots fired. In fact, Communist regimes are among the most successful democratizers of the past thirty years, often outperforming their authoritarian neighbors in important areas of human development, such as education for females, basic health, and recreation—a contrast underscored by comparing the non-Communist and former Communist Islamic populations of Central Asia. Communism's demise is still far from producing a global consensus that America's political and economic model is the best alternative for everyone.

Chapter Four

1. Johnson (2004).

2. Zegart (1999, p. 253).

3. Hirsh (2003, p. 91).

4. Hook (2005).

5. "Evaluations are unlikely to be critical of existing operations, since all parties could lose in the short run. It should come as no surprise that AID Project Evaluation Summaries are quite general and conciliatory in tone" (Guess 1987, p. 107).

6. A liberal vision for foreign aid is articulated in Lumsdaine (1993).

7. Ruttan (1996, p. 332).

8. Ibid., p. 22.

9. See Brainard (2007), "A Unified Framework for U.S. Foreign Assistance" and "Organizing U.S. Foreign Assistance to Meet Twenty-First Century Challenges" (pp. 1–66).

10. There is little direct correlation between aid expenditures by the United States and reductions in infant mortality and other basic indicators of human development. This failure can generally be attributed to public choices made in the recipient countries and could probably only be influenced by the outside if aid were directly targeted on the basis of its contribution to supporting liberal political regimes. The rules governing aid transfers generally prohibit such explicit political motivation (Boone 1996). Boone found that liberal political regimes exhibit 30 percent lower infant mortality rates than the least free regimes.

11. For more information on the subject of the welfare effects of winning coalition size, see Bueno de Mesquita and others (2003) and Bueno de Mesquita and Root (2000).

12. In *The White Man's Burden,* William Easterly (2006) explains that massive aid-based development plans are futile, but he accepts the rationale for foreign aid as given: to better the human condition in poor countries by alleviating poverty. It fails, he asserts, because it is guided by bad economic policy—state-led as opposed to market-centered approaches, the big push over gradualism. My view is that aid is motivated by foreign policy and therefore subordinated by policy planners to judgments about security. But security is related to the progress of development among our alliance partners, so that good development policy is also good foreign policy. Aid has never enjoyed a consensus on development, as Easterly infers; still today it is not led by a consensus, not because no one is paying attention to the plight of the world's poorest people or to the ravages of poverty they face. The institutions that govern aid were not originally designed to fulfill the current function, and their intellectual and political legacy as diplomatic tools of the cold war affects performance.

13. Perkins (2006).

14. Zegart (1999, p. 85).

15. Kissinger (1979, p. 30).

16. Rosati and Twing (1998, p. 47).

17. Zegart (1999, p. 239).

18. Ruland (2005, p. 232).

19. Hoffman (1983, p. 26).

Chapter Five

1. Melanson (2005, p. 37).

2. Robert Packenham (1973) has written, "But the United States was 'born equal'; it needed no profound social revolution to become so" (p. 135). In a similar vein,

Louis Hartz (1955) has written, "It is the absence of the experience of social revolution which is at the heart of the American dilemma" (p. 306).

3. Antipathy toward violent revolution, Packenham (1973) concludes, stems from America's "experiences and beliefs . . . [which] have made it difficult for Americans to perceive, understand, and appreciate the positive role that radicalism and revolution, with the intense conflict and violence that often attend them, play under certain circumstances in other countries" (p. 138).

4. In many cases, extreme secular ideologies such as state socialism were employed to transcend tribal ties, but most frequently multiethnic rivalry ended with the domination of one part of the population by another.

5. Douglass North (1990, 1993) has argued in a number of influential books and articles that economic development will elude a society weak in formal institutions to facilitate cooperation and trust or lacking informal institutions or values that underpin mutual understanding.

6. Montgomery (1962, p. 151).

7. On the record of U.S. nation building, see Minxin Pei and Sara Kasper (2003). They identify sixteen attempts at nation building (not counting the Philippines) and qualify four as successes: Japan 1945–52, West Germany 1945–49, Panama 1989, and Grenada 1983. Their definition of success is limited to the ability to sustain democracy in the ten years that followed U.S. withdrawal. The criteria being applied include economic growth—hence Grenada and Panama are excluded. Critics point out that Cuba shows up three times, and Panama, the Dominican Republic, and Haiti twice each. Cambodia hardly qualifies, and South Korea is omitted.

8. After the Treaty of Westphalia, in 1648, wars between states were no longer directly fought and resolved for the private benefit of elite families.

9. See Root (1985) and de Tocqueville (1960).

10. Weber (1947, pp. 324–40); Perrow (1986, pp. 1–48).

11. Root (2006, pp. 128–34).

12. Ibid., pp. 174–77.

13. The battle to eliminate slavery is a common experience that the United States shares with many developing nations and could have been a common reference point. The revocation of slavery in the United States, despite the existence of the Bill of Rights, was only the first step in the struggle for civil rights.

14. Przeworski (2000).

15. Harries (1986, pp. 3–7).

16. Without social consensus, societies are unable to mobilize and coordinate resources to build large enterprises. Instead of investing in productive capacity, individuals make investments to protect their assets from possible social conflict. Systemic social and economic divisions make it difficult to achieve broad-based consensus about the quantity and quality of public goods, on government expenditures, and on revenue collection. Without agreement on the amount of nontraded social or "public" goods—roads, education, police, defense, or courts of law—social development as well as the economy stagnates.

Disparities in wealth contribute to uncertainty that threatens domestic peace with revolutions or strikes that can rupture policy continuity and destabilize the macro-economy with antimarket reversals of policy. In Latin America, for example, frequent policy reversals have undermined the credibility of market reforms and triggered sociopolitical stalemates that prevent Latin American society from resolving debates about the level and distribution of taxation and spending. Social polarization that is devastating to sound public finance is one reason support for democracy is unsteady in the region, and it is why the dispossessed in many Latin American countries are willing to accept a return of authoritarian leaders in exchange for more public goods (Root 2006).

17. Political parties are unlikely to emerge that can convey information to voters about whether politicians have fulfilled promises to create a better policy environment; instead voters can only judge politicians by their particular promises to provide private tangible benefits.

18. Collier (2007).

19. United Nations Development Program (2008).

20. Institutions can also fail. Banking systems collapse, and hyperinflation and economic breakdowns cause social institutions to realign.

21. Montgomery (1962, p. 17).

22. An example of an ultimatum game is the following. A wealthy retiree is sitting on an airplane and announces to the passenger in the next seat that he can have 10,000 dollars if he in turn can find a way to divide it with the person to his left. The second person makes an offer to share 1,000 of the 10,000 dollars but it is rejected. No deal is struck, and so both parties are worse off. The game's outcome implies that people will reject an offer, even one that provides a financial gain, if the offer is perceived as being unfair.

23. James S. Coleman (1990), states that "social capital is productive, making possible the achievement of certain ends that would not be attainable in its absence. . . . In a farming community . . . where one farmer got his hay [baled] by another and where farm tools are extensively borrowed and lent, the social capital allows each farmer to get his work done with less physical capital in the form of tools and equipment" (p. 167).

24. France did not experience massive out-migration from rural sectors in part because during the French Revolution land was distributed among the peasantry, reducing rural migration overseas and to domestic urban centers.

25. See Singh and Day (1975) and Day (2004). "Theories of steady state convergence that reign in economic studies do not offer accurate accounts of how societies behave or how they experience change. Social behavior is characterized by multipolarity and dynamic irregularity. The more general condition of social organizations such as the market, the polity, and the household is disequilibrium. Models of economic growth that assume linear progression from one steady state to another distort the complex multiphase sequencing that make[s] up interacting adapting processes" (Day 2004, pp. 59–140).

26. Campos and Root (1996).

27. Ibid.

28. Economic liberalism in the wrong hands could be a rationalization for weak states that succumbed to corruption and domination by elites, and economic liberals could end up overlooking the distributional consequences of poverty that triggered discontent. Definitive but unjust property-rights assignments as in Argentina and in Latin America generally compensate absentee rights holders, who do not have to be efficient. The polarization of economic rights produces polarization in politics. Governments that trade economic power for political support by reserving access to opportunities for cronies of the political regime produce short-term stability at the risk of long-term violent disruption. The insight of the Nobel Prize winner Ronald Coase that connects property rights to social welfare is hardly applicable in such environments. Neoliberalism, by failing to recognize inappropriate top-down allocation, frequently perpetuated existing injustices.

29. Beinhocker (2006, pp. 287–89).

30. An analysis of "tagging" and the distinction between discriminatory and equity norms appears in Axtell, Epstein, and Young (2000) and in Epstein (2006, pp. 176–98). They underscore the difference between explaining the conditions that trigger the emergence of norms and explaining the equilibrium conditions that sustain them. The authors conclude that equity norms are more sustainable, although discriminatory norms can produce property rights systems that can be long-lived. The primacy of property rights to economic performance is emphasized by Douglass North (1990, 1993) and Hernando de Soto (1989, 2002).

31. Legitimacy fails more quickly once long-standing repression is released. Moderate reductions may have a dramatic catalyzing effect and serve as large-scale tipping devices, such as those that caused the French, Russian, and Iranian revolutions (Epstein 2006, pp. 262–63). An atmosphere of laxity and endemic corruption in the Philippines and Thailand seems to be less of a provocation since a sudden decline in standards cannot be attributed to any particular set of actors. Endemic corruption does not seem to be an effective catalyst for action because the legitimacy of the state is only incrementally diminished by more corruption.

Chapter Six

For Chinese names and places we adopt the pinyin system for the most part, with a few exceptions, such as Sun Yat-sen, Chiang Kai-shek, Kuomintang, Soong Mayling, T. V. Soong, and H. H. Kung, for which we use the Wade-Giles transliterations. These exceptions were made because we did not want to burden the readers with a new set of names that they are not familiar with.

1. A view that diverges even further from the American mainstream was expressed by John P. Davies Jr., a State Department official who spent considerable time in China. In his report to Washington, he stated that he believed the United

States should not fear a Communist takeover of China, but should cooperate with the Communists:

> The United States is the greatest hope and the greatest fear of the Chinese Communists. They recognize that if they receive American aid, even if only on an equal basis with Chiang, they can quickly establish control over most if not all of China, perhaps without civil war. For most of Chiang's troops and bureaucrats are opportunists who will desert the Generalissimo if the Communists appear to be stronger than the Central Government. We are the greatest fear of the Communists because the more aid we give Chiang exclusively the greater the likelihood of his precipitating civil war and the more protracted and costly will be the Communist unification of China. So the Chinese Communists watch us with mixed feeling. If we continue to reject them and support an unreconstructed Chiang, they see us becoming their enemy. But they would prefer to be friends. Not only because of the help we can give them but also because they recognize that our strategic aims of a strong, independent and democratic China can jibe with their nationalist objectives. (Quoted in Kubek 1963, p. 235)

2. Luce (1941).

3. Koen (1960, p. 63).

4. Morgenthau and Thompson (1982, p. 206).

5. For example, MacArthur (1964) complained, "For some unaccountable reason, the Communists were not looked upon with disfavor by the State Department, who labeled them 'agrarian reformers'" (p. 320).

6. A case in point was the persecution of the State Department officials and career diplomats John Patton Davies Jr., John Carter Vincent, and John Stewart Service.

7. Struggles with his former warlord allies Yan Xishan and Feng Yuxiang in 1930 resulted in 250,000 casualties and nearly bankrupted the Kuomintang government.

8. Officially known as the Chinese Soviet Republic, the Jiangxi Soviet existed from 1931 to 1934 in Ruijin, Jiangxi Province, before the city was encircled by Chiang's army and the Communist troops were forced to retreat in what became known as the Long March.

9. Payne (1969, p. 150).

10. He Yingqin, commander of the Kuomintang armies in northern China, signed an agreement with Yoshijiro Umezu (1938–1939), the general officer commanding the First Army and vice minister of war. Umezu is one of fourteen Japanese class-A war criminals interred at Yasukuni Shrine. The Japanese invasion of Manchuria began in 1931 after the September 18 Incident (known in the West as "the Mukden Incident"), in which a bomb planted by Japanese secret agents destroyed a Japanese express train near Shenyang. In July 1937, Japan launched an all-out war on mainland China.

11. Quoted in Terrill (1999, pp. 172–73).

12. Ibid., pp. 173–74.

13. The largest casualty estimate is from the Kuomintang government, which claimed 430,000 victims, including 230,000 civilians and 110,000 military personnel. The city of Nanjing claims 300,000 deaths, according to the entrance to the Nanjing Massacre Memorial Hall. The Japanese scholar Horo Tomio reports 200,000 soldier and civilian casualties, excluding battlefield deaths. For casualty estimates, see Honda (1999, p. 285). For the mainland perspective, see Xu (1995).

14. In South Anhui in January 1941, Kuomintang troops ambushed the Communist forces, killing 10,000.

15. Barrett (1970, p. 19) and Spence (1990, pp. 464–69).

16. Tuchman (1970, p. 378).

17. Ibid., p. 531.

18. Ibid., p. 378.

19. The three-year mission, commanded by Colonel David Barrett, arrived in Yan'an in July 1944 and hosted both the Patrick Hurley and George Marshall diplomatic missions. The views of Barrett were rejected under pressure from the pro-Chiang China lobby in Washington. The colonel was denied a promotion when Patrick Hurley charged him with undermining efforts to unite the Communists and the Nationalists.

20. Moise (1994, p. 98).

21. Barrett (1970, p. 91).

22. In 1945–1946, when compared to the smaller Communist forces, Chiang's army lacked neither equipment nor personnel (see table 6-1).

23. Niu (2005). Niu Jun is a researcher with the Beijing-based Chinese Academy of Social Sciences.

24. This statement was reported slightly differently in a *Time* article, "China: 'You Shall Never Yield . . . ,'" (December 6, 1948, p. 29), in which Chiang claimed, "The Japanese are like a terrible skin disease; but Communism is a cancer."

25. Jespersen (1996) explores Americanized images of China.

26. For China's land distribution see Chevrier (2004, p. 77).

27. "Battle of China," *Time*, June 1, 1942, p. 20.

28. Macdonald (1992, p. 78).

29. As a supplement to the feature story on Chiang Kai-shek published in *Time* (see note 27), the magazine ran a brief story titled "No Bitterness" (*Time*, June 22, 1942, p. 4) in the form of a letter from a reader.

30. Dai Li was head of the Juntong, the Bureau of Investigation and Statistics of the Military Affairs Commission. Dai Li, "the only man that was allowed in the Generalissimo's bedroom armed at any time of day or night," was often compared to Himmler. Dai's secret arrests and assassinations of Communists and left-wing intellectuals during the 1930s and 1940s are discussed in Wakeman (2003).

31. Spence (1990, p. 417). Dai Li assassinated the leader of the Chinese League for the Protection of Civil Rights in 1933 and the editor of a Shanghai major newspaper

in 1934, both leading figures in opposing Chiang's political programs for China. On the Young Generals' Plot, which involved two hundred to six hundred officers and resulted in Dai Li's execution of sixteen generals, see Tuchman (1970, p. 455).

32. The murder of Shi Liangcai was a case in point. Documentation exists that Chiang had ordered the murder of the leader of the League for the Protection of Human Rights, which was not Communist-affiliated. Shi was murdered for his involvement in the league and for his condemnation of the government's education policy (Wakeman, 2003, pp. 179–82).

33. "China: 'I Am Very Optimistic,'" *Time*, September 3, 1945, p. 31.

34. Wakeman (2003, pp. 344–46). *Time* explained Chiang's lack of resistance against Japan as "turning the Christian other cheek." When Chiang was kidnapped by his two generals in 1936, *Time* depicted General Zhang Xueliang as a drug addict, and it ignored overtures by the Communists to form a united front with Chiang against the Japanese. See Jespersen (pp. 24–44).

35. Esherick (2003, pp. 40–41).

36. Luard (1965, p. 114).

37. Bhutto (1969, p. 33).

38. Terrill (1999, pp. 173; 239); Yuan (2005, pp. 309–12).

39. Terrill (1999, p. 218).

40. Ibid.

41. Niu (2005).

42. Morgenthau and Thompson (1982, p. 205).

43. The United States and Britain relinquished concessions and privileges they had extorted from China shortly after Pearl Harbor. China under Chiang was made one of the five permanent members of the United Nations. Yet the mainland was bitterly divided into two ideologically antagonistic governments and some warlords still controlled part of the periphery after World War II.

44. In 1981, Mao was voted 70 percent "good" and 30 percent "negative" by a Chinese Communist Party resolution. A 1994 survey of more than 6,000 Chinese found that Mao was their favorite national political leader (40 percent), followed by his longtime deputy, Zhou Enlai (26.6 percent), and the reform initiator Deng Xiaoping (10 percent). For Mao's popularity among Chinese people in the economic-reform era, see Tim Healy and David Hsieh's article "Mao Now," *Asia Week*, September 6, 1996 (www.pathfinder.com/asiaweek/96/0906/cs1.html).

45. See the account of General Wedemeyer, reported in Koen (1960, pp. 103–4), in which the general alludes to "conditions . . . that may have precluded the fulfillment of many of our commitments" (U.S. Senate, 80th Congress, 1st Session, Committee on Appropriations, Hearings, December 17, 1947).

46. "Relief: Thunder," *Time*, July 22, 1946, p. 27. The United Nations Relief and Rehabilitation Administration (UNRRA) was an organization founded in 1943 in Washington to give assistance to areas liberated from the Axis forces. Each of the forty-four founding members contributed funds amounting to 2 percent of national

income in 1943, but the United States funded close to half the organization's budget. During the organization's existence, China, along with Czechoslovakia, Greece, Italy, Poland, and Yugoslavia, were the primary beneficiaries until March 31, 1949.

47. Rawski (1989).

48. Of 229 banks 181 were closed.

49. "China: Opening Doors," *Time*, July 9, 1945, p. 39.

50. "China: Three Changes," *Time*, August 13, 1945, p. 43.

51. For an analysis of China's economic growth from the late nineteenth century to the Pacific War in World War II, see Rawski (1989).

52. Rawski (1989) confirms that "Chinese governments remained fiscally weak during the entire period preceding the Pacific War. The inability of China's political authorities to gain control over substantial financial resources meant that important economic magnitudes were determined mainly within the private sector" (pp. 31–32). Huang (2000) reports that to compensate for its administrative weakness, the Kuomintang depended upon various types of organized crime.

53. Tuchman (1970, pp. 529–30); Spence (1990, pp. 484–91).

54. Tuchman (1970, pp. 529–30).

55. Tuchman (1970) points out: "American forces were actively helping to restore French rulers in Indochina against a strong movement for independence. In charters and declarations American aims were democratic but in practice the executants opted for the old regime. In China the decision was not merely futile; it aligned America in popular eyes with the oppressor and landlord and tax collector, it disheartened the liberal forces and violently antagonized the future rulers" (p. 527).

56. Ibid., p. 526.

57. A highly stereotyped image of international affairs culminated in the purges inspired by Joseph McCarthy, who declared that eighty-one officials in the State Department were Communist sympathizers who had contributed to the Communist victory in China. Pro-Communist magazines were shut down and John Service's officers were sacked, compromising the ability of the State Department to benefit from independent judgment.

58. Terrill (1999, p. 221).

59. Ibid., p. 171.

60. China's experience resembles that of Europe during the period of the religious wars, which produced perspectives favorable to state power, such as that of Thomas Hobbes (2006) expressed in *Leviathan*.

61. Esherick (2003, p. 58).

Chapter Seven

1. Kolko (1988, p. 25). United States Department of State/*Foreign Relations of the United States, 1958–1960. South and Southeast Asia*, Volume XV (1958–60), p. 1096.

2. Manglapus (1976) has written, "The Spaniards must also take the responsibility for another reputed Filipino disqualification for democracy, namely, the admitted

but often exaggerated incapacity of the millions of land-bound share-cropping tenants to vote independently of their landlords. The Spanish government institutionalized the *datu* [local leaders] into the *Cabeza de Barangay* [head of the communes], the hereditary instrument of the central government. The communal lands were transformed into public domain available for private titling by the *Cabezas*" (pp. 51–52).

3. By contrast, the Japanese elite was the enemy, so MacArthur dissolved prewar monopolies and redistributed wealth by promoting social economic reforms. Thus, he hoped to deprive the elite of the resources for another series of conquests. As in Japan, Taiwan, and South Korea, he wanted to create support for the new pro-American regimes through land reform.

4. MacArthur (1964, pp. 235–36).

5. Not surprisingly, the island's elite families, such as the successful businessman Andres Soriano and the future president Manuel Roxas (1946–48), stood at MacArthur's side and did not seek social reforms or wish to settle scores with collaborators. At the outbreak of World War II, Roxas joined the Philippine army as a major and was assigned a post as liaison officer between MacArthur and the Philippines Armed Forces. In April 1944 he became chair of the Economic Planning Board in the José Laurel cabinet and was in charge of procuring and distributing rice. MacArthur affirmed that it was the job of local authorities to determine the treatment of collaboration charges.

6. "Shortly after World War II a Communist guerrilla army, the Hukbong Magpalayang Bayan (HMB), or People's Liberation Army, became a serious threat to the new Philippine Republic. The Huks, as they are commonly known, controlled large parts of the sugar cane– and rice-growing areas of Central Luzon and carried out military and political operations in other parts of the islands. Like their Communist counterparts in Vietnam and Malaya, the Huks began as an anti-Japanese guerrilla army. In fact, *Huk* originally referred to *Hukbalahap,* a contraction of a phrase meaning People's Army Against the Japanese. As the military arm of the Communist Party, however, their ambitions always exceeded mere anti-Japanese activities" (Mitchell 1969).

7. The U.S. view was that military problems and economic-political problems were intertwined. It was in this context that Edward Lansdale was sent to Manila to assist with the suppression of the Huk rebellion, encourage a pro-American attitude in the people, and strengthen government forces to maintain internal order. The notion was that a Huk victory would discredit the United States and that suppressing the Huks would require more than military measures.

8. See Cullather (1994, pp. 96–123).

9. Cortes (1999).

10. Jawaharlal Nehru wrote of the Bandung participants: "A tightly knit group represented, if I may say so, the United States policy. This consisted chiefly of Turkey, Pakistan, Iraq, and Lebanon. Also, of course, the Philippines and Thailand. These two were at least somewhat moderate in their expression. The other four were quite aggressive and sometimes even offensive." Letter from Nehru to Edwina Mountbatten, quoted in Claude Arpi, "Was Bandung in Vain?" (www.rediff.com/news/2005/apr/22claude.htm).

11. Brands (1992, p. 268).

12. Ibid.

13. Ibid., p. 276.

14. U.S. officials required the lifting of those trade barriers in exchange for postwar reconstruction aid, but they did not exact a quid pro quo in trade.

15. Between 1945 and 1958, the Philippines received U.S. economic aid worth over a billion dollars, more than any other country in East Asia (Cullather 1994, p. 184). This aid allowed the government to escape insolvency.

16. Cullather (1994, p. 77).

17. Ferdinand Marcos, quoted in Celoza (1997, p. 100).

18. Balisacan and Hill (2003, p. 49).

19. Lappé, Collins, and Kinley (1980, p. 21).

20. Jeane Kirkpatrick (1982), Reagan's ambassador to the UN, made the case that the United States was suffering from a double standard at the hands of its critics; the Soviets could deal with dictators and suffer no loss of prestige.

21. Bonner (1987, p. 442).

22. Kissinger (1986, p. 61).

23. Brands (1992, p. 341).

24. Guess (1987, p. 188).

25. Herrin and Pernia (2003).

26. Celoza (1997, p. 99).

27. Cullather (1994, p. 186).

28. Brands (1992, p. 261).

29. Herrin and Pernia (2003, p. 305).

30. Secretary of State Colin Powell called her act "bowing to terrorists." Other U.S. officials warned that the concession would encourage further political kidnappings.

31. The fate of Angelo de la Cruz became a celebrated issue in the Philippines because it exposed the limits of the nation's geopolitical alignment with the United States. The weakness of Arroyo's political mandate was also exposed. Unable to do much for the poor, she had won election two months earlier with only 40 percent of the vote. The crux of her insecurity is captured by Richard Paddock, a reporter, writing in the *Los Angeles Times* (see "Hostage Freed after Philippine Troops' Departure," July 21, 2004, and "Philippines Completes Iraq Pullout," July 20, 2004): "The De la Cruz crisis has been one of Arroyo's toughest tests since 2001 when, as vice president, she assumed office with the ouster of President Joseph Estrada. Many of Estrada's supporters—poor workers like de la Cruz—have never accepted her legitimacy as president. If Arroyo permitted De la Cruz to be beheaded, she faced the possibility of street protests that could topple her presidency just over a month after she was elected to her first term."

32. Salisbury (1976a, p. xiii).

33. The post-Marcos Senate rejected the lease extension of the bases in 1991. Many observers reflected that the senators who opposed the bases were registering their

hostility to the support handed to his dictatorship. Ironically, it was the eruption of Mount Pinatubo that destroyed Clark Air Force Base and that also sped up the closure of Subic Bay Naval Base.

34. Inequality is especially detrimental to cooperation because it is the perceived outcome of the policies of a dishonest dictator. This perception triggered the growth of an armed opposition during the Marcos years. After the restoration of democracy, corruption and high-level influence peddling continued to project the same absence of integrity at the head of government. But it is harder to pinpoint a direct culprit.

35. Political party competition follows traditional networks of bribery, and preexisting social inequality corrupted the governing institutions down to the local level. Instead of working for wholesale reform, each incumbent indulges in subjugating, cajoling, and buying the support of rivals. These practices eat up government revenues without generating new resources for mounting a developmental push similar to that in South Korea and Taiwan in the 1960s. Of the country's misfortunes, a CIA report of August 10, 1950, declared that "at the base of these is an irresponsible ruling class which exercises economic and political power almost exclusively in its own interests" (Brands 1992, p. 236).

36. Buss (1977).

37. Manglapus (1976) concludes, "So let there be social revolution. Let it fight injustice, give hope. Let it produce wealth, but also close the gap between those who enjoy the wealth and those who do not. Let it not surrender to the simplistic idea that the only problem in Asia is productivity, 'the enlarging of the pie,' and that exploitation of man by man will resolve itself with this enlargement. Let it persevere until the millions of Asia are released from the bonds of retarding traditions, feudal tenancy, and centralized power. Let America help to fire it, but do not make it an American revolution. Let it be so universal in meaning, so pregnant with hope for all races, that each nation will take it for its own" (p. 69).

38. "Slightly less than 14 percent of [the] world['s] population lives in middle-income countries, and 6.7 percent of individuals in the world have incomes that place them among the world middle class." Milanovic (2006, p. 131).

39. See Root (2006, pp. 226, 231–34). That theory was formalized in the work of Robert Barro. Barro (1997) argues that if median voters are poor, opposition to private investment policies is probable; growth-oriented policies will arouse opposition from capital-poor groups.

Chapter Eight

1. Herring (1979, p. 47).
2. Ibid.
3. South Vietnam failed to prosper, even with $26 billion in military and economic aid over the twenty-year period. The country's advantages—untapped natural resources, a productive agricultural sector, one of the highest farm-to-person ratios in

Asia, and access to advanced technology—did not ensure national prosperity or balanced economic development. See Buttinger (1967, pp. 920–22); Hoan (1958); Lindholm (1959, p. 338).

4. South Vietnam existed as an independent entity from 1627 to 1778.

5. Diem subverted the agreements by insisting on free elections and free speech in each zone before the elections. Herring (1979) explains, "With American assistance, a 'national' referendum was hastily arranged between Diem and Bao Dai. Diem secured 98.2 percent of the vote, winning more than 605,000 votes from the 405,000 registered voters in Saigon" (p. 59). Despite the rigged outcome, he was hailed as one of Asia's champions of democracy.

6. Buttinger (1967, p. 945).

7. Shaplen (1965, p. 134). This attitude also extended to the military establishment. Kahin notes that "much of the army's support is based on personal loyalty to the President who, bypassing formal organization, often deals directly with young field commanders and military chiefs of province" (Kahin 1959, p. 346).

8. Montgomery (1962, pp. 69–70). Diem did not trust his own officials, and his unwillingness to delegate even minor matters to subordinate officials caused even routine administrative matters to be referred to him such as passports, property transfers to foreigners, sales of surplus military supplies, and even divorces. Also, in some instances, regime elites created institutions that were designed to be ineffective, such as regulations governing private enterprise, in order to support patron-client structures.

9. Fall (1963, p. 253).

10. Scigliano (1964, p. 60).

11. Initially, Diem seemed so successful that he earned accolades as "Vietnam's George Washington," but concentration of power and wealth among the army and the bureaucracy dispossessed so many ethnic and religious groups that his policies unleashed civil war within the South.

12. Scigliano (1964, p. 80).

13. Halberstam (1965, p. 66).

14. Buttinger (1967, pp. 960–63).

15. Fall (1963, p. 253).

16. Jumper (1957, p. 51).

17. Buttinger (1967, p. 951); Jumper (1957).

18. Scigliano (1964, p. 76).

19. Writing in 1964, Scigliano observed, "Thus, the Diem regime has assumed the aspect of a carpetbag government in its disproportion of Northerners and Centralists, in the ease of access to high positions granted officials from the Hue area, and in its Catholicism. These imbalances have been a source of support for Diem and a foundation for a strong anti-Communist policy. The vehement anti-Communist programs of the government have been carried out by the Department of Information (later reduced to general directorate status), which is packed with Northern Catholics" (p. 54).

20. Buttinger (1967, p. 947); Duncanson (1968, pp. 228–31); Scigliano (1964, pp. 60–61).

21. Roy Jumper observed in 1957, "In the absence of political parties with grass roots, the bureaucracy began to fulfill a number of functions that in the West are normally performed by political parties and other representative organizations. . . . During the campaign [to cement Diem's formal title of leadership] . . . entire administrative services were closed so that civil servants could distribute campaign literature and join . . . campaign parades" (p. 57); this shows how the Diem regime used its client base of civil servants to build political support, in the absence of a legitimate political base.

22. Duncanson (1968, pp. 229–30); Mansfield (1963); Kahin (1959, p. 384).

23. Buttinger (1967, p. 933); Catton (2002, p. 54); Wiegersma and Medley (2000, p. 72).

24. Diem's contract program, which established a ceiling of 25 percent of the crop, was resisted by tenants who were paying no rent at all. That these officials took the best lands is exhibited not only by the emphasis on properly compensating landlords for land obtained by the government for redistribution but also through the exemption of land not used to cultivate rice and of Catholic church holdings, both of which were substantial and were held by key bases of support for the Diem regime (Scigliano 1964, pp. 121–23; Buttinger 1967, p. 933).

25. Gabriel Kolko (1994) writes, "For it was Diem's land program, not the Party, which led inevitably to renewed conflict in South Vietnam. The moment he abolished the legal standing of the Viet Minh's land reforms, he unleashed social discontent and created actual and potential enemies. This was particularly true where the Revolution's land reforms had gone the furthest" (p. 93).

26. Wiegersma and Medley (2000, p. 78).

27. Zasloff (1962, p. 333).

28. "In 1954, about 40 percent of the land planted to rice was owned by about 2,500 persons—by a quarter of one percent of the rural population. Rent alone commonly took 50 percent of the tenant's crop and sometimes more; he either provided his own fertilizer, seeds, man- and draft-power, and equipment, rented them at extra costs or he could be ejected from his leasehold at the landlord's whim" (Scigliano 1964, p. 120; see also Gittinger 1959, pp. 1, 50).

29. Scigliano (1964, p. 198–99, 203–5); Montgomery (1962, pp. 72, 118, 147–48).

30. Disagreement between the United States and the GVN occurred during negotiations to devalue the piaster, Diem's disbanding of the independent National Union Front, the restoration of damaged public facilities, and a program to distribute seeds to rural areas. Once allocations were set, the programs were allowed to function by Congress despite the failure of GOSV to comply. See Montgomery (1962, pp. 72–73), Scigliano (1964, pp. 200–201, 209), and Guess (1987, pp. 210, 216).

31. Streeb (1994).

32. Buttinger (1967, p. 1182).

33. Nolting (1988, pp. 3, 15).

34. They range from negligence to a concern for faster social reforms to a disagreement over enlarging the American presence.

35. Chinese business intermediaries played a similar role in providing the economic support for the Suharto dictatorship in neighboring Indonesia.

36. These efforts were too late, as capable villagers did not want to become targets for assassination and the new village councils could not overcome the corruption of village chiefs.

37. Kolko (1994, p. 381).

38. Southeast Asia in general and Vietnam in particular had little intrinsic value to America's well-being. The value of South Vietnam came from the fear that the loss of Vietnam would lead to the loss of Indochina, followed by Indonesia and the Philippines, which would turn Japan away from the world system toward accommodation with the Communist bloc.

39. Scigliano (1964, p. 215) stated that two U.S. ambassadors and several other officials had expressed this opinion to him.

40. Kolko (1994, p. 219).

41. Scigliano (1964, p. 155–56).

42. Nguyen (1987, p. 45).

43. Buttinger (1967, p. 966).

44. Kissinger (1969, p. 106).

45. Girling (1980, p. 45).

46. Kolko (1994, p. 224).

47. Wiegersma and Medley (2000, p. 75).

48. Girling (1980, p. 45).

49. Taylor (1961).

50. The U.S. government eventually exerted heavy pressure on Diem to devalue the piaster and was finally successful in 1962, but even the new rate of sixty piasters to the dollar was overvalued.

51. Rent was created by the fact that a licensed importer could, for thirty-five piasters, purchase a dollar's worth of goods, then sell them on the Vietnamese market for the value of the goods in piasters, which was substantially higher.

52. Montgomery (1962, p. 91).

53. Ibid.

54. Fall (1967, p. 284).

55. Also, it should be noted that the GVN's tax effort was not markedly better in the peaceful period (1955–1960) than in the years of heightened security threat (1961–1964), suggesting that security issues were not a prime cause of ineffective tax collection (Dacy 1986, p. 223).

56. Kurer (1997, pp. 132–33).

57. Ibid., pp. 43, 200.

58. North (1990, p. 13).

59. Keeler (1993); MacIntyre (2003, pp. 106–7); North (1993, pp. 62–65); Kurer (1997, pp. 13, 15).

60. Kolko (1994, p. 460).

61. Montgomery (1962, p. 91).

62. Compared to before the recession started (Dacy 1986, p. 19).

63. Dacy (1986, pp. 16–19, 75); Le (1975); Nguyen (1987, pp. 288–89, 311).

64. Nguyen (1987, p. 284).

65. U.S. Congress, Senate Committee on Foreign Relations (1974, p. 8).

66. Ibid., p. 30.

67. Americans share a set of founding myths that conform to the self-image shared by most non–African Americans. Part of the common ground is a language of liberty and freedom that makes Americans different from all other nationalities. This shared standard of civic ethics establishes legitimacy for the state and produces a conducive environment for trade and investment. Americans' ideal state of freedom is mirrored in a civil state that reflects and overlaps with their identity as individuals who control their own destiny. On the meaning of "American Exceptionalism," Joseph Ferrie (2005) has written, "One of the most significant is the belief that in the United States history is not destiny: without a hereditary aristocracy or caste system or controls on internal migration, Americans are less constrained than others by their family background in shaping their own lives" (p. 199).

68. The cultural unity of Americans typically finds expression in the inaugural speeches of presidents that tend to be virtually interchangeable invocations of a shared historical experience and space. When an American president speaks of freedom or liberty in an inaugural address, he enacts a ritual that tells us precious little about the actual policies of a particular administration. He is engaging in a ritual affirmation of American identity by defining a shared value system.

69. Turchin (2003, p. 75).

70. Colonialism in South Vietnam did not produce a strong or coherent economic elite. This made South Vietnam different from the Philippines, where a strong precolonial elite existed that controlled the economy and the loyalties of the agrarian population.

71. Easterly (2002, pp. 245–46, 258–59); Burnside and Dollar (2000).

72. Marcos nationalized 300 businesses, from the largest to the most trivial, showering loans on his followers without proper due diligence, only to reschedule the loans to help those same cronies avoid foreclosure. In 1983, the American Embassy in the Philippines issued a thirty-six-page report about government involvement in the Philippine economy. "During martial law Marcos had issued 688 presidential decrees and 283 letters of instruction, which injected the government into the economy in one form or another. There was not only a National Steel Corporation but also a National Stud Farm. . . . The government owned outright or controlled more than 300 companies, engaging in everything from coal mining to the making of polyester to the production of mosquito coils. Many had been privately owned until taken over by the government. By 1983 the government had control of between 75 and 80 percent of all the country's financial assets" (Scott 1972, p. 12). Increasing government control over production and enterprise provided opportunities to enforce regulations and to allocate resources needed by regime loyalists to control key sectors of the economy.

73. See Buttinger (1967, p. 968); Musloff (1963); Scigliano (1964, p. 199); Taylor (1961).

74. Fall (1967, p. 298).

75. Kurer (1997, p. 48). This would include both laws that limit the scope or exercise of executive power and countervailing political forces, such as an independent judiciary, the central bank, the legislature, or the bureaucracy.

76. Kurer (1997, p. 71).

77. Campos and Root (1996) and Root (1996).

78. Rostow (1985).

79. Moyar (2006, pp. xiii, 2–7).

80. Even if the United States had stayed and routed North Vietnam, it still would not have solved the dilemma of establishing a legitimate government in the South.

81. Bak (1996, p. 123).

Chapter Nine

Carter is quoted in J. A. Bill, *The Eagle and the Lion: The Tragedy of American-Iranian Relations.*

1. A third category of failure can be found in the conflicts between the NSC and the State Department, which biased much Cold War diplomacy, but this topic will not be covered here.

2. Initially, when the Islamic Republic was declared, a number of U.S. analysts welcomed it, believing that the population would now be better inoculated against Soviet influence.

3. One of the reasons for the emergence of a revolutionary clergy was that centralization had weakened the hold landlords had over local mosques.

4. Security analysts feared that Mossadegh had ties of dependency and affinity with Iran's Communist Tudeh Party, and that this would produce a rapprochement with the Soviets.

5. The shah's father was removed from power because of his pro-German sentiments.

6. Immediate financial assistance went to the shah in 1955, 1957, and 1958 for his support of the Eisenhower Doctrine, the Baghdad Pact, and CENTO, respectively, making the aid packages appear to be a bribe for Iran's cooperation with U.S. strategic goals.

7. As a nationalistic attempt to fight against British and Soviet imperialism, Muhammad Mossadegh, then prime minister, demanded that Iran gain complete ownership and control over the country's oilfields. Washington was initially supportive of Mossadegh's objectives, and President Truman facilitated negotiating the McGhee-Mossadegh Proposal, a fifty-fifty profit-sharing scheme between Britain and Iran. Britain declined the proposal, asserting that the nationalization of the oil fields in Iran would lead other Middle Eastern countries to follow suit.

8. Pollack (2004, p. 88).

9. Even supporters such as Eisenhower expressed concern that Pahlavi was paying too much attention to military strength and insufficient attention to economic

and social development. In a telegram from Secretary of State Dulles to the Department of State on January 25, 1958 (Keefer 2005, p. 533), Dulles stated that increased military assistance to the shah seriously strained Iran's economic welfare:

> The Shah, who considers himself a military genius, is determined to build up the military forces of Iran. . . . This of course will throw an increased economic burden upon the country and further unbalance an already unbalanced budget. This threatens both her development program to which most of the oil revenues are dedicated and also threatens inflation.
>
> The governmental ministers are mostly concerned with the economic problems of the country but are unable to cope with these in the face of the Shah's military obsessions. . . . All of this has been building up to quite a climax with hints that unless I gave explicit assurances of far greater military and economic aid the Shah might announce withdrawal of Iran from the Baghdad Pact with a neutralist policy to follow involving cooperation with both the Soviet Union and Free World in accordance with the Egyptian and Indian pattern.

Nevertheless Dulles recommended compliance with the shah's military, out of fear that Iran would renounce its support of the Baghdad Pact in favor of neutrality to U.S.-Soviet relations.

10. Bill (1988, p. 99).

11. Seitz (1980).

12. Sick (1985, p. 12).

13. Ibid., pp. 10–12. Khomeini was arrested in October 1963 and remained in prison for nearly eight months. In October 1964, after another clash with the government, Khomeini was exiled to Turkey.

14. Ibid., p. 11.

15. Library of Congress, Federal Research Division, "Iran: State and Society, 1964–74," Country Studies Series (www.country-data.com/cgi-bin/query/r-6388.html).

16. On June 27, 1968, Johnson wrote to the U.S. ambassador, Armin Meyer, that "my relationship with His Majesty has been one of the real pleasures of my Administration"; on June 16, 1964, Johnson also said to the businessman David Lilienthal, "Dave, what is going on in Iran is about the best thing going on anywhere in the world" (see Bill 1988, pp. 174, 178). The shah made four visits to the United States during Johnson's tenure.

17. Despite the fact that from 1953 to 1963 the proportion of economic and military aid from the United States to Iran was roughly the same, this funding enabled the Shah to expand the portion of Iran's budget allocated toward military production disproportionately (Abrahamian 1982, p. 435). Furthermore, after 1963, military aid entirely overtook U.S. overseas economic assistance. From 1950 to 1970, Iran received $1.8 billion in military grant aid. "During the 1970s, Iran became the single largest buyer of American arms. . . . Roughly 27% of the Shah's budget went to defense, and that budget quadrupled in size between 1973–74 and again between 1976–77" (Rubin 1981, pp. 123, 158).

18. Sick (1985, p. 19).

19. Halliday, 1980, p. 72. The shah's expenses were mostly on weapons procurement, which resulted in a major bonanza for U.S. arms procurers.

20. Sick (1985, p. 20).

21. The reason for Carter's moral capitulation reflected the fact that "the shah's policies directly benefited the United States. Vance himself listed five such positive policies: (1) the shah provided important economic assistance to countries in the area; (2) he helped reduce tensions in southwest Asia; (3) his forces had helped to defeat an insurgency in Oman; (4) he was 'a reliable supplier of oil to the West'; he had, in fact, refused to join the 1973 Arab oil embargo; and (5) he was Israel's primary source of oil. Thus, 'we decided early on that it was in our national interest to support the shah so he could continue to play a constructive role in regional affairs'" (Bill 1988, pp. 226–27).

22. Ibid., p. 228.

23. Looney (1982).

24. Gasiorowski (1991, p. 135).

25. The shah had the power to distribute licenses and foreign capital, offer tax holidays and low bank rates, impose high tariffs, and prohibit certain imports. Such control allowed him to promote the large and frequently inefficient businesses of wealthy aristocrats or to champion unsustainable economic growth of elitist consumerism (Abrahamian 1982, p. 437; Keddie 2003, p. 158). Pahlavi took advantage of cheap bank loans and invested the money in similar businesses. In particular, the Pahlavi Foundation, set up in the guise of a charitable fund, in reality took in money and reinvested it in companies so that the shah owned shares in as many as 207 companies, in every sector of the economy. He used his administrative power to become the pivotal player in the economy and accumulated a fortune on the magnitude of $5 billion to $20 billion (Abrahamian 1982, p. 437).

26. An extreme example was that the government tried to modernize Tehran's bakeries by replacing local bread with French and English processed bread. This ignored consumer taste and was nutritionally deficient. A more practical policy would have been to modernize traditional bread making rather than supplant it with bread nobody wanted.

27. The government invested U.S. aid in hydroelectric dams that were never finished because of insufficient funding (Amuzegar 1993, p. 125–27; Katouzian 1981, p. 204). Public investment in manufacturing was wasted on unproductive projects, such as the development of chemical-fertilizer plants, which were shut down within six months of their establishment (Katouzian 1981, p. 204). Such projects were criticized as serving upper-class society at the expense of the nation's poor majority. From 1953 to 1963, consumer-based growth, rather than industrial growth, represented the majority of economic activity (Looney 2006, p. 32).

28. Even though Iran's extraction of raw materials increased, the overall productivity of its manufacturing base declined, as most production was devoted to

consumer goods rather than capital investment (Keddie 2003, pp. 158–60; Looney 2006, pp. 32, 75).

29. The population of Tehran nearly doubled, from 2,719,730 in 1966 to 4,496,259 in 1976 (Abrahamian 1982, p. 431).

30. World Bank (1983, pp. 44, 148–49).

31. The shah initiated the Green Revolution in 1963 after receiving a donation from President Kennedy of $85 million; the United States insisted in return that the shah liberalize his rule through instituting necessary land reform. This meant extending property rights to peasants and introducing aid and modern capital equipment to assist local farmers in agricultural production (Abrahamian 1982, p. 422). Although the Green Revolution had appealing objectives, its implementation was disastrous for local farmers. Agricultural aid only went to a small number of large agricultural businesses owned by wealthy landlords and elites, thus causing the small farming businesses to be neglected. Such large farm businesses included farm corporations and agribusinesses—corporations owned by multinational firms. Furthermore, the government introduced price controls on wheat and grain products sold in the cities. This move further decreased agricultural revenues for small farmers. The direction of aid toward farm corporations and agribusinesses, and declining crop revenues eventually compelled many peasants to sell their land to these agribusinesses, usually for an unreasonably small amount of money, and move to shanty cities and towns, where they encountered further job uncertainties and poverty (Keddie 2003, pp. 152–54). Many of the grand Ayatollah's foot soldiers allegedly came from this social stratum.

32. Campos and Root (1996).

33. Michael Ross (2001) argues that oil wealth stunts political pluralism. Oil-rich regimes do not have to listen to their people because they do not depend on tax revenues. They can relieve social pressures by employing oil revenues as patronage. Governments can repress opposition and prevent the formation of independent groups that would demand rights.

34. Gasiorowski (1991).

35. Robert Moss, "Who's Meddling in Iran?" *New Republic,* December 2, 1978, pp. 15–18.

36. The Marxist-Leninist Tudeh and Fedai Khalq were among those who hoped that a Socialist revolution had begun, but only Khomeini had an extensive network of followers throughout the country.

37. After the shah's departure, the intelligentsia was the first to hold positions of high authority, but in short order, their lack of an adequate institutional base rendered their tenure in office unstable.

38. In this vein, see Looney (2006).

39. Islamic Republic of Iran (1999, p. 5).

40. Ibid., p. 139.

41. Ibid., p. 16.

42. Ibid., p. 5.

43. Ibid., p. 16.

44. Ibid., p. 15.

45. Citizens elect the president, the deputies to the Islamic Consultative Assembly, and members to local Islamic Councils. The Assembly elects jurists to the Council of Guardians. Citizens also have the right to approve constitutional amendments by referendum. The Supreme Leader, the highest authority, is elected by the Assembly of Experts. Coordinating the three branches of government—executive, legislative, and judiciary—and determining general policies and plans, including the five-year development plans, are the responsibilities of the Supreme Leader.

46. Pollack (2006).

47. Many commentators suggest that East Asia followed a course of growth with equity because of its presumed ethnic homogeneity, but this does not explain the region's differences with Iraq.

Chapter Ten

Reischauer is quoted in Eustace Seligman's *What the United States Can Do about India*; Tariq Azim Khan is quoted in David E. Sanger and David Rohde, "U.S. Is Likely to Continue Aid to Pakistan," *New York Times*, November 5, 2007.

1. Cohen and Chollet (2007, pp. 7–19).

2. Bhutto (1969, p. 53).

3. Kaul (1980, p. 99).

4. The United States provided India with nearly $10 billion in aid between 1951 and the early 1970s. During this period, India was the largest single recipient of U.S. economic assistance, receiving 36 percent of U.S. foreign aid. In 1971, bilateral aid virtually ceased, except for a limited amount sent under Public Law 480, the Food for Peace Program, and was not resumed until 1978. Subsequent allocations never reached earlier levels (U.S. Congress, House Ways and Means Committee 2004).

5. Prasad (1979, p. 71). On April 26, 1942, Gandhi was quoted as saying, "We know what American aid means. It amounts in the end to American influence, if not for American Rule, added to British" (Bhutto 1969, p. 37).

6. Chandrasekhar (1965, p. 64); *Congressional Record,* June 28, 1952, p. 8551.

7. Merrill (1990, p. 13).

8. See Farooq Sulehria, "Emperors and Dictators," Labor Party of Pakistan website (www.laborpakistan.org/articles/pakistan/dictatoremperor.php).

9. Merrill (1990, p. 96).

10. Bhutto (1969, p. 43).

11. Ibid., p. 44.

12. Chandrasekhar (1965, pp. 61–62).

13. Allende in Chile, Bhutto in Pakistan, and Sukarno in Indonesia were among the many third world leaders who, like Nehru, believed socialism was compatible with democracy.

14. This notion is articulated by the economist Robert Barro (1997).

15. Seligman (1956, p. 25).

16. Cited in Merrill (1990, p. 38).

17. Ibid., p. 44.

18. Palmer (1984, p. 125).

19. Korbel (2002).

20. Seligman (1956, p. 33).

21. SEATO prominently influenced the intercountry aid allocations in 1955. In Pakistan and Thailand, especially, aid was related to enhancing military capabilities.

22. Cohen (1980, p. 104).

23. Merrill (1990, p. 106).

24. Gopal (1975–1984).

25. The political scientist A. Organski originated the theory of power transitions. Power transition theory relates the cyclic nature of war to power in international relations and appeared originally in Organski's textbook, *World Politics* (1958). According to this theory, John Kenneth Galbraith was correct, that the closer India and Pakistan came to parity, the more likely they would be to engage in war. As two countries approach parity, the more relations will become adversarial. The median voter theory upon which power transition theory is based holds that as two parties with widely divergent beliefs or preferences approach parity, they become more confrontational, more willing to challenge each other (see Tammen and others 2000).

26. Phillips and Poplai (1958, p. 89).

27. Wolf (1960, p. 204).

28. India conducted its first nuclear test in 1974.

29. On August 10, 1971, the *New York Times* editorialized: "The incredible United States decision to keep supplying arms aid and the aid to Pakistan in spite of the ruthless Pakistani crack-down on autonomy-seeking Bengalis, and especially on Bengali Hindus, has handed Moscow a major foreign policy coup" (cited in Palmer 1984, p. 48).

30. Quoted in Merrill (1990, p. 104).

31. Looney (2001).

32. Bhutto (1969, p. 151).

33. Cohen and Chollet (2007, p. 7–19).

34. National Commission on Terrorist Attacks upon the United States (2004).

35. On October 6, 2007, nearly eight years to the day since taking control of Pakistan in a bloodless coup, President Pervez Musharraf was overwhelmingly reelected. On October 12, 1999, then General Pervez Musharraf had ousted Prime Minister Nawaz Sharif, who fled to Saudi Arabia rather than face corruption charges at home. Eight years later, to ensure cooperation from the country's largest political party, Musharraf dropped corruption charges against the twice-ousted former Prime Minister Benazir Bhutto, allowing her to lead her party in the 2007 parliamentary elections. The rules that bar candidates from serving a third term were ignored for Bhutto. But Nawaz Sharif, also ejected twice on corruption charges, was excluded, his attempt to return home in late September 2007 thwarted. History will note that having toppled one corrupt politician to gain power, President Musharraf made a deal

with another to hold on to power. When asked about the legitimacy of the 2007 vote, Musharraf replied, "If the majority votes for something, it is the rule of the day, that's democracy. There is no problem." See Kamlan Haider, "Musharraf Sweeps the Vote," *Reuters,* October 6, 2007.

36. Secretary of Defense Robert Gates emphasized the need to be "mindful not to do anything that would undermine ongoing counter-terrorism efforts." Such statements have left Pakistanis with little reason to doubt that the war against terror is about America's security, not Pakistan's security.

37. David E. Sanger and David Rohde, "U.S. Is Likely to Continue Aid to Pakistan," *New York Times,* November 5, 2007.

38. As in the other examples, a commitment trap has ensued, with Musharraf believing Washington needs him more than he needs Washington. This leaves the United States with little leverage over decisions, despite its considerable support of the military budget. Musharraf gains his leverage by manipulating the perceived lack of alternatives. Of course, alternatives will not materialize so long as he is allowed to prevent all meaningful political expression among secular alternatives.

39. Wright and Witte (2007).

40. Siddiqa (2007).

41. Asian Development Bank (2004).

42. Most of the $10 billion in U.S. assistance Pakistan received in the five years after September 11, 2001, was channeled through the military (Cohen and Chollet 2007, pp. 7–19). "The majority of the $10 billion, 57 percent, has gone toward Coalition Support Funds, money intended to reimburse U.S. partners for their assistance in the war on terrorism. Roughly 18 percent, or $1.8 billion, has gone toward security assistance. The Pakistanis have spent the majority of this money on purchases of major weapons systems. Another 16 percent has gone toward budget support as direct cash transfer to the government of Pakistan with few real accountability mechanisms built in. This leaves less than 10 percent for development and humanitarian assistance, including the U.S. response to the October 2005 earthquake. Education . . . comes in at only $64 million per year for more than 55 million school-aged children or $1.16 per child per year" (Cohen and Chollet 2007, p. 11–12). Roads, electricity and schools in Baluchistan would have better served both the purposes of development and the mitigation of extremism.

43. A belief that Islamic tendencies make the Pakistani population hostile and unfit for modernity restrains Western enthusiasm for local democratic movements. A stagnant view of Islam during the cold war led many Western observers to mistakenly assume religion would inoculate the region against socialism.

44. Shahid and Shahid (2007, p. 374).

45. General Musharraf finds himself in the uncomfortable position of needing to remind the West of the dangers posed by Islamist groups while at the same time tethering those groups to the military. He cannot afford to either completely eradicate or domesticate the extremist danger, for this would eliminate the raison d'être for military rule. Validating the perception that extremism must be reckoned with, Musharraf

endears himself and the military regime to the West by convincing it that for the time being democracy must be traded for stability (Grare 2007).

46. An *Atlantic Monthly* poll (December 2006) of U.S. Pakistani experts conceded that Pakistan must be perceived "as a partner who is not always helpful, but as least as good as the likely alternatives." Again the military has convinced the U.S. that if it is abandoned many tears will be shed. As one respondent put it, "The widely shared and often articulated belief that 'after Musharraf the deluge' allows him to limit any pressure the United States attempts to apply to get him to more fully cooperate with the United States in the fight against terrorist groups."

Chapter Eleven

Gaddis, in *Strategies of Containment,* reports Roosevelt's use of this proverb.

1. Maliki's defiance of U.S. wishes includes a long list of governance failures, according to a classified memo by National Security Adviser Stephen J. Hadley, the text of which was published by the *New York Times.* These failures could precipitate the dissolution of the regime, plunging Iraq into civil war. "Text of Security Advisor's Iraq Memo," *New York Times,* November 29, 2006 (www.nytimes.com/2006/11/29world/middleest/29mtext.html?). Hadley observed that "removal of Iraq's most effective commanders on a sectarian basis and efforts to ensure Shi'a majorities in all ministries—when combined with the escalation of sectarian killings by Shi'a militias such as the Jaish al-Mahdi's—all suggest a campaign to consolidate Shi'a power in Baghdad." Maliki, Hadley added, was unable "to take action against the interests of his own Shi'a coalition and for the benefit of Iraq as a whole." He concluded that "the reality on the streets of Baghdad suggests Maliki is either ignorant of what is going on, misrepresenting his intentions, or that his capabilities are not yet sufficient to turn his good intentions into action." The Maliki regime failed to foster cross-sectarian cooperation, divide up the oil revenues, establish regional governments, or establish criteria for national reconciliation. Yet President Bush praised Maliki for being the right guy to govern Iraq, for representing the weak but liberal mainstream of Iraqi society.

2. The theoretical link between aid and dependency was considered by David Baldwin (1985): "Other things being equal, the greater the donor's gain from the aid relationship, the more dependent he is on maintaining the relationship and the less able he is to make credible threats to forgo it" (pp. 306–08). Thomas Schelling (1960, p. 11) has theorized that common interests weaken the credibility of a threat.

3. Marshall got both parties to agree to a cease-fire while he attempted to persuade Chiang Kai-shek to convene an assembly with Communist leaders. Unfortunately, military confrontations between the Nationalists and the Communists continued, and the Kuomintang limited the veto powers of the Communists, reaffirming the presidential power of Chiang Kai-shek so that a genuine cabinet system could not be formed and provincial autonomy was rejected. Democratic reconstruction was undermined by assassinations of leftists. Nationalist troops amassed for an assault on Manchuria despite the cease-fire. The National Assembly failed, and in January 1947,

Marshall announced the failure of his mission. Nevertheless, on August 10, 1946, President Truman wrote a letter to Chiang stating: "American faith in the peaceful and democratic aspirations of the Chinese people has not been destroyed by recent events, but has been shaken."

4. In Rubin (1980, p. 42).

5. Macdonald (1992).

6. There was no risk of losing South Korean support for the war against the north in the 1950s, but there was a chance that a democratic Korea in the 1970s might not support Korean participation in the Vietnam War.

7. Keohane (1971).

8. Cited in Macdonald (1992, p. 45).

9. Thomas Sowell, "Diversity's Oppressions: Why Iraq Has Proven to Be So Hard to Pacify," *Wall Street Journal*, October 30, 2006 (www.opinionjournal.com/editorial/feature.html?id=110009170).

10. Max Boot, "Many Dead Ends in Iraq," *Los Angeles Times*, November 8, p. A43.

Chapter Twelve

Wilson is quoted in Louis Brandeis, *Other People's Money and How the Bankers Use It*, chapter 10.

1. The liberalizing role played by the commercial middle classes during modernization is a central idea of Lipset (1959).

2. Anatoly Chubais's privatization program aimed to foment a *bourgeois revolution* by creating a class with a direct interest in rapid economic growth but privatization has not produced demands for political representation in large part because the Russian state survives on rents generated by mineral exports. Since the state captures the bulk of these rents it does have to build mechanisms for taxation and consent. See Boycko (1995) and Shleifer and Treisman (2000, p. 1–20).

3. Mandelbaum (2007, p. 114–15).

4. Pastor (1999, p. 342–43).

5. An analogous argument that links the overthrow of European absolutism to the rise of the commercial bourgeoisie originates in the theory that the French Revolution was the triumph of capitalism over feudalism. The argument for the bourgeois origin of liberal democracy has been revised by historians who have shown that it was not the interests of a single social class that caused the edifice of European absolutism to collapse. Representatives of all social classes were instrumental in the outcome. An entire generation of French historians, led by the Briton Alfred Cobban, the Frenchman François Furet, and the American George Taylor, played roles in laying to rest one of the most persistent dogmas in the history of democratic idealism.

6. In the ideal democratic marketplace, all consumers have access to the same information; traders organize as if each had access to all of the economy's information. Large and liquid financial markets, broad property-rights protection, corporate disclosure, and third-party audits allow individual traders to engage in profitable risk

arbitrage: when efficient market conditions are met, the price system will guide the economy toward market efficiency. Open information access will allow competitive resource allocation to occur as if directed by an invisible hand. The small actors pool their capital and invest in the projects of strangers, often guided by institutional intermediaries. Pooling, by harnessing the power of the law of large numbers, allows optimally efficient financing of projects by directing capital to its highest value. As markets mature, the quest for outside funds leads corporate managers to submit to outside monitoring and control in order to raise capital from publicly managed institutions. The efficiency of capital markets motivates corporate governance to become more transparent. The stakeholders—management, shareholders, labor, and consumers—have an interest in ensuring that the laws are enforced and that mandates exist to ensure adequate funding of public agencies responsible for enforcing the rules. In such settings, Adam Smith's intuition might be applicable and private wealth and social agendas could be complementary. Wilson's political ideals extend Adam Smith's economic vision.

However, much contemporary research has revealed that this simple view of competitive markets misrepresents managerial incentives. We know that markets are only responsible for a part of all possible economic exchanges; many of the most important contributions to growth come from the innovations by traders to surmount the informational gaps of the market. Joseph Stiglitz (2003), for example, has argued that market economy models that focus on prices provide poor descriptions of actual economies because they inadequately treat information problems. Once informational asymmetries between market participants are recognized, we observe that the principles of competitive markets are destabilized by the gap between de facto and de jure rights; in no society are property rights perfectly assigned.

Sandford Grossman points out that if markets were completely informationally efficient, there would be no role for traders who specialize in market information; intermediaries such as Merrill Lynch, Goldman Sachs, or Morgan Stanley would have no productive role to play. In fact, however, absent such specialization, trade would collapse. Since trade depends upon information that is privately collected, it is unrealistic to assume that market prices fully reveal all necessary information. Completely competitive market prices would reduce the incentives for the production of information, and many markets would simply close or not come into existence at all if uninformed traders could ride on the efforts of informed traders. Yet it is the gospel of such idealized notions of markets that inspires faith in economic growth as the stimulus for global democracy.

7. Root (2006, chapter 3); Rajan and Zingales (2006).

8. See Reich (2007) and Stiglitz (2003).

9. Greif (2006).

10. The complexity of business organizations that flourish under conditions of uncertainty does not necessarily correspond with a country's wealth. Some rich countries, such as the oil economies of the Middle East, have highly underdeveloped market institutions, and state actors that control natural resources display little interest in

encouraging private opportunities or championing strong market institutions. Where market institutions are rudimentary, traders depend on blood ties to organize trade. Illegal transactions often thrive because members of the same extended family will rarely cooperate with state authorities against the interests of their clan. Mafias fill in where market formality breaks down, further voiding state institutions of legitimacy.

11. Khanna and Rivkin (2001) explore the advantages conferred by family ownership, examining affiliated firms in fourteen nations. They emphasize the insurance, or risk-mitigating, logic of taking coordinated action, finding that affiliated firms share both benefits and costs.

12. Khanna and Palepu (2000) and Khanna and Rivkin (2001) explain that affiliation compensates for poorly functioning market institutions. In a similar vein, Leff (1976, 1978) writes about how group organization reduces market frictions.

13. In the U.S. automobile industry, for example, the Ford family controls Ford Motors and has no interest or shares in its competitors Chrysler and General Motors. Ford is an exception. In the United States, *family firm* generally means a small firm. Most large firms enjoy diffuse rather than concentrated family ownership. Typically, in the United States one firm or family does not own shares in rivals, is not controlled by insider voting, and is professionally managed, in sharp contrast to the conditions in most emerging markets, where concentrated family ownership is the norm.

14. Morck, Wolfenzon, and Yeung (2005).

15. Seeking to prevent a few families united by caste from spreading their influence over the entire economy, India's first prime minister, Jawaharlal Nehru, promoted state ownership of India's industrial and financial wealth, protecting state-owned corporations from internal and external competition and small firms from large enterprises. However, his approach to balancing competition and cooperation ended as a vehicle for politicians to funnel jobs and projects to their backers.

16. The pattern was introduced to the region during the pre-World War II period by Japan. In most of Asia today, firm ownership structures vest control rights in the hands of a few minority owners who invest very little of their own wealth to command an overwhelming percentage of their nation's listed assets; see Root (2006, pp. 64–73).

17. Few developing countries are attracted by the American idea of regulating monopoly power in order to control it. Introducing U.S.-style antitrust laws is not feasible where strong vested interests will interfere with implementation. In the face of entrenched inequality, government commitment to maintain a competitive marketplace is rarely credible.

18. Fisman (2001). In Indonesia, an important component of the share price of well-connected firms can be positively attributed to political connections. Mara Faccio (2002, p. 369–86) reports that the shares of certain companies increase noticeably when a shareholder becomes prime minister.

19. A number of cross-country studies reveal that Anglo and American corporations surpass their rivals around the world in accountability, predictability, transparency, and shareholder participation. Most Anglo and American corporations are owned by shareholders, not by wealthy families. Corporate boards are selected in a

relatively transparent manner. They disseminate information about their activities, their liabilities, and their assets openly, and they are bound by rules that protect shareholder rights and ensure third-party audits of company accounts. One of the most important results of this activism is the creation of a democratic marketplace of information accessible to shareholders, labor, consumers, and the public at large, which includes access to essential data about firm assets, liabilities, and ownership. Transparent corporate governance practices reflect the interventions of several generations of political activism on the part of shareholders, labor, and consumers.

20. Reich (2007).

21. The fallacy of this perspective, which attributed the rise of democracy to the rise of the middle classes, is well documented by social historians of the French Revolution. Yet patient historical analysis of the social origins of the French Revolution has conclusively revealed that the commercial middle classes were not the great catalysts of political change that modernization theorists predicted. The most studied democratic transition in history has revealed that the French commercial classes of the eighteenth century were not more responsive as a group to the drumbeat of democracy than were the nobility or the peasantry. The French monarchy itself, as Alexis de Tocqueville wrote in his classic study of Old Regime France, triggered a demand for egalitarian social conditions by inadvertently inculcating democratic norms through the expansion of a kingdom-wide bureaucracy and court system, and by endowing peasant communities with the tools to challenge traditional hierarchy by offering access to both the king's administration and his justice. See Root (1985).

22. Bueno de Mesquita and Downs (2005) argue that consumption of material goods can substitute for political freedom.

23. Li and Reuveny (2003).

24. Boix and Garicano (2001).

25. Hiscox and Kastner (2004) have found that democracies that open themselves to trade without social insurance are prone to failure. Authoritarian regimes that open to trade but do not spend on redistribution are less vulnerable to political challenge and failure.

26. Williams (1976, p. 54),

Chapter Thirteen

Jefferson is quoted in Abraham D. Sofaer, "The Presidency, War, and Foreign Affairs: Practice under the Framers," *Law and Contemporary Problems,* vol. 40, no. 2, p. 22.

1. This group typically had to vie for influence with advisers who were grounded in domestic politics. As the cold war consensus broke down and domestic policy debates became more acrimonious and public opinion more polarized, the relative importance of domestic policy credentials increased.

2. The U.S. helped defeat the leftist Huks, who had fought against the Japanese invaders. See Thompson (1975).

3. Rogowski (2000).

4. Summers (1982, p. 183).

5. Macdonald (1992, p. 24).

6. During the Cold War, Southeast Asia enjoyed high priority because of its importance in securing democracy against Communism. The U.S. intervention in Korea was undertaken because of perceived security risks. The war in Vietnam offered few economic benefits to offset its costs. In the Philippines, U.S. decisionmaking always waived considerations about economic interests. U.S. businesses operating in the Philippines frequently complained that the U.S. embassy assigned their investments low priority compared with military security questions.

7. Guess (1987, p. 91).

8. Guess (1987, preface).

9. Feinberg (1983, p. 79).

10. Jervis and Snyder (1993).

Chapter Fourteen

1. Westad (2005, p. 380–81). Opposition was growing within the Soviet Union as a result of the rising costs of an interventionist foreign policy that added pressure to a stagnating economy.

2. Ibid., pp. 381, 383, 387.

3. Gilman (2003).

4. Micklethwait and Wooldridge (2004, pp. 295–300, 303–08) attribute differences between Europe and the United States on matters of diplomacy and security to American exceptionalism. Two cataclysmic events—the end of the Cold War and September 11—were catalysts that triggered already existing exceptional tendencies. Americans are traditionally keen on limiting the size of the state and are relatively indifferent to inequality. Both of these characteristics influence the U.S. views on development policy. Americans tend to be optimistic about their own chances for social mobility and to repudiate class warfare.

5. In a chapter called "America's Fatwas," Alice H. Amsden writes (2007, pp. 127–37) that during the 1980s, U.S. developmental policy went from permissive to ideological, imposing rigid and inappropriate limits to intellectual inquiry and policy advice.

6. Holland (1995, 1998).

7. Japanese still dream of a democracy based on policy competition rather than on subsidies and cronies. The coherence and predictability of policy have been largely driven by the bureaucracy, but transparency to voters remains weak.

8. South Korea and Japan did not have to confront the possibility of internal ethnocentric polarization aggressively, but that possibility did exist in Malaysia, Singapore, Indonesia, Thailand, and Taiwan.

9. Medley, pp. 65, 70.

10. Ibid., pp. 39–40.

11. Ibid., pp. 39–40, 69–70.

12. Wiegersma and Medley (2000).

13. Hook (2005, pp. 381–83) points out that the Universal Declaration of Human Rights adopted by the United Nations in 1948 incorporates social and economic rights into its definition of human rights, whereas the United States adheres to a more narrowly defined notion of political liberty and civil rights.

14. Root (2006, pp. 221–45).

15. Satter (2003).

16. Wintrobe (2007) offers a systematic theory of the difference between tyrannies and totalitarian states and illustrates how the right policy varies according to a dictatorship's type. For example, sanctions reduce repression in totalitarian regimes but increase it in tin-pot regimes. He concludes that the right policy is not always obvious, even if the United States pursues idealistic objectives such as reducing repression.

17. "In autocracies, leaders do not have to satisfy a majority; they have more latitude to do what they want with the economic surplus they control. . . . In fact, the variance in economic growth rates between autocracies is about twice what it is for democracies" (Bueno de Mesquita and Root, 2000, p. 6).

18. Contrary to popular belief, the transition to democracy generally reduces governance as measured by governmental effectiveness, rule of law, and anticorruption because most transitional, young democracies have inadequate safeguards against capture by wealthy and well-organized minorities (Kaufmann, 2005).

19. The link between democratic social conditions and the well-being of democratic practices was an essential insight of Tocqueville, which he expressed in *Democracy in America*. Family farming was a foundation on which egalitarian social norms could consolidate. Another initial condition that allowed American democracy to survive and overcome the ossification of class was the frontier, which allowed new groups to emerge that accrued the resources necessary to alter the status quo.

20. Epstein and others (2006).

21. I thank Ray Bowen for making this suggestion at the Mercatus Center manuscript conference, George Mason University (May 12, 2007).

22. Similar concerns were voiced by the authors of a study conducted by the Massachusetts Institute of Technology, Center for International Studies, "The Objectives of United States Economic Assistance Programs," Foreign Aid Program: Compilation of Studies and Surveys, prepared under the direction of the Special Committee to Study the Foreign Aid Program, 85th Cong., 1st sess., 1957, Senate Doc. no. 52.

23. Development agencies such as the World Bank do not generally support policing in borrowing-member countries, and the Defense Department has other priorities. Within the U.S. aid establishment, budgets for technical assistance to local police forces are divided among several government agencies and are often highly inadequate for sustained training.

24. As reported in "Petraeus on Vietnam's Legacy," *Washington Post*, January 14, 2007.

25. Inglehart and Welzel (2005) discuss how discrepancies between culture and institutions create pressures for regime change: "The stability of political regimes depends on the degree of congruence between political institutions and mass values:

political institutions must be consistent with the citizens' value orientation or they will not be seen as legitimate, and their stability will be low. The greater the incongruence between mass values and political institutions, the more unstable the regime will be" (p. 186).

26. Baldwin (1985, pp. 306–07).

27. Schelling (1960, p. 11).

28. Under the spell of neoconservatism, the Bush administration did less than its recent predecessors to expand and strengthen the international trading system.

29. The belief in critical self-organization may prove as illusionary as the belief that unfettered markets are a sure way to efficiency (Page, 2001, pp. 25–48).

30. Baldwin (1985, pp. 325–34).

31. Root (2006, chapter 12).

32. Root (2006, chapter 2).

33. Campos and Root (1996).

34. See Paulson and Townsend (2001) and Townsend and Ueda (2001, 2003).

35. Root (1996).

36. The social organization and systems of household risk sharing that characterize preindustrial societies undergo shifts that destroy social capital. Many members of the population lose access to traditional safety networks. Although a large number of groups are left without compensation, the perceived socioeconomic gap may be wider than the actual one. In Latin America, privatization is perceived as reducing employment and creating inequality, but econometric data reveal a more balanced outcome.

37. Chua (2004).

38. Bizot (2004, pp. 34–35).

39. Ibid.

40. Tammen and others (2000).

References

Abrahamian, E. 1982. *Iran between Two Revolutions.* Princeton University Press.

Acheson, Dean. 1969. *Present at the Creation: My Years at the State Department.* New York: Norton.

Alesina, Alberto, and David Dollar. 2000. "Who Gives Foreign Aid to Whom and Why?" *Journal of Economic Growth* 5, no. 1(March): 33–63.

Amsden, Alice H. 2007. *Escape from Empire: The Developing World's Journey through Heaven and Hell.* MIT Press.

Amuzegar, J. 1993. *Iran's Economy under the Islamic Republic.* London: I. B. Tauris.

Asia Foundation. 2004. *Public Perceptions of U.S.-Philippine Relations.* Washington, D.C.

Asian Development Bank. 2004. *Technical Assistance to the Islamic Republic of Pakistan for Implementing Public Safety Reforms in Four Districts of the Province of Punjab.* December 2004, www.adb.org/Documents/TARs/PAK/tar-pak-38576.pdf.

Auty, Richard M. 1993. *Sustaining Development in Mineral Economies: The Resource Curse Thesis.* New York: Routledge.

Axelrod, R. 1984. *The Evolution of Cooperation.* New York: Basic Books.

Axtell, R., J. M. Epstein, and H. P. Young. 2000. "The Emergence of Classes in a Multi-Agent Bargaining Model." Working Paper. Brookings Institution.

Bacevich, Andrew J. 2002. *American Empire: The Realities and Consequences of U.S. Diplomacy.* Harvard University Press.

Bak, Per. 1996. *How Nature Works: The Science of Self-Organized Criticality.* New York: Springer-Verlag.

Baldwin, David A. 1985. *Economic Statecraft.* Princeton University Press.

Balisacan, A. M., and H. Hill. 2003. *The Philippine Economy: Development, Policies, and Challenges.* Oxford University Press.

Barrett, David D. 1970. *Dixie Mission: The United States Army Observer Group in Yenan, 1944.* University of California–Berkeley, Center for Chinese Studies.

Barro, Robert J. 1997. *Determinants of Economic Growth: A Cross-Country Empirical Study.* MIT Press.

Beinhocker, E. D. 2006. *The Origin of Wealth: Evolution, Complexity, and the Radical Remaking of Economics.* Boston: Harvard Business School Press.

Berman, Sheri. 2003. "Islamism, Revolution, and Civil Society." *Perspective on Politics* 1, no. 2: 257–72.

Bhutto, Z. A. 1969. *The Myth of Independence.* Oxford University Press.

Bill, J. A. 1988. *The Eagle and the Lion: The Tragedy of American-Iranian Relations.* Yale University Press.

Bizot, François. 2004. *The Gate.* New York: Vintage.

Blum, W. 2000. *Rogue State: A Guide to the World's Only Superpower.* Monroe, Me.: Common Courage Press.

Boix, Charles, and Luis Garicano. 2001. "Democracy, Inequality and Country-Specific Wealth." University of Chicago. Typescript (www.yale.edu/leitner/pdf/PEW-Boix.pdf).

Bonner, Raymond. 1987. *Waltzing with a Dictator: The Marcoses and the Making of American Policy.* New York: Times Books.

Boone, Peter. 1996. "Politics and the Effectiveness of Foreign Aid." *European Economic Review* 40, no. 2: 289–329.

Boycko, M., and others. 1995. *Privatizing Russia.* MIT Press.

Brainard, Lael, ed. 2007. *Security by Other Means: Foreign Assistance, Global Poverty, and American Leadership.* Brookings.

Brandeis, Louis. 1995. *Other People's Money and How the Bankers Use It* (New York: Bedford Books/St. Martin's Press, 1995; originally published 1914).

Brands, H. W. 1992. *Bound to Empire: The United States and the Philippines.* Oxford University Press.

Bueno de Mesquita, Bruce, and G. W. Downs. 2005. "Development and Democracy." *Foreign Affairs* 84, no. 5: 77–88.

Bueno de Mesquita, Bruce, and Alastair Smith. 2007. "Foreign Aid and Policy Concessions." *Journal of Conflict Resolution* 51, no. 2: 251–84.

Bueno de Mesquita, Bruce, Alastair Smith, Randolph M. Siverson, and James D. Morrow. 2003. *The Logic of Political Survival.* MIT Press.

Bueno de Mesquita, Bruce, and Hilton Root. 2000. *Governing for Prosperity.* Yale University Press.

Burnside, C., and David Dollar. 2000. "Aid, Policies, and Growth." *American Economic Review* 90, no. 4: 847–68.

Bush, George W. 2005. Speech given at the National Endowment for Democracy, Washington, D.C., October 6, www.presidentialrhetoric.com/speeches/10.06.05.html.

Buss, Claude A. 1977. *The United States and the Philippines: Background for Policy.* Washington: American Enterprise Institute.

Buttinger, J. 1967. *Vietnam: A Dragon Embattled.* New York: Praeger.

Campos, Jose Eduardo, and Hilton L. Root. 1996. *The Key to the Asian Miracle: Making Shared Growth Credible.* Brookings.

Catton, P. 2002. *Diem's Final Failure: Prelude to America's War in Vietnam.* University Press of Kansas.

Celoza, A. F. 1997. *Ferdinand Marcos and the Philippines: The Political Economy of Authoritarianism.* Westport, Conn.: Praeger.

Center for Defense Information. 2007. "U.S. Arms Exports and Military Assistance in the 'Global War on Terror.'" Press release, September 27.

Chandrasekhar, S. 1965. *American Aid and India's Economic Development.* New York: Praeger.

Chevrier, Yves. 2004. *Mao and the Chinese Revolution.* Northampton, Mass.: Interlink Publishing Group.

Chua, Amy. 2004. *World on Fire: How Exporting Free Market Democracy Breeds Ethnic Hatred and Global Instability.* New York: Anchor Books.

Cohen, C., and Derek Chollet. 2007. "When $10 billion Is Not Enough: Rethinking U.S. Strategy toward Pakistan." *Washington Quarterly* 30, no. 2(2007): 7–19.

Cohen, Stephen P. 1980. "South Asia and U.S. Military Policy." In Lloyd I. Rudolph and Susanne Hoeber Rudolph, eds., *The Regional Imperative: U.S. Foreign Policy towards South Asian States under Presidents Johnson and Nixon.* Atlantic Highlands, N.J.: Humanities Press.

Coleman, James S. 1990. *Foundations of Social Theory.* Harvard University Press.

Collier, Paul. 2007. *The Bottom Billion: Why the Poorest Countries Are Failing and What Can Be Done about It.* Oxford University Press.

Collins, John M. 1998. *Military Geography for Professionals and the Public.* Washington: National Defense University Press.

Cortes, R., ed. 1999. *Philippine Presidents 100 Years.* Quezon City, Philippines: New Day Publishers.

Cottam, R. 1977. *Foreign Policy Motivation: A General Theory and a Case Study.* University of Pittsburgh Press.

Cullather, N. 1994. *Illusions of Influence: The Political Economy of United States–Philippines, 1942–1960.* Stanford University Press.

Dacy, D. C. 1986. *Foreign Aid, War, and Economic Development: South Vietnam, 1955–1975.* Cambridge University Press.

Day, R. H. 2004. *The Divergent Dynamics of Economic Growth: Studies in Adaptive Economizing, Technological Change, and Economic Development.* Cambridge University Press.

Destler, I. M. 1998. "Foreign Economic Policy Making under Bill Clinton." In James M. Scott, ed., *After the End: Making U.S. Foreign Policy in the Post–Cold War World.* Duke University Press.

De Dios, E., and P. Hutchcroft. 2003. "Political Economy." In A. Balisacan and H. Hill, eds., *The Philippine Economy: Development, Policies, and Challenges.* Oxford University Press.

De Soto, Hernando. 2002. *Other Path: The Economic Answer to Terrorism.* New York: Basic Books.

———. 1989. *Other Path: The Invisible Revolution in the Third World.* London: Tauris.

Dickson, B. 2003. *Red Capitalists in China: The Party, Private Entrepreneurs and Prospects for Political Change.* Cambridge University Press.

Duncanson, D. 1968. *Government and Revolution in Vietnam.* Oxford University Press.

Easterly, William. 2002. *The Elusive Quest for Growth.* MIT Press.

———. 2006. *The White Man's Burden: Why the West's Efforts to Aid the Rest Have Done So Much Ill and So Little Good.* New York: Penguin.

Edwards, George, and others. 2000. *Government in America: People, Politics and Policy.* New York: Longman.

Epstein, D., R. Bates, J. Goldstone, I. Kristensen, and S. O'Halloran. 2006. "Democratic Transitions." *American Journal of Political Science* 50, no. 3: 551–69.

Epstein, Joshua. M. 2006. *Generative Social Science: Studies in Agent-Based Computational Modeling.* Princeton University Press.

Esherick, J. W. 2003. "Ten Theses on the Chinese Revolution." In *Twentieth-Century China: New Approaches.* London, New York: Routledge.

Faccio, Mara, and L. H. P. Lang. 2002. "The Ultimate Ownership of Western European Corporations." *Journal of Financial Economics.* 65, no. 3: 365–95.

Fall, Bernard. 1963. *The Two Viet-Nams: A Political and Military Analysis.* New York: Praeger.

Feinberg, R. E. 1983. *The Intemperate Zone: The Third World Challenge to U.S. Foreign Policy.* New York: Norton.

Ferrie, J. P. 2005. "The End of American Exceptionalism? Mobility in the United States since 1850." *Journal of Economic Perspectives,* 19, no. 3: 172–99.

Fisman, R. 2001. "Estimating the Value of Political Connections." *American Economic Review* 91, no. 4: 1095–1102.

Gaddis, John Lewis. 2005. *Strategies of Containment: A Critical Appraisal of American National Security Policy during the Cold War.* Oxford University Press.

Gasiorowski, M. 1991. *U.S. Foreign Policy and the Shah: Building a Client State in Iran.* Cornell University Press.

Gause, F. G., III. 2005. "Can Democracy Stop Terrorism?" *Foreign Affairs* 84, no. 5: 62–76.

Gilman, Nils. 2003. *Mandarins of the Future: Modernization Theory in Cold War America.* Johns Hopkins University Press.

Girling, John L. S. 1980. *America and the Third World: Revolution and Intervention.* London: Routledge & Kegan Paul.

Gopal, S. 1975–1984. *Jawaharlal Nehru: A Biography.* 3 vols. Harvard University Press.

Grare, Frederic. 2006a. "Islam, Militarism, and the 2007–2008 Elections in Pakistan." Carnegie Paper 70. Washington: Carnegie Endowment for International Peace, July.

———. 2006b. "Pakistan: The Myth of an Islamist Peril." Policy Brief No. 45. Washington: Carnegie Endowment for International Peace, February.

———. 2007. "Rethinking Western Strategies toward Pakistan: An Action Agenda for the United States and Europe." Washington: Carnegie Endowment for International Peace.

Greif, A. 2006. *Institutions and the Path to the Modern Economy: Lessons from Medieval Trade.* Cambridge University Press.

Grimmett, Richard F. 2007. "Conventional Arms Transfers to Developing Nations, 1999–2006." Report prepared for U.S. Congress. Washington: Congressional Research Service, September 26.

Grossman, Sanford. 1976. "On the Efficiency of Competitive Stock Markets Where Traders Have Diverse Information." *Journal of Finance* 31, no. 2: 573–85.

Guess, G. M. 1987. *The Politics of United States Foreign Aid.* New York: St. Martin's Press.

Halberstam, David. 1965. *The Making of a Quagmire.* New York: Random House.

Halliday, F. 1980. "The Gulf between Two Revolutions: 1958–1979." *Merip Reports* 83 (February): 6–15.

Hammond, Scott J., Kevin R. Hardwick, and Howard Leslie Lubert. 2007. *Classics of American Political and Constitutional Thought.* Indianapolis: Hackett.

Harries, Owen. 1986. "The Idea of a Third Force." *National Interest* 3 (Spring): 3–7.

Harrison, Selig S. 1981. *In Afghanistan's Shadow: Baluch Nationalism and Soviet Temptations.* Washington: Carnegie Endowment for International Peace.

Hartz, Louis. 1955. *The Liberal Tradition in American Politics.* New York: Harcourt Brace.

Herrin, A. N., and E. M. Pernia. 2003. "Population, Human Resources, and Employment." In A. Baliscan and H. Hill, eds., *The Philippine Economy: Development, Policies, and Challenges.* Oxford University Press.

Hirsh, Michael. 2003. *At War with Ourselves: Why America Is Squandering Its Chance to Build a Better World.* Oxford University Press.

Herring, G. C. 1996. *America's Longest War: The United States and Vietnam, 1950–1975.* New York: McGraw-Hill.

Hiscox, Michael, and Scott Kastner. 2004. "Trade Policy Openness, Government Spending, and Democratic Consolidation: A Preliminary Analysis." Paper presented at the annual meeting of the International Studies Association. Quebec, Le Centre Sheraton Hotel (March 17). Available at www.allacademic.com/meta/p73404_index.html.

Hoan, B. 1958. "The Consequences of the Geneva Peace for the Vietnamese Economy." *Far Eastern Economic Review* 18: 753–57, 839–42.

Hobbes, Thomas. 2006. *Leviathan.* Mineola, N.Y.: Dover.

Hoffman, Stanley. 1983. *Dead Ends: American Foreign Policy in the New Cold War.* Cambridge, Mass.: Ballinger.

Holland, John H. 1995. *Hidden Order: How Adaptation Builds Complexity.* Reading, Mass.: Addison-Wesley/Helix Books.

———. 1998. *Emergence: From Chaos to Order.* Reading, Mass.: Addison-Wesley/Helix Books.

Holsti, O. R. 1998. "Public Opinion and U.S. Foreign Policy after the Cold War." In James M. Scott, ed., *After the End: Making U.S. Foreign Policy in the Post–Cold War World.* Duke University Press

Honda, K. 1999. *The Nanjing Massacre*. Armonk, N.Y.: M. E. Sharpe.

Hook, Steven W. 2005. *U.S. Foreign Policy: The Paradox of World Power*. Washington: CQ Press.

Huang, H. L. 2000. "The Chiang Kai-shek Regime and State Crime in China and Taiwan, 1927–1975." Ph.D. dissertation, University of Kansas.

Inglehart, Ronald, and Christian Welzel. 2005. *Modernization, Cultural Change and Democracy: The Human Development Sequence*. Cambridge University Press.

Islamic Republic of Iran. 1999. *United Nations in the Islamic Republic of Iran and Plan and Budget Organization of the Islamic Republic of Iran: 1999*. Human Development Report of the Islamic Republic of Iran. Tehran: Government of Iran.

Jervis, Robert, and Jack L. Snyder. 1993. *Coping with Complexity in the International System*. Boulder: Westview.

Jespersen, T. C. 1996. *American Images of China: 1931–1949*. Stanford University Press.

Johnson, Chalmers. 2004. *The Sorrows of Empire: Militarism, Secrecy, and the End of the Republic*. New York: Henry Holt.

Jumper, Roy. 1957. "Mandarin Bureaucracy and Politics in South Vietnam." *Pacific Affairs* 30: 47–58.

Kahin, G. 1959. *Government and Politics of Southeast Asia*. Cornell University Press.

Kalantari, Behrooz. 2005. "Eastern Public Management: A Cultural Approach to Developmental Administration." *Public Organization Review* 5, no. 2 (June 2005): 125–38.

Katouzian, H. 1981. *The Political Economy of Modern Iran: Despotism and Pseudo-Modernism 1926–1976*. New York: Palgrave Macmillan.

Kaufmann, D., and others. 2005. "Measuring Governance Using Cross-Country Perceptions Data." In S. Rose-Ackerman, ed., *Handbook of Economic Corruption*. Washington: World Bank.

Kaul, T. N. 1984. "The Kissinger Years: Indo-American Relations: New Delhi." In Norman D. Palmer, ed., *The United States and India: The Dimensions of Influence*. New York: Praeger.

Keddie, N. R. 2003. *Modern Iran: Roots and Results of Revolution*. Yale University Press.

Keefer, Philip, and Razvan Vlaicu. 2005. "Democracy, Credibility and Clientelism." Working Paper 3472. Washington: World Bank.

Keeler, John T. S. 1993. "Opening the Window for Reform: Mandates, Crises and Extraordinary Policymaking." *Comparative Political Studies* 25 (January 1993): 433–86.

Kegley, C. W., Jr., and S. W. Hook. 1991. "U.S. Foreign Aid and U.N. Voting: Did Reagan's Linkage Strategy Buy Deference or Defiance?" *International Studies Quarterly* 35, no. 3: 295–312.

Kennan, George F. 1947. "The Sources of Soviet Conduct." *Foreign Affairs* 25: 575–76.

Kennedy, John F. 1960. *The Strategy of Peace*. New York: Harper.

Keohane, Robert O. 1971. "The Big Influence of Small Allies." *Foreign Policy* (Spring 1971): 161–82.

Kerry, Richard. 1990. *The Star-Spangled Mirror: America's Image of Itself and the World.* Lanham, Md.: Rowman & Littlefield.

Khanna, T., and J. W. Rivkin. 2001. "Estimating the Performance Effects of Business Groups in Emerging Markets." *Strategic Management Journal* 22, no. 1: 45–74.

Khanna, T., and K. Palepu. 2000. "Is Group Affiliation Profitable in Emerging Markets? An Analysis of Diversified Indian Business Groups." *Journal of Finance* 55, no. 2: 867–93.

Kinzer, Stephen. 2006. *Overthrow: America's Century of Regime Change from Hawaii to Iraq.* New York: Times Books.

Kirkpatrick, Jeane J. 1982. *Dictatorships and Double Standards: Rationalism and Reason in Politics.* New York: Simon & Schuster.

Kissinger, Henry A. 1969. *American Foreign Policy: Three Essays.* New York: Norton.

———. 1979. *White House Years.* Boston: Little Brown.

———. 1986. "Can We Toss All Dictators to the Wind?" *Newsday,* March 11.

Kochanek, S. A. 1974. *Business and Politics in India.* University of California Press.

Koen, R. 1960. *The China Lobby in American Politics.* New York: Macmillan.

Kolko, Gabriel. 1994. *Anatomy of a War: Vietnam, the United States, and the Modern Historical Experience.* New York: New Press.

———. 1988. *Confronting the Third World: United States Foreign Policy 1945–1980.* New York: Pantheon Books.

Korbel, Josef. 2002. *Danger in Kashmir.* Oxford University Press.

Kubek, A. 1963. *How the Far East Was Lost: American Policy and the Creation of Communist China, 1941–1949.* Chicago: Henry Regnery.

Kurer, Oskar. 1997. *The Political Foundations of Development Policies.* Lanham, Md.: University Press of America.

Kuziemko, I., and Eric Werker. 2006. "How Much Is a Seat on the Security Council Worth? Foreign Aid and Bribery at the United Nations." *Journal of Political Economy* 114, no. 5: 905–30.

Laird, Melvin. 2005. "Iraq: Learning the Lessons of Vietnam." *Foreign Affairs* 84, no. 6: 22–43.

Lappé, Frances Moore, Joseph Collins, and David Kinley. 1980. *Aid as Obstacle: Twenty Questions about Our Foreign Aid and the Hungry.* San Francisco: Institute for Food and Development Policy.

Le, Trong H. 1975. "Survival and Self-Reliance: A Vietnamese Viewpoint." *Asia Survey* 15: 281–300.

Leff, Nathaniel H. 1976. "Capital Markets in the Less Developed Countries: The Group Principle." In R. McKinnon, ed., *Money and Finance in Economic Growth and Development.* New York: Marcel Dekker.

———. 1978. "Industrial Organization and Entrepreneurship in the Developing Countries: The Economic Groups." *Economic Development and Cultural Change* 26, no. 4: 661–75.

Li, Longgeng. 2003. "Renmin Jiefang Zhanzheng (People's liberation war)." In *Zhongguo Jindai Xiandai Shi,* edited by Hongzhi Wang and Mingxun Shi (China's

Modern and Contemporary History). Beijing: Renmin Jiaoyu Chubanshe (People's Educational Press).

Li, Q., and R. Reuveny. 2003. "Economic Globalization and Democracy: An Empirical Analysis." *British Journal of Political Science* 33: 29–54.

Lindholm, R., ed. 1959. *Vietnam: The First Five Years*. Michigan State University Press.

Lipset, Seymour M. 1959. "Some Social Requisites of Democracy: Economic Development and Political Legitimacy." *American Political Science Review* 53, no. 1 (March 1959): 69–105.

Looney, R. E. 1982, *Economic Origins of the Iranian Revolution*. Oxford: Pergamon Press.

———. 2001. "Pakistan's Economy: Achievements, Progress, Contraints, and Prospects," in H. Malik (ed.), *Pakistan: Founders' Aspirations and Today's Realities*. Oxford University Press.

———. 2006. "The Iranian Economy: Crony Capitalism in Islamic Garb." *Milken Institute Review* (First Quarter): 28–37.

Luard, E. 1965. "Chinese Attitudes to the West." In Iyer Raghavan, ed., *The Glass Curtain between Asia and Europe*. Oxford University Press.

Luce, Henry R. 1941. "The American Century." *Life,* February 17, 1941, pp. 61–65.

Lumsdaine, David Halloran. 1993. *Moral Vision in International Politics: The Foreign Aid Regime, 1949–1989*. Princeton University Press.

MacArthur, Douglas. 1964. *Reminiscences*. New York: McGraw-Hill.

Macdonald, D. J. 1992. *Adventures in Chaos: American Intervention for Reform in the Third World*. Harvard University Press.

MacFarlane, A. 1978. *Origins of English Individualism: The Family, Property, and Social Transition*. Cambridge University Press.

MacIntyre, A. 2003. *The Power of Institutions*. Cornell University Press.

Madison, James. 1787. *Federalist Paper Number 10*. "The Same Subject Continued: The Union as a Safeguard against Domestic Faction and Insurrection." *New York Packet,* November 23.

Mandelbaum, M. 2007. *Democracy's Good Name: The Rise and Risks of the World's Most Popular Form of Government*. New York: PublicAffairs.

Manglapus, R. S. 1976. *The Silenced Democracy*. New York: Orbis Books.

Mann, J. 2004. *The Rise of the Vulcans: The History of Bush's War Cabinet*. New York: Viking Press.

Mansfield, M. 1963. "Vietnam and Southeast Asia: A Report to the Committee on Foreign Relations." Washington: Government Printing Office.

Marshall, Monty G., and Keith Jaggers. 2006. *Polity IV Project: Political Regime Characteristics and Transitions 1800–2004*. Center for Global Policy, George Mason University, Arlington, Va., and Center for International Development and Conflict Management, University of Maryland, College Park (www.cidcm.umd.edu/polity).

Melanson, R. A. 2005. *American Foreign Policy since the Vietnam War: The Search for Consensus from Richard Nixon to George W. Bush*. Armonk, N.Y.: M. E. Sharpe.

Melanson, R. A., and D. Meyers. 1987. *Reevaluating Eisenhower: American Foreign Policy in the 1950s*. University of Illinois Press.

Merrill, D. 1990. *Bread and the Ballot: The United States and India's Economic Development, 1947–1963*. University of North Carolina Press.

Micklethwait, John, and Adrian Wooldridge. 2004. *The Right Nation: Conservative Power in America*. New York: Penguin.

Milanovic, Branko. 2005. *Measuring International and Global Inequality* (Princeton University Press).

Mitchell, Edward J. 1969. "Some Econometrics of the Huk Rebellion." *American Political Science Review* 63, no. 4 (December 1969): pp. 1159–71.

Moise, E. E. 1994. *Modern China: A History.* 2nd ed. London and New York: Longman.

Montgomery, J. D. 1962. *The Politics of Foreign Aid: American Experience in Southeast Asia.* New York: Praeger.

Morck, R., D. Wolfenzon, and B. Yeung. 2005. "Corporate Governance, Economic Entrenchment and Growth." *Journal of Economic Literature* 53: 655–720.

Morgenthau, Henry. 1962. "A Political Theory of Foreign Aid." *American Political Science Review* 56, no 2.: 301–9.

Morgenthau, Henry J., and K. W. Thompson. 1982. *In Defense of the National Interest: A Critical Examination of American Foreign Policy.* Lanham, Md.: University Press of America.

Moyar, Mark. 2006. *Triumph Forsaken: The Vietnam War, 1954–1965.* Cambridge University Press.

Musloff, L. 1963. *Public Enterprise and Development Perspectives in South Vietnam.* Michigan State University Press.

National Commission on Terrorist Attacks upon the United States. 2004. *The 9/11 Commission Report.* Washington.

Niu, J. 2005. "Guomindang and CCP Policies toward the United States during the Period of the Marshall Mediation" (http://niujun.coldwarchina.com/ywlz/lw/000295.htm).

Nolting, F. 1988. *From Trust to Tragedy.* New York: Praeger.

North, Douglass. 1990. *Institutions, Institutional Change and Economic Performance.* Cambridge University Press.

———. 1993. "Toward a Theory of Institutional Change." In W. Barnett and others, eds., *Political Economy: Institutions, Competition and Representation.* Cambridge University Press.

Nguyen, Tuan A. 1987. *South Vietnam: Trial and Experience.* Ohio University Press.

Odom, W. E., and R. Dujarric. 2004. *America's Inadvertent Empire.* Yale University Press.

Organski, A. F. K. 1958. *World Politics.* New York: Knopf.

Packenham, R. 1973. *Liberal America and the Third World, Political Development Ideas in Foreign Aid and Social Science.* Princeton University Press.

Page, B., and M. Bouton. 2006. *The Foreign Policy Disconnect: What Americans Want from Our Leaders but Don't Get.* University of Chicago Press.

Page, Scott E. 2001. "Self-Organization and Coordination." *Computational Economics* 18: 25–48.

Palmer, N. D., ed. 1984. *The United States and India: The Dimensions of Influence.* New York: Praeger.

Pastor, Robert A. 1999. "The Role of Electoral Administration in Democratic Transitions: Implications for Policy and Research." *Democratization* 6, no. 4 (Winter 1999): 1–27.

Paulson, Anna L., and Robert M. Townsend. 2004. "Entrepreneurship and Financial Constraints in Thailand." *Journal of Corporate Finance,* vol. 10, no. 2: 229–62.

Payne, Robert. 1969. *Chiang Kai-shek.* New York: Weybright & Talley.

Pei, M., and S. Kasper. 2003. "Lessons from the Past: The American Record on Nation Building." Policy brief. Washington: Carnegie Endowment for International Peace.

Perkins, J. 2006. *Confessions of an Economic Hit Man.* New York: Penguin.

Perrow, Charles. 1986. *Complex Organizations: A Critical Essay.* 3rd ed. New York: Random House.

Pollack, Kenneth M. 2004. *The Persian Puzzle: The Conflict between Iran and America.* New York: Random House.

———. 2006. "Iran: Three Alternative Futures." *Middle East Review of International Affairs* 10, no. 2 (June 2006) (http://meria.idc.ac.il/journal/2006/issue2/jv10no2a5.html).

Powell, Colin L. 1995. *My American Journey.* New York: Random House.

Prasad, Devki Nandan. 1979. "Food for Peace: The Story of US Food Assistance to India." In D. Merrill, ed., 1990, *Bread and the Ballot: The United States and India's Economic Development, 1947–1963.* University of North Carolina Press.

Przeworski, Adam. 2000. *Democracy and Development: Political Institutions and Well-Being in the World, 1950–1990.* Cambridge University Press.

Putnam, R., R. Leonardi, and R. Y. Nanetti. 1993. *Making Democracy Work: Civic Traditions in Modern Italy.* Princeton University Press.

Rajan, R., and L. Zingales. 2006. "The Persistence of Underdevelopment: Institutions, Human Capital or Constituencies?" NBER Working Paper 12093. Cambridge, Mass.: National Bureau of Economic Research.

Rawski, T. 1989. *Economic Growth in Prewar China.* University of California Press.

Reich, Robert B. 2007. *Supercapitalism: The Transformation of Business, Democracy, and Everyday Life.* New York: Knopf.

Rielly, John E. 1995. *American Public Opinion and U.S. Foreign Policy.* Chicago Council on Foreign Relations.

Rogowski, Ronald. 1989. *Commerce and Coalitions: How Trade Affects Domestic Political Alignments.* Princeton University Press.

Root, Hilton L. 1985. *Peasants and King in Burgundy: Agrarian Foundations of French Absolutism.* University of California Press.

———. 1994. *The Fountain of Privilege: Political Foundation of Markets in France and England.* University of California Press.

————. 1996. *Small Countries, Big Lessons: Governance and the Rise of East Asia.* Oxford University Press.

————. 2006. *Capital and Collusion.* Princeton University Press.

Rosati, J. A. 1987. *The Carter Administration's Quest for Global Community: Beliefs and Their Impact on Behavior.* University of South Carolina Press.

Rosati, J., and S. Twing. 1998. "The Presidency and U.S. Foreign Policy." In J. M. Scott, ed., *After the End: Making U.S. Foreign Policy in the Post–Cold War Environment.* Duke University Press.

Ross, Michael L. 1999. "The Political Economy of Resource Curse." *World Politics* 51(1): 297–322.

————. 2001. "Does Oil Hinder Democracy?" *World Politics* 53, no. 4: 325–61.

Rostow, Walt Whitman. 1985. *Eisenhower, Kennedy, and Foreign Aid.* University of Texas Press.

Rubin, B. 1981. *Paved with Good Intentions: The American Experience and Iran.* New York: Viking Press.

Ruland, J. 2005. "Conclusion and Perspectives: U.S. Policy towards the Global South after September 11, 2001." In J. Ruland and others, eds., *U.S. Foreign Policy toward the Third World: A Post–Cold War Assessment.* Armonk, N.Y.: M. E. Sharpe.

Ruttan, V. W. 1996. *United States Development Assistance Policy: The Domestic Politics of Foreign Economic Aid.* Johns Hopkins University Press.

Sachs, Jeffrey, and M. Warner. 1995. "Natural Resource Abundance and Economic Growth." NBER Working Paper 5398. Cambridge, Mass.: National Bureau of Economic Research.

————. 2001. "The Curse of National Resources." *European Economic Review* 45: 827–38.

Sala-i-Martin, Xavier, and Arvind Subramanian. 2003. "Addressing the Natural Resource Curse: An Illustration from Nigeria." NBER Working Paper 9804. Cambridge, Mass.: National Bureau of Economic Research.

Salisbury, Harrison E. 1976a. Preface to *The Silenced Democracy,* by R. S. Manglapus. New York: Orbis Books.

————. 1976b. *Travels through America.* New York: Walker.

Satter, David. 2003. *Darkness at Dawn: The Rise of the Russian Criminal State.* Yale University Press.

Scigliano, R. 1964. *South Vietnam: Nation under Stress.* Boston: Houghton Mifflin.

Scott, James C. 1972. *Comparative Political Corruption.* Englewood Cliffs, N.J.: Prentice-Hall.

Seitz, J. L. 1980. "The Failure of U.S. Technical Assistance in Public Administration: The Iranian Case." *Public Administration Review* 40, no. 5 (September–October): 407–13.

Seligman, E. 1956. *What the United States Can Do about India.* New York University Press.

Shahid, M. Imtiaz, and Memoona Shahid. 2007. *An Advance Study in Pakistan Affairs.* Lahore: Advance Publishers.

Shaplen, R. 1965. *The Lost Revolution*. New York: Harper & Row.

Shleifer, A., and Daniel Treisman. 2000. *Without a Map: Political Tactics and Economic Reform in Russia*. MIT Press.

Sick, G. 1985. *All Fall Down: America's Tragic Encounter with Iran*. New York: Random House.

Siddiqa, A. 2007. *Military Inc: Inside Pakistan's Military Economy*. Pluto Press.

Singh, I., and R. H. Day. 1975. "Factor Utilization and Substitution in Economic Development: A Green Revolution Case Study." *Journal of Development Studies* 11, no. 3(April 1975): 155–77.

Sofaer, Abraham D. 1976. "The Presidency, War, and Foreign Affairs: Practice under the Framers." *Law and Contemporary Problems*, 40, no. 2, Presidential Power: Part 1 (Spring).

Spence, J. D. 1990. *The Search for Modern China*. New York: Norton.

Spulber, N. 1997. *Redefining the State: Privatization and Welfare Reform in Industrial and Transitional Economies*. Cambridge University Press.

———. 2003. *Russia's Economic Transitions: From Late Tsarism to the New Millennium*. Cambridge University Press.

Stohl, Rachel. 2007. *U.S. Arms Exports and Military Assistance in the "Global War on Terror."* Washington: Center for Defense Information.

Strayer, Joseph R. 1970. *On the Medieval Origins of the Modern State*. Princeton University Press.

Streeb, K. 1994. *A Fragmented Effort: Ngo Dinh Diem, The United States Military and State Department and the Strategic Hamlet Program 1961–1963*. George Mason University Press.

Stiglitz, Joseph. 2003. *Globalization and Its Discontents*. New York: Norton.

Summers, Harry G., Jr. 1982. *On Strategy: A Critical Analysis of the Vietnam War*. Novato, Calif.: Presidio Press.

Talbot, Phillips, and S. L. Poplai. 1958. *India and America: A Study of Their Relations*. New York: Harper & Bros.

Tammen, R., and others. 2000. *Power Transitions: Strategies for the 21st Century*. New York: Chatham House.

Tarnoff, Curt, and Larry Nowels. 2004. "Foreign Aid: An Introductory Overview of U.S. Programs and Policy." Report prepared for U.S. Congress. Washington: Congressional Research Service, April 15.

Taylor, M. 1961. "South Vietnam: Lavish Aid, Limited Progress." *Pacific Affairs* 34 (Autumn): 242–56.

Terrill, R. 1999. *Mao: A Biography*. Stanford University Press.

Thompson, W. Scott. 1975. *Unequal Partners: Philippine and Thai Relations with the United States, 1965–75*. Lexington, Mass.: Lexington Books.

Tocqueville, Alexis de. 1960. *Democracy in America*. 2 vols. New York: Vintage.

Toffler, Alvin. 1984. *Future Shock*. New York: Bantam.

Townsend, Robert M., and Kenichi Ueda. 2001. "Transitional Growth with Increasing Inequality and Financial Deepening." IMF Working Paper WP/01/108. Washington: IMF, Research Department.

———. 2003. "Financial Deepening, Inequality, and Growth: A Model-Based Quantitative Evaluation." IMF Working Paper WP/01/193. Washington: IMF, Research Department.

Tuchman, Barbara. W. 1970. *Stillwell and the American Experience in China, 1911–45.* New York: Macmillan.

Turchin, P. 2003. *Historical Dynamics: Why States Rise and Fall.* Princeton University Press.

United Nations in the Islamic Republic of Iran and Plan and Budget Organization of the Islamic Republic of Iran. 1999. Human Development Report of the Islamic Republic of Iran, 1999.

United Nations Development Program. 2001. *Human Development Report 2001: Making New Technologies Work for Human Development.* New York: Oxford University Press.

———. 2008. *Human Development Report 2007/2008.* New York: Palgrave Macmillan.

United States Congress, Senate Committee on Foreign Relations. 1974. *Vietnam May 1974.* Government Printing Office.

United States Department of State. 1958–1960. *Foreign Relations of the United States, 1958–1960: South and Southeast Asia.* Volume 15. Washington: State Department.

United States Government Accountability Office. 2007. "Stabilizing Iraq: DOD Cannot Ensure That U.S.-Funded Equipment Has Reached Iraqi Security Forces." Report to Congressional Committees, July, Washington, D.C.

U.S. Congress, House Ways and Means Committee. 2004. *Green Book: Background Material and Data on Programs within the Jurisdiction of the House Committee on Ways and Means.* Washington: Government Printing Office.

Vogel, T. K., and E. A. Witte. 2005. "America Should Ditch Its Tyrant Friends." *International Herald Tribune,* August 15.

Wakeman, F., Jr. 2003. *Spymaster: Dai Li and the Chinese Secret Service.* University of California Press.

Weber, Max. 1947. *The Theory of Social and Economic Organization.* New York: Free Press.

Westad, O. A. 2005. *The Global Cold War.* Cambridge University Press.

Wheeler, John Archibald. 1994. *At Home in the Universe.* Woodury, N.Y.: American Institute of Physics.

Wiegersma, Nan, and Joseph E. Medley. 2000. *U.S. Economic Development Policies towards the Pacific Rim: Success and Failures of US Aid.* New York: St. Martin's Press.

Williams, William A. 1972. *America Confronts a Revolutionary World, 1776–1976.* New York: William Morrow.

Wintrobe, Ronald. 1998. *The Political Economy of Dictatorship.* Cambridge University Press.

———. 2007. "Dictatorship: Analytical Approaches." In Carles Boix and Susan Stokes, eds., *Oxford Handbook of Comparative Politics.* Oxford University Press.

Wolf, C., Jr. 1960. *Foreign Aid: Theory and Practice in Southern Asia.* Princeton University Press.

World Bank. 1983. *World Tables.* Volume 2. 3rd ed. Johns Hopkins University Press.

———. 2002. *Transition—The First Ten Years: Analysis and Lessons for Eastern Europe and the Former Soviet Union.* Washington: World Bank.

Wright, Robin, and Griff Witte. 2007. "Pakistan Election Poses Challenges for U.S." *Washington Post,* October 6, 2007, p. A18 (www.washingtonpost.com/wp-dyn/content/article/2007/10/05/AR2007100502480.html).

Wrong, D. 1979. *Power: Its Forms and Bases.* Oxford: Basil Blackwell.

Xu, Z. 1995. *Lest We Forget: Nanjing Massacre, 1937.* Beijing: Chinese Literature Press.

Yuan, Nansheng. 2005. *Si Dalin, Mao Zedong yu Jiang Jieshi* [Stalin, Mao Zedong, and Chiang Kai-shek]. Changsha: Hunan Renmin Publishing House.

Zasloff, J. 1962. "Rural Resettlement in South Vietnam: The Agroville Program." *Pacific Affairs* 35, no. 4: 327–40.

Zegart, A. B. 1999. *Flawed by Design: The Evolution of the CIA, JCS, and NSC.* Stanford University Press.

Index

143, 196–97; U.S. overthrow of government in, 27–28; World War II and, 125, 135. *See also* Middle East; Persian Gulf War, First

Iran—individual participants: Khomeini, Ruhollah (Ayatollah), 126, 127, 136–37, 243n13; Mossadegh, Muhammad, 123–25, 242n7; Pahlavi, Mohammad Reza Shah, 122–24, 125–26, 127–32, 133–34, 137, 143–44, 174, 175, 242n9, 244n21, 244n25, 245n31. *See also mentioned individuals by name*

Iran-Contra hearings (Tower Commission; *1986*), 48

Iranian Revolution (*1979*), 36

Iran-Iraq War. *See* Persian Gulf War, First

Iran, shah of. *See* Iran; Pahlavi, Mohammad Reza Shah

Iraq: al Qaeda and, 35, 179; casualties of the Iraq war, 192; CENTO and, 153; domino theory and, 176–77; economic issues of, 134, 180, 193; Islamists in, 36; Maliki, Nuri al-, and, 173, 175, 179, 210, 249n1; Philippines and, 98; U.S. foreign policies and, 18, 32, 34, 35, 176–79, 194; U.S. overthrow of government in, 27–28, 226n7; U.S. withdrawal from, 176–77; weapons in, 222n17. *See also* Commitment traps; Hussein, Saddam; Middle East; Persian Gulf War, Second

Islam and Islamists: anti-Americanism and, 149; Bush, George W., and, 34; Middle Eastern political organizations of, 24; radicalization of, 169; sharia and, 136; U.S. foreign policies and, 12, 24–25, 123, 169, 226n8. *See also* Iran; Jihad and jihadists; Khomeini, Ruhollah; Pakistan; Muslim countries

Israel, 36, 52. *See also* Arab-Israeli War; Middle East

Japan: China and, 73–75; democracy and democratization in, 215; economic issues in, 64, 119, 133; industrialization of, 214; invasion of Manchuria, 73–74; political legitimacy in, 118; post-World War II, 17, 57, 205; pre-World War II, 57; social organization in, 57–58; U.S. foreign aid and, 193; World War II and, 191; Yalta Conference and, 79

JCS. *See* Joint Chiefs of Staff

Jiangxi Soviet Republic (China), 74, 231n8

Jihadism and jihadists, 34–36, 176–77. *See also* Islam and Islamists; Pakistan; War on terror

Jinnah, Muhammad Ali. *See* Pakistan

Johnson, Lyndon B., 44, 122–24

Johnson (Lyndon B.) administration, 176

Joint Chiefs of Staff (JCS; U.S.), 43, 49–50, 147

Jordan, 17, 24–25

Kashmir, 152–53, 154, 158. *See also* India; Pakistan

Kazakhstan, 38–39, 187

Kennan, George, 37

Kennedy, John F.: India and, 146, 148; Iran and, 125, 174, 175; NSC and, 48; Pakistan and, 148; South Korea and, 174; South Vietnam and, 103, 108

Kennedy (John F.) administration, 48, 91, 113, 126

Kenya, 17

Kerry, John, 31

Kerry, Richard, 26

Khomeini, Ruhollah (Ayatollah; Iran), 36. *See also* Iran

Kirkpatrick doctrine, 93–94, 143

Kirkpatrick, Jeane, 93, 143, 214

Kissinger, Henry, 48–49, 52, 94, 113, 210

KMT. See Kuomintang

Military issues. *See* Armed forces; Arms race; Arms sales; Joint Chiefs of Staff; *individual countries*
Mondale, Walter, 93
Montgomery, John D., 56, 62–63
Morgenthau, Hans, 78
Morocco, 24–25, 34
Mossadegh, Muhammad, 28. *See also* Iran
Moss, Robert, 134
Multilateral organizations, 208
Multinational corporations, 181, 182, 185
Musharraf, Pervez. *See* Pakistan
Muslim countries, 38–39, 147–48, 153. *See also* Islam and Islamists; *individual countries*
Muslim League, 153, 166
Myanmar (Burma), 17, 38, 185
Myth of Independence (Bhutto), 77

Napoleon, 58
National Commission on Terrorist Attacks upon the United States, 158
National Endowment for Democracy, 34
National Front for the Liberation of South Vietnam (NLF), 105, 109
Nationalism, 82, 106, 107, 124, 185, 194. *See also individual countries*
Nationalist Party (China). *See* Kuomintang
Nationalist Party (Philippines), 89, 92
National Liberation Front (South Vietnam), 104
National Security Act of *1947,* 49, 192
National Security Council (NSC; U.S.), 43, 48, 49, 152, 196, 208
Nazism, 21
Nehru, Jawaharlal, 77, 151, 153. *See also* India
Neoconservatives, 211, 256n28
Netherlands, 131, 151
New Deal (U.S.), 205–06

Newsday, 94
New York Times, 104, 155
New Zealand, 153
Nhu, Ngo Dinh, 105
Nicaragua, 27–28, 32, 64, 143–44, 197. *See also* Sandanistas
9/11 Commission Report (U.S.), 158
Nixon, Richard M.: China and, 85; foreign policy and, 52; Marcos, Ferdinand, and, 194; Pahlavi, Mohammad Reza Shah, and, 122–24, 126–27; Pakistan and, 148; reorganization efforts of, 43
Nixon (Richard M.) administration, 111, 126, 127
NLF. *See* National Front for the Liberation of South Vietnam
Nolting, Frederick, 108
Nonaligned movement, 148–49, 150, 153. *See also* India
North America. *See* United States
North Korea. *See* Korea, North
North Vietnam. *See* Vietnam, North
NSC. *See* National Security Council

October War of *1973* (Arab-Israel), 48
Office of Management and Budget (OMB), 11
Oil issues: Iranian oil, 124–26, 130, 132, 133, 141, 242n9, 244n21; Iraqi oil, 177, 210; in the Middle East, 251n10; political pluralism, 245n33, 249n1. *See also* Iran
OMB. *See* Office of Management and Budget
Overseas Development Assistance (U.S.), 25

Page, B., 19, 20–21
Pahlavi, Mohammad Reza Shah (shah of Iran), 28, 36, 52, 63, 83, 174, 223n1. *See also* Iran
Pahlavi, Reza Shah, 124

Pakistan: alliance curse in, 8–9; arms sales to, 10–11; bureaucratic and social organization in, 59; corruption in, 156–57, 164–65, 166, 167; democratization and constitution of, 5, 149, 157, 159, 160–61, 163–67; economic issues in, 64, 65, 134, 143–44, 156–57, 161–63, 165, 167, 214; extremism in, 159–65, 166–67, 168, 169; human resource development in, 38; Islamists in, 158, 164, 167–68, 169, 248n43; military and arms issues in, 153–55, 159, 161–62, 164, 167, 168; reforms in, 8, 162–64, 165–67; social and cultural issues of, 157, 160–61, 164, 217

Pakistan—foreign relations: anti-Americanism in, 17, 47, 159–60, 166–67, 169; Bush (George W.) administration and, 33; China and, 155; India and, 154–55, 159; relationship with the U.S., 145, 148, 152–53, 155–57, 159, 167–69; terrorists and terrorism in, 157–59, 160, 162, 164, 165, 166; U.S. foreign aid to, 5, 8, 24–25, 47, 145, 146, 148, 149, 150f, 153, 157–58, 165, 194, 247n29, 248n42; U.S. foreign policies and, 13, 18, 32, 52, 57, 152, 166–69, 191, 192; U.S. support of dictators in, 34. *See also* Kashmir

Pakistan—individual participants: Ayub Khan, Mohammad, 156; Bhutto, Benazir, 159, 257n35; Bhutto, Zulfikar, 77, 148, 157, 166; Jinnah, Muhammad Ali, 147–48, 153, 169; Musharraf, Pervez, 149, 158–61, 162–64, 166, 167, 247n35, 248n45. *See also mentioned individuals by name*

Palestine, 36
Palestinian Authority, 18, 24
Panama, 27–28, 32
Park Chung-hee, 151, 174

Pastor, Robert, 181
Patron-client regimes: economic issues and, 188; incentives and rewards of, 60–61; Iran, 193; maintenance of commitment credibility and, 210; Pakistan, 212; Philippines, 193; political order and, 204, 212; South Vietnam, 114, 117, 118; supporting reform in client states, 174–76
Pentagon Papers (U.S.), 104
Peoples Party (Pakistan), 166
Persian Gulf War, First (Iraq-Iran; *1980–88*), 136, 137, 174
Persian Gulf War, Second (Iraq-Kuwait; *1990–91*), 32, 33
Petraeus, David, 209
Philippines: Communism and Communists in, 94, 191; corruption and fraud in, 5, 87–88, 89, 90, 91, 92, 93, 94, 98–100, 118, 222n7, 237n34, 237n35; democratization of, 5, 87–88, 93, 94, 99, 100–01; economic issues of, 64, 65, 88, 91–92, 94, 95–100, 117, 134, 191, 193, 241n72; government of, 117, 118; historical timeline of, 87; Huk insurgency in, 89, 90, 91, 235n6, 235n7; independence and occupation of, 87; instability in, 60, 194; Islamic insurgency in, 88, 97–98; nationalism in, 194; patrimonial state in, 92–94; People Power Revolutions in, 88; power asymmetries in, 60; social and cultural issues of, 86–87
Philippines—foreign relations: American vision of law and order in, 94–97; anti-Americanism in, 26, 89, 94; clientelism in, 88–91, 117, 118; historical timeline of, 87; SEATO and, 153; Spanish rule of, 88, 234n2; U.S. alliances with, 3, 90, 92, 95, 97–98; U.S. foreign aid and, 25, 47, 89, 93, 97, 191, 194, 236n15; U.S.